interactive
SCIENCE

Some raccoons live in hollow trees. Their flexible legs help them run down the outside of these trees headfirst.

PEARSON

Glenview, Illinois • Boston, Massachusetts • Chandler, Arizona • Upper Saddle River, New Jersey

Authors

You are an author!

You are one of the authors of this book. You can write in this book! You can take notes in this book! You can draw in it too! This book will be yours to keep.

Fill in the information below to tell about yourself. Then write your autobiography. An autobiography tells about you and the kinds of things you like to do.

Name ....

School ....

Town, State ....

Autobiography ....

....

....

....

....

....

....

My Photo

ISBN-13:   978-0-328-52099-2
ISBN-10:   0-328-52099-3
           22 19

ON THE COVER
Some raccoons live in hollow trees. Their flexible legs help them run down the outside of these trees headfirst.

Program Authors

DON BUCKLEY, M.Sc.
*Information and Communications Technology Director,
The School at Columbia University, New York, New York*
Mr. Buckley has been at the forefront of K–12 educational technology for nearly two decades. A founder of New York City Independent School Technologists (NYCIST) and long-time chair of New York Association of Independent Schools' annual IT conference, he has taught students on two continents and created multimedia and Internet-based instructional systems for schools worldwide.

ZIPPORAH MILLER, M.A.Ed.
Associate Executive Director for Professional Programs and Conferences, National Science Teachers Association, Arlington, Virginia
Associate executive director for professional programs and conferences at NSTA, Ms. Zipporah Miller is a former K–12 science supervisor and STEM coordinator for the Prince George's County Public School District in Maryland. She is a science education consultant who has overseen curriculum development and staff training for more than 150 district science coordinators.

MICHAEL J. PADILLA, Ph.D.
Associate Dean and Director, Eugene P. Moore School of Education, Clemson University, Clemson, South Carolina
A former middle school teacher and a leader in middle school science education, Dr. Michael Padilla has served as president of the National Science Teachers Association and as a writer of the National Science Education Standards. He is professor of science education at Clemson University. As lead author of the *Science Explorer* series, Dr. Padilla has inspired the team in developing a program that promotes student inquiry and meets the needs of today's students.

KATHRYN THORNTON, Ph.D.
Professor and Associate Dean, School of Engineering and Applied Science, University of Virginia, Charlottesville, Virginia
Selected by NASA in May 1984, Dr. Kathryn Thornton is a veteran of four space flights. She has logged more than 975 hours in space, including more than 21 hours of extravehicular activity. As an author on the *Scott Foresman Science* series, Dr. Thornton's enthusiasm for science has inspired teachers around the globe.

MICHAEL E. WYSESSION, Ph.D.
Associate Professor of Earth and Planetary Science, Washington University, St. Louis, Missouri
An author on more than 50 scientific publications, Dr. Wysession was awarded the prestigious Packard Foundation Fellowship and Presidential Faculty Fellowship for his research in geophysics. Dr. Wysession is an expert on Earth's inner structure and has mapped various regions of Earth using seismic tomography. He is known internationally for his work in geoscience education and outreach.

Instructional Design Author

GRANT WIGGINS, Ed.D.
President, Authentic Education, Hopewell, New Jersey
Dr. Wiggins is a co-author with Jay McTighe of *Understanding by Design, 2nd Edition* (ASCD 2005). His approach to instructional design provides teachers with a disciplined way of thinking about curriculum design, assessment, and instruction that moves teaching from covering content to ensuring understanding.
UNDERSTANDING BY DESIGN® and UbD® are trademarks of ASCD, and are used under license.

Planet Diary Author

JACK HANKIN
Science/Mathematics Teacher, The Hilldale School, Daly City, California Founder, Planet Diary Web site
Mr. Hankin is the creator and writer of Planet Diary, a science current events Web site. Mr. Hankin is passionate about bringing science news and environmental awareness into classrooms.

Activities Author

KAREN L. OSTLUND, Ph.D.
Advisory Council, Texas Natural Science Center, College of Natural Sciences, The University of Texas at Austin
Dr. Ostlund has more than 35 years of experience teaching at the elementary, middle school, and university levels. She was Director of WINGS Online (Welcoming Interns and Novices with Guidance and Support) and Director of the UTeach | Dell Center for New Teacher Success at the University of Texas at Austin. She served as Director of the Center for Science Education at the University of Texas at Arlington, President of the Council of Elementary Science International, and on the Board of Directors of the National Science Teachers Association. As an author of *Scott Foresman Science*, Dr. Ostlund was instrumental in developing inquiry activities.

ELL Consultant

JIM CUMMINS, Ph.D.
Professor and Canada Research Chair, Curriculum, Teaching and Learning Department at the University of Toronto
Dr. Cummins focuses on literacy development in multilingual schools and the role of technology in learning. *Interactive Science* incorporates research-based principles for integrating language with the teaching of academic content based on his work.

Reviewers

Program Consultants

William Brozo, Ph.D.
Professor of Literacy, Graduate School of Education, George Mason University, Fairfax, Virginia.
Dr. Brozo is the author of numerous articles and books on literacy development. He co-authors a column in The Reading Teacher and serves on the editorial review board of the Journal of Adolescent & Adult Literacy.

Kristi Zenchak, M.S.
Biology Instructor, Oakton Community College, Des Plaines, Illinois
Kristi Zenchak helps elementary teachers incorporate science, technology, engineering, and math activities into the classroom. STEM activities that produce viable solutions to real-world problems not only motivate students but also prepare students for future STEM careers. Ms. Zenchak helps elementary teachers understand the basic science concepts, and provides STEM activities that easy are to implement in the classroom.

Content Reviewers

Brad Armosky, M.S.
Texas Advanced Computing Center
University of Texas at Austin
Austin, Texas

Alexander Brands, Ph.D.
Department of Biological Sciences
Lehigh University
Bethlehem, Pennsylvania

Paul Beale, Ph.D.
Department of Physics
University of Colorado
Boulder, Colorado

Joy Branlund, Ph.D.
Department of Earth Science
Southwestern Illinois College
Granite City, Illinois

Constance Brown, Ph.D
Atmospheric Science Program
Geography Department
Indiana University
Bloomington, Indiana

Dana Dudle, Ph.D.
Biology Department
DePauw University
Greencastle, Indiana

Rick Duhrkopf, Ph. D.
Department of Biology
Baylor University
Waco, Texas

Mark Henriksen, Ph.D.
Physics Department
University of Maryland
Baltimore, Maryland

Andrew Hirsch, Ph.D.
Department of Physics
Purdue University
W. Lafayette, Indiana

Linda L. Cronin Jones, Ph.D.
School of Teaching & Learning
University of Florida
Gainesville, Florida

T. Griffith Jones, Ph.D.
College of Education
University of Florida
Gainesville, Florida

Candace Lutzow-Felling, Ph.D.
Director of Education
State Arboretum of Virginia & Blandy Experimental Farm
Boyce, Virginia

Cortney V. Martin, Ph.D.
Virginia Polytechnic Institute
Blacksburg, Virginia

Sadredin Moosavi, Ph.D.
University of Massachusetts Dartmouth
Fairhaven, Massachusetts

Klaus Newmann, Ph.D.
Department of Geological Sciences
Ball State University
Muncie, Indiana

Scott M. Rochette, Ph.D.
Department of the Earth Sciences
SUNY College at Brockport
Brockport, New York

Ursula Rosauer Smedly, M.S.
Alcade Science Center
New Mexico State University
Alcade, New Mexico

Frederick W. Taylor, Ph.D.
Jackson School of Geosciences
University of Texas at Austin
Austin, Texas

Chapter 1

The Nature of Science

This scientist is recording observations.

myscienceonline.com

 Untamed Science
Watch the Ecogeeks as they learn about the nature of science.

Got it? 60-Second Video
Watch and learn about the nature of science.

Envision It!
See what you already know about the nature of science.

Memory Match
Mix and match vocabulary practice.

 I Will Know...
See how the key concepts about the nature of science come to life.

Chapter 2

Technology and Design

This satellite is technology that helps people communicate.

myscienceonline.com

Untamed Science
Ecogeeks answer your questions about technology and design.

Got it? 🕑 **60-Second Video**
Review lessons about technology and design in 60 seconds!

Explore It! Animation
Quick and easy online experiments about technology and design

Investigate It! Virtual Lab
Investigate how materials affect a boat's design and function.

MY PLANET DIARY
Find out more about technologies that improve car safety.

Unit B
Life Science

Chapter 3
Plants and Animals

To survive and grow, these plants need sunlight, water, carbon dioxide, and nutrients from the soil.

myscienceonline.com

Untamed Science
Watch the Ecogeeks learn about plants and animals.

Got it? **60-Second Video**
Lessons about plants and animals reviewed in a minute!

Envision It!
See what you already know about plants and animals.

Explore It! Animation
Quick and easy online experiments about plants and animals

Vocabulary Smart Cards
Mix and match plants and animals vocabulary.

Ecosystems

Animals get energy by eating plants or other animals.

myscienceonline.com

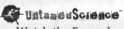

Untamed Science
Watch the Ecogeeks as they learn about ecosystems.

Got it? 60-Second Video
Watch a one-minute video summarizing ecosystem topics.

Envision It!
Find out what you already know about ecosystems.

I Will Know...
See what you've learned about ecosystems.

Explore It! Animation
Explore ecosystems in a new way.

Unit C
Earth Science

Chapter
5

Earth's Resources

Salt water can cause weathering that changes Earth's surface.

myscience**on**Line.com

UntamedScience
Watch the Ecogeeks as they learn about Earth's resources.

Got it? 60-Second Video
Watch and learn about Earth's resources.

Envision It!
Find out what you already know about Earth's resources.

Explore It! Animation
Explore Earth's resources in a new way!

I Will Know...
See what you've learned about Earth's resources.

Chapter 6

Earth and Space

Earth's rotation causes day to change into night and night to change into day.

myscienceonline.com

Untamed Science
Go on an Earth and space adventure with the Ecogeeks!

Got it? 60-Second Video
Review each lesson on Earth and space in 60 seconds!

Envision It!
See what you already know about Earth and space.

Explore It! Animation
Quick and easy online experiments about Earth and space

I Will Know...
See how key concepts of each Earth and space lesson are brought to life!

Unit D
Physical Science

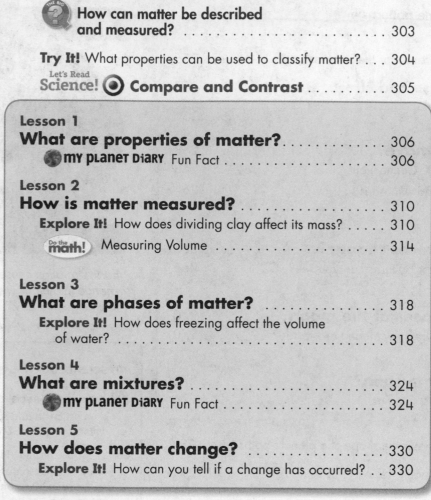

Matter

Water can exist as a solid, a liquid, or a gas.

myscienceonline.com

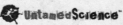Untamed Science
Watch the Ecogeeks as they learn about matter.

Got it? 60-Second Video
Watch and learn about matter.

Envision It!
See what you already know about matter.

Memory Match
Mix and match vocabulary on matter.

 I Will Know...
See how the key concepts about matter come to life.

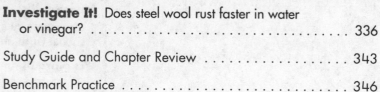

Energy and Heat

You use many different forms of energy, such as light and electrical energy, every day.

mʏscienceonLine.com

Untamed Science
Ecogeeks answer your questions about energy and heat.

Got it? **60-Second Video**
Review lessons about energy and heat in 60 seconds!

Explore It! Animation
Quick and easy online experiments about energy and heat

Investigate It! Simulation
Investigate which material is the better heat conductor.

mʏ pLaneT DiaʀY
Learn fun facts about glow sticks and how guitars produce sound.

Chapter 9

Electricity and Magnetism

Wind turbines use electromagnets to transform energy of motion into electricity.

myscienceonline.com

Untamed Science
Watch the Ecogeeks learn about electricity and magnetism.

Got it? **60-Second Video**
Lessons about electricity and magnetism reviewed in a minute!

Envision It!
See what you already know about electricity and magnetism.

Explore It! Animation
Quick and easy online experiments about electricity and magnetism

Vocabulary Smart Cards
Mix and match electricity and magnetism vocabulary.

Chapter 10

Motion

*The force of the cyclists
pushing on the pedals helps
their bikes move.*

myscienceonline.com

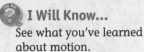

🐟 **Untamed Science**
Watch the Ecogeeks as they
learn about motion.

Got it? ⏱ **60-Second Video**
Watch one-minute videos for
each motion lesson!

Envision It!
Find out what you already
know about motion.

❓ **I Will Know...**
See what you've learned
about motion.

◀ **Explore It!** Animation
Explore motion in a
new way!

"This is your book. You can write in it!"

interactive SCIENCE

Big Question

At the start of each chapter you will see two questions—an **Engaging Question** and a **Big Question.** Just like a scientist, you will predict an answer to the Engaging Question. Each Big Question will help you start thinking about the Big Ideas of science. Look for the symbol throughout the chapter!

WHERE did these drops come from?

The Water Cycle and Weather

Chapter 7

Try It! How can water move in the water cycle?

Lesson 1 What is the water cycle?

Lesson 2 What is the ocean?

Lesson 3 What is weather?

Lesson 4 How do clouds and precipitation form?

Lesson 5 What is climate?

Investigate It! Where is the hurricane going?

It has not rained, but after spending the night resting, this fly was covered with droplets in the morning.

Predict Where do you think this water came from?

_____

How does water move through the environment?

Let's Read Science!

You will see a page like this toward the beginning of each chapter. It will show you how to use a reading skill that will help you understand what you read.

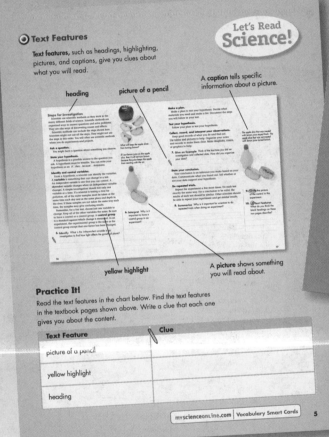

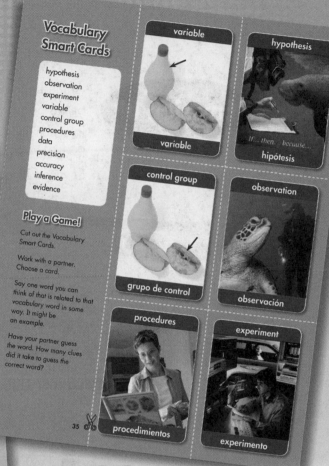

Vocabulary Smart Cards

Go to the end of the chapter and cut out your own set of **Vocabulary Smart Cards.** Write a sentence, draw a picture, or use a vocabulary strategy to learn the word. Play a game with a classmate to practice using the word!

Look for **MyScienceOnline.com** technology options.
At MyScienceOnline.com you can immerse yourself in virtual environments, get extra practice, and even blog about current events in science.

"Engage with the page!"

interactive SCIENCE

Envision It!

At the beginning of each lesson, at the top of the page, you will see an **Envision It!** interactivity that gives you the opportunity to circle, draw, write, or respond to the Envision It! question.

Lesson 1
What are forces?

Envision It!

Tell why the metal ring on the string does not fall.

I will know some forces that cause objects to move.

Words to Know
force
contact force
friction
non-contact force
gravity

my planet diary

/// MISCONCEPTION ///

You may have seen video clips of astronauts floating around in a spacecraft. People often think astronauts have no weight at all in space. In fact, they do. Most astronauts work just 300 km above ground. This is relatively close to Earth. At that height, they are only a few pounds lighter. They seem to float because their spacecraft is moving along with them. However, the spacecraft and the astronauts are both in fact falling, just like a skydiver. They don't crash because they are also moving forward fast enough to follow the curvature of the Earth.

Which everyday activities do you think would be easier in orbit?

464   myscienceonline.com   my planet diary

Forces

When one object pushes or pulls another object, the first object is exerting a force on the second one. A **force** is a push or pull that acts on an object.

Every force has a strength, or magnitude. This strength is measured in units called newtons (N). A force also has a direction. The direction of a force can be described by telling which way the force is acting. The dog is pushing the ball with a force of around 2 N.

Forces can change the way objects move. When an object begins to move, it is because a force has acted on it. When an object is already moving, forces can make it speed up, slow down, or change direction.

1. ⊙ **Main Idea and Details** Use the graphic organizer below to list two details and the main idea found in the last paragraph of the text.

Detail	Detail

Main Idea

The direction of the arrow shows that the dog is pushing, not pulling.

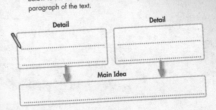

myscienceonline.com   Envision It!   465

my planet diary

My Planet Diary interactivities will introduce you to amazing scientists, fun facts, and important discoveries in science. They will also help you to overcome common misconceptions about science concepts.

After reading small
chunks of information,
stop to check your
understanding. The
visuals help teach about
what you read. Answer
questions, underline
text, draw pictures,
or label models.

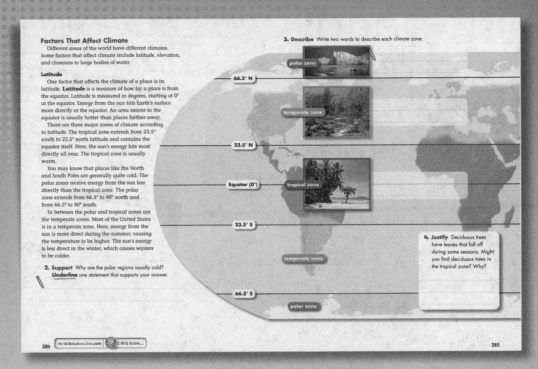

Factors That Affect Climate

Different areas of the world have different climates.
Some factors that affect climate include latitude, elevation,
and closeness to large bodies of water.

Latitude

One factor that affects the climate of a place is its
latitude. **Latitude** is a measure of how far a place is from
the equator. Latitude is measured in degrees, starting at 0°
at the equator. Energy from the sun hits Earth's surface
more directly at the equator. An area nearer to the
equator is usually hotter than places farther away.

There are three major zones of climate according
to latitude. The tropical zone extends from 23.5°
south to 23.5° north latitude and contains the
equator itself. Here, the sun's energy hits most
directly all year. The tropical zone is usually
warm.

You may know that places like the North
and South Poles are generally quite cold. The
polar zones receive energy from the sun less
directly than the tropical zone. The polar
zone extends from 66.5° to 90° north and
from 66.5° to 90° south.

In between the polar and tropical zones are
the temperate zones. Most of the United States
is in a temperate zone. Here, energy from the
sun is more direct during the summer, causing
the temperature to be higher. The sun's energy
is less direct in the winter, which causes winters
to be colder.

2. Support Why are the polar regions usually cold?
Underline one statement that supports your answer.

3. Describe Write two words to describe each climate zone.

polar zone
66.5° N
temperate zone
23.5° N
Equator (0°)   tropical zone
23.5° S
temperate zone
66.5° S
polar zone

4. Justify Deciduous trees
have leaves that fall off
during some seasons. Might
you find deciduous trees in
the tropical zone? Why?

284   mysciencenonline.com   I Will Know...   285

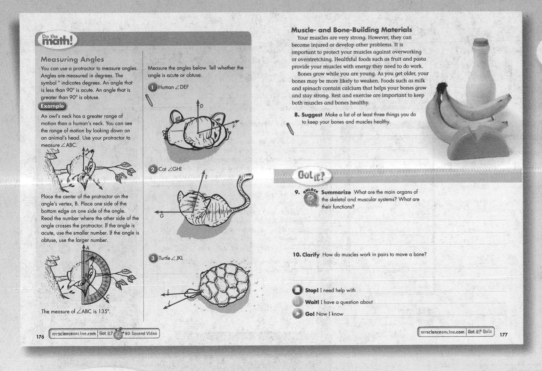

Do the math!

Measuring Angles

You can use a protractor to measure angles.
Angles are measured in degrees. The
symbol ° indicates degrees. An angle that
is less than 90° is acute. An angle that is
greater than 90° is obtuse.

Example

An owl's neck has a greater range of
motion than a human's neck. You can see
the range of motion by looking down on
an animal's head. Use your protractor to
measure ∠ABC.

Place the center of the protractor on the
angle's vertex, B. Place one side of the
bottom edge on one side of the angle.
Read the number where the other side of the
angle crosses the protractor. If the angle is
acute, use the smaller number. If the angle is
obtuse, use the larger number.

The measure of ∠ABC is 135°.

Measure the angles below. Tell whether the
angle is acute or obtuse.

1 Human ∠DEF

2 Cat ∠GHI

3 Turtle ∠JKL

Muscle- and Bone-Building Materials

Your muscles are very strong. However, they can
become injured or develop other problems. It is
important to protect your muscles against overworking
or overstretching. Healthful foods such as fruit and pasta
provide your muscles with energy they need to do work.

Bones grow while you are young. As you get older, your
bones may be more likely to weaken. Foods such as milk
and spinach contain calcium that helps your bones grow
and stay strong. Rest and exercise are important to keep
both muscles and bones healthy.

8. Suggest Make a list of at least three things you do
to keep your bones and muscles healthy.

Got it?

9. Summarize What are the main organs of
the skeletal and muscular systems? What are
their functions?

10. Clarify How do muscles work in pairs to move a bone?

Stop! I need help with

Wait! I have a question about

Go! Now I know

176   mysscienceonline.com   Got it?   60-Second Video

mysscienceonline.com   Got it? Quiz   177

Got it?

At the end of each
lesson you will have a
chance to evaluate your
own progress! After
answering the **Got it?**
questions, think about
how you are doing. At
this point you can stop,
wait, or go on to the next
lesson.

Do the math!

Scientists commonly use math as a tool to help them answer science
questions. You can practice skills that you are learning in math class right
in your *Interactive Science* Student Edition!

"Have fun! Be a scientist!"

interactive SCIENCE

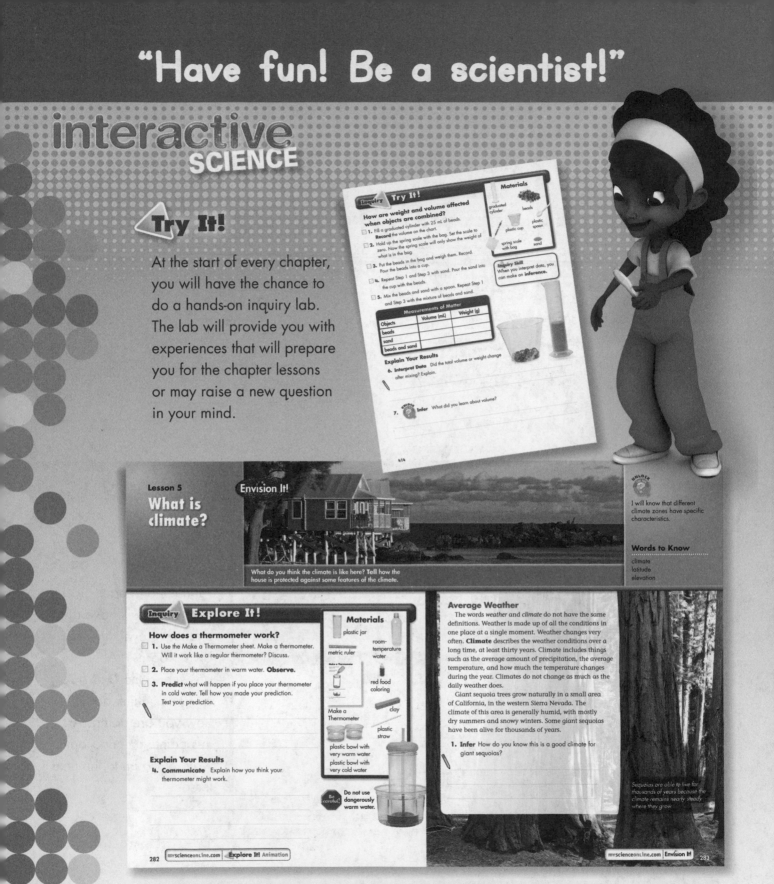

Try It!

At the start of every chapter, you will have the chance to do a hands-on inquiry lab. The lab will provide you with experiences that will prepare you for the chapter lessons or may raise a new question in your mind.

Explore It!

Before you start reading the lesson, **Explore It!** activities provide you with an opportunity to first explore the content!

Design It!

STEM activities are found throughout core and ancillary materials.

The **Design It!** activity has you use the engineering design process to find solutions to problems. By identifying the problem, doing research, and developing possible solutions, you will design, construct, and test a prototype for a real world problem. Communicate your evidence through graphs, tables, drawings, and prototypes and identify ways to make your solution better.

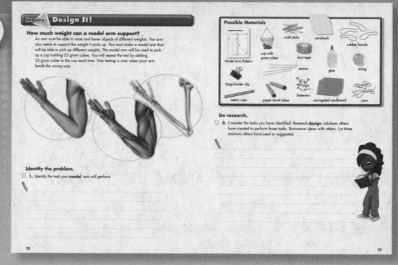

Investigate It!

At the end of every chapter, a Directed Inquiry lab gives you a chance to put together everything you've learned in the chapter. Using the activity card, apply design principles in the Guided version to Modify Your Investigation or the Open version to Develop Your Own Investigation. Whether you need a lot of support from your teacher or you're ready to explore on your own, there are fun hands-on activities that match your interests.

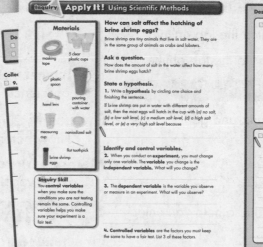

Apply It!

At the end of every unit, an Open Inquiry lab gives you a chance to explore science using scientific methods.

"Go online anytime!"

interactive SCIENCE

Here's how you log in...

1 Go to www.myscienceonline.com.

2 Log in with your username and password.

Username:

Password:

3 Click on your program and select your chapter.

Check it out!

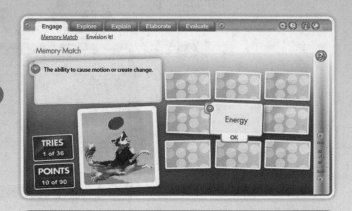

Watch a Video!

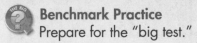 **Untamed Science™** Join the Ecogeeks on their video adventure.

Got it? **60-Second Video** Review each lesson in 60 seconds.

Go Digital for Inquiry!

Explore It! Simulation Watch the lab online.

Investigate It! Virtual Lab Do the lab online.

Show What You Know!

Got it? Quiz Take a quick quiz and get instant feedback.

Benchmark Practice Prepare for the "big test."

Writing for Science Write to help you unlock the Big Question.

Get Excited About Science!

The Big Question Share what you think about the Big Question.

my PLANET DIARY Connect to the world of science.

Envision It! Connect to what you already know before you start each lesson.

Memory Match Play a game to build your vocabulary.

Get Help!

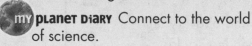 **my SCIENCE COACH** Get help at your level.

Science, Engineering, and Technology

Where is the scientist?

The Nature of Science

Try It! How do scientists make observations?

Lesson 1 What questions do scientists ask?

Lesson 2 How do scientists use tools?

Lesson 3 How do scientists answer questions?

Lesson 4 How do scientists draw conclusions?

Investigate It! What affects how many times a pendulum swings?

Scientists observe the natural world. Through observation they can learn about things such as what kinds of plants and animals live in an area. They can also learn how those plants and animals interact.

Predict What do you think these student scientists might ask about this environment? Why?

How will they adapt to the new enviornment

What is science?

Materials

stapler or other
classroom object

How do scientists make observations?

☑ **1. Observe** a stapler or another object your teacher selects.

☑ **2.** Write 10 true statements about the object.

1. _____

2. _____

3. _____

4. _____

5. _____

6. _____

7. _____

8. _____

9. _____

10. _____

> **Inquiry Skill**
> Based on your careful **observations** you can make true statements.

☐ **3.** Work in a group. Put an ✗ by the true statements that were written by more than one person.

Explain Your Results

4. **UNLOCK THE BIG ?** How did working in a group help you make better **observations**?

_____

_____

_____

_____

_____

⊙ Text Features

Text features, such as headings, labels, pictures, and captions, give you clues about what you will read.

A **heading** tells what the content that follows is about.

A **picture** shows something you will read about.

A **caption** tells specific information about a picture.

Lightning Lab

Investigations

Scientists do investigations to help them find answers to their questions. An **investigation** is a careful way of looking for something. Scientists use process skills in science investigations. You already use many of these skills in your daily life whenever you answer questions or solve problems. You will use them in a more organized way as you do science activities.

Observe

Science often starts when a person observes something. For example, someone could visit a cave and observe the shapes of the cave walls. The person may then wonder how those shapes formed. Observations are made with the senses and with tools. Observations lead to questions that start an investigation. However, scientists continue making observations throughout an investigation.

Research

After scientists ask a question, they do research by studying reference materials. Reference materials include encyclopedias, books, magazines or journals, the Internet, and more. Scientists often write articles that appear in scientific journals. Other scientists read the articles. This helps scientists learn what others have already discovered.

When scientists use information from a reference material, they keep track of where the information came from. They write down the name of the book or article and the name of the person who wrote it. It is important for others to be able to find the reference material the scientists used.

3. **Underline** the information you would need to write down about an article in a scientific journal.

4. **Apply** Look at the cave photos on this page. What research might you want to do before exploring a cave?

This scientist is studying cave formations.

Lightning Lab

Testing Observations
Working by yourself, explore the properties of different rocks. Write down your observations. Then work together as a class. Discuss the observations of others. Write down what you learned as a class that you did not discover on your own.

8 myscienceonLine.com | Got it? | 60-Second Video

picture of a pencil

Practice It!

Find the text features in the textbook page shown above.
Write a clue that each one gives you about the content.

Feature	Clue
caption	tells me that a scientist is shown in the picture
picture of a pencil	
Lightning Lab	

What questions do scientists ask?

Envision It!

Tell what questions scientists might ask about this rock structure.

my pLaneT DiaRY

Science Stats

The Paiute name for it is Paxa Uipi. You know it as the Grand Canyon. The Grand Canyon is located in the state of Arizona.

It is 446 kilometers long and ranges in width from 180 meters to nearly 29 kilometers. It is, on average, 1.6 kilometers deep. The canyon walls reveal layer after colorful layer of rock, nearly 40 of them. The oldest rock, at the bottom of the canyon, is the Vishnu schist. It is approximately 1.7 billion years old.

The Grand Canyon is clearly a wonder of the natural world. People from all over the world come to see this beautiful place.

Examine the statistics listed above. What questions might they make you want to ask about the Grand Canyon?

....

....

I will know what questions scientists ask. I will know how scientists find answers to their questions.

Words to Know

inquiry
investigation

Questions

Science includes **inquiry,** or the process of asking questions and searching for answers. Scientists ask questions about what they observe in the natural world. Someone looks at something carefully and asks about it. For example, a scientist studying Earth might think of a number of questions to ask. *How do islands form? What kinds of rock are on Earth's surface?*

Scientists first study what other scientists have already learned about the answers to their questions. Then scientists do experiments and make observations to find answers. They keep records of their observations and experiments. Keeping records can help them share what they learn with others.

1. ◉ **Text Features** Complete the chart to explain some of the features on this page.

2. **Ask Questions** What question do you think these scientists might be trying to answer?

Feature	Clue
heading	The heading tells that the paragraph is about questions.
picture	*see how scientist use tools when asking quistions*

Investigations

Scientists do investigations to help them find answers to their questions. An **investigation** is a careful way of looking for something. Scientists use process skills in science investigations. You already use many of these skills in your daily life whenever you answer questions or solve problems. You will use them in a more organized way as you do science activities.

Observe

Science often starts when a person observes something. For example, someone could visit a cave and observe the shapes of the cave walls. The person may then wonder how those shapes formed. Observations are made with the senses and with tools. Observations lead to questions that start an investigation. However, scientists continue making observations throughout an investigation.

Research

After scientists ask a question, they do research by studying reference materials. Reference materials include encyclopedias, books, magazines or journals, the Internet, and more. Scientists often write articles that appear in scientific journals. Other scientists read the articles. This helps scientists learn what others have already discovered.

When scientists use information from a reference material, they keep track of where the information came from. They write down the name of the book or article and the name of the person who wrote it. It is important for others to be able to find the reference material the scientists used.

3. **Underline** the information you would need to write down about an article in a scientific journal.

4. **Apply** Look at the cave photos on this page. What research might you want to do before exploring a cave?

....

....

This scientist is studying cave formations.

Lightning Lab

Testing Observations
Working by yourself, explore the properties of different rocks. Write down your observations. Then work together as a class. Discuss the observations of others. Write down what you learned as a class that you did not discover on your own.

Experiment

Scientists use their observations and research to come up with possible answers to their questions. Then they design and run tests to try to confirm those answers. These tests are called experiments. Scientists record their observations during experiments. The results of an experiment may match the earlier answer or provide a different answer. The results of their experiments are added to their earlier observations and research.

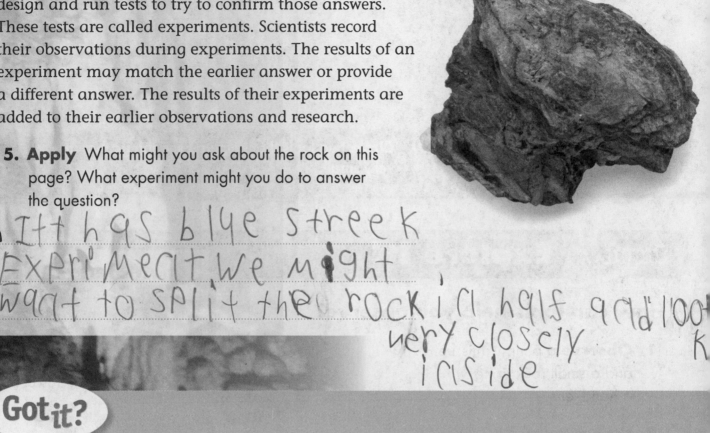

5. **Apply** What might you ask about the rock on this page? What experiment might you do to answer the question?

Itt has blue streek Experiment,we might want to split the rock in half and look very closely inside

Got it?

6. **Ask Questions** What would you like to know about land features in your state? Write a question.

....

7. **Judge** Why might some reference materials be better than others?

....

8. **Infer** Why might scientists repeat experiments?

....

....

⬛ **Stop!** I need help with ....

⏸ **Wait!** I have a question about ....

▶ **Go!** Now I know ....

How do scientists use tools?

Envision It!

Circle two tools that help you see things that are very small.

Inquiry **Explore It!**

How can tools help you observe?

☑ **1. Observe** a penny, a tissue, and a small rock using a hand lens.

☑ **2.** Use a microscope to observe the penny and the tissue.

Materials

penny

microscope

small rock

piece of tissue

hand lens

Explain Your Results

3. Draw a Conclusion Which tool worked better for **observing** each object? Explain.

....

....

....

....

....

Be careful! **Handle microscopes with care.**

myscienceonline.com | **Explore It!** Animation

I will know how to use tools to do science. I will know how to do science safely.

Word to Know

tool

Tools

Scientists use many different kinds of tools. A **tool** is an object or device used to perform a task. The tool you use depends on the task. Tools can help you measure objects or gather information. You can measure volume, temperature, length, distance, mass, and more with the proper tools. Measurements give you exact observations that you can share with others. Scientists choose different tools based on how exact they need their measurements to be.

1. **Underline** two things that tools help you do.

2. **Infer** (Circle) the measurement that is more exact.
   about 5 cm
   5.3 cm

weight

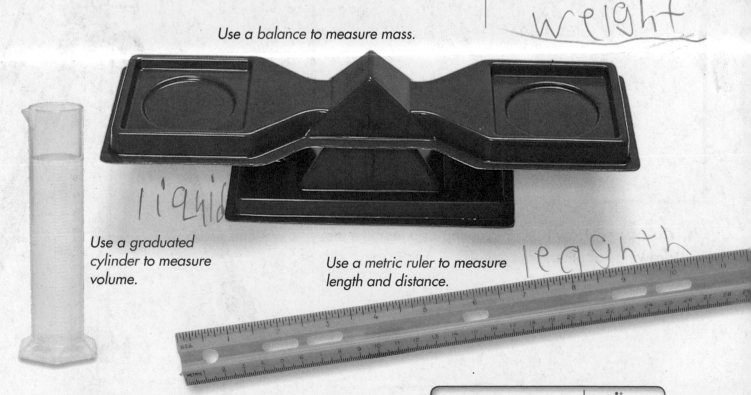

Use a balance to measure mass.

liquid

Use a graduated cylinder to measure volume.

Use a metric ruler to measure length and distance.

length

More Tools

Tools can serve many purposes as you conduct science experiments and investigations. Some tools help with observations, helping you to see things that are very small or very far away in more detail.

Other tools, such as a computer, can help analyze or visualize data. Computers with access to the Internet can help you find information collected by others. A computer can also help you create presentations to communicate your results to others.

Use a hand lens to make objects appear larger. This allows you to see more detail than you could with just your eyes.

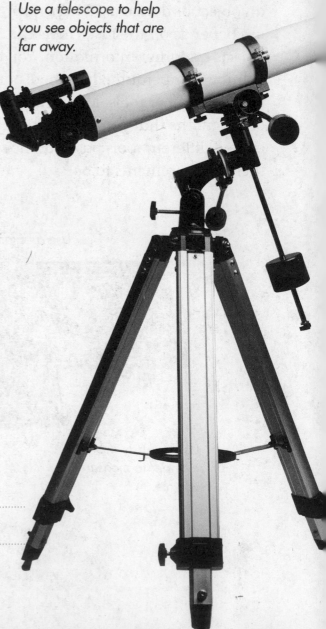

Use a telescope to help you see objects that are far away.

3. **Apply** Use a hand lens to observe a leaf. Draw what you see.

4. **Compare** How is your drawing of a leaf like the drawings of others?

....

....

myscienceonline.com   THE BIG ?   I Will Know...

Use a computer to analyze data.

5. Explain Tell another way you use a computer.

Microscopes use several lenses to make objects appear much larger. Use microscopes to see things in greater detail.

Lightning Lab

Compare Measurements

Use a metric ruler to measure the length of your pencil in centimeters. Record your measurement. Have a partner do the same. Compare your results. Discuss reasons why your measurements might be different. Repeat your measurements using a U.S. standard ruler.

6. Apply Tell what you would look at with a microscope.

Use a thermometer to measure temperature.

Compare Observations

Scientists make observations many times to make sure their data are accurate. Data are the facts you collect as you observe. Scientists record their findings, and then compare their data with the observations of other scientists. Even though groups of scientists may use different tools to observe, their data should be similar.

Comparing your results with others is important. Sometimes there are errors in how observations are made. Sometimes the tool being used has a flaw. Sometimes a scientist misses an important detail.

7.  **Text Features** Why do you think some of the words in the captions are purple?

8. Infer Why do you think people with long hair need to tie it back when they do a science experiment?

....

....

....

9. Identify Suppose you are doing an activity with vinegar and baking soda. (Circle) the safety rules that apply.

Safety

Scientists know that they must work safely when doing experiments and using tools. You need to be careful when you do science activities too. Always follow these safety rules.

Science Safety Rules

- Read the activity carefully before you start.
- Listen to the teacher's instructions. Ask questions about things you do not understand.
- Keep your work area neat and clean. Clean up spills right away.
- Never taste or smell any substance unless directed to do so by your teacher.
- Handle sharp items and other equipment carefully.
- Use chemicals carefully. Dispose of chemicals properly.
- Help keep plants and animals that you use safe.
- Tell your teacher if there is an accident or if you see anything that looks unsafe.
- Wash your hands well when you are finished.
- Wear safety goggles and gloves when necessary.
- Tie back long hair.

10. Explain What do these students need to do to be safe?

....

....

myscienceonline.com | Got it? 60-Second Video

Following safety rules keeps you and others from getting hurt. Some chemicals can damage your skin or eyes. Safety goggles and gloves can protect you from these chemicals. If you are working with something that is sharp or moves quickly, safety goggles will protect your eyes. Gloves can protect your hands.

11. Write The students below are following safety rules. Explain how each student is protected.

Got it?

12. Summarize How can tools help you do science?

13. UNLOCK THE BIG ? **Judge** Why is it important for scientists to compare their observations with the observations of others?

⬛ **Stop!** I need help with

⏸ **Wait!** I have a question about

▶ **Go!** Now I know

Lesson 3
How do scientists answer questions?

Tell what question you have about the starfish.

What helps scientists answer questions?

Scientists try to find answers to questions by following certain principles. In an investigation, they change only one thing, measure how something else changes, and keep everything else the same. Think about these principles as you try to answer this question: How does temperature affect how much salt dissolves?

☑ **1.** To a cup of cold water, add 1 level spoonful of salt and stir until it dissolves. Repeat until the salt no longer dissolves. **Record** how many spoonfuls you added before it stopped dissolving.

☑ **2.** Repeat Step 1 but change from cold water to warm water.

Explain Your Results

3. Identify the one thing you changed.

....

4. Identify what you **measured.**

....

5. Identify one thing you made sure not to change.

....

Materials

plastic cup of very cold water
plastic cup of warm water

salt   spoon

Data Table

	Number of Spoonfuls of Salt
Cold Water	
Warm Water	

mysienceonLine.com | **Explore It!** Animation

I will know some different scientific methods scientists use to answer questions.

Words to Know

scientific methods
hypothesis
evidence
three-dimensional
two-dimensional

Tell how you could find an answer to your question.

Scientific Methods

Scientists use scientific methods as they work. **Scientific methods** are organized ways to answer questions and solve problems. Scientific methods help scientists draw conclusions. Scientists do not always use the same methods. They do not follow the methods in rigid order. Scientists record their method so it can be repeated accurately. You will use scientific methods when you do experiments.

Scientific methods include experiments, observations, surveys, and sampling. In a survey, scientists ask people a number of questions and then analyze the answers. A survey might help scientists find the source of an illness, for example. Sampling is another way of collecting data. Scientists may take samples of a population. They might catch, test, and release birds to see if they are healthy.

1. **Underline** the definition of *scientific methods*.

2. **Evaluate** Cross out the statement that is not true.

   Surveys are one type of scientific method.

   ~~The scientific method follows a rigid order.~~

   Scientists make careful observations.

3. **Ask Questions**
   Suppose the scientist in the picture below wants to see how petrels care for their young. What scientific methods can she use to answer her question?

   observerving the petrels

This scientist studies the habits of petrels.

A Bouncing-Ball Experiment

Science begins with an observation. For example, you may notice that a ball bounces differently in different rooms. These two pages show a series of steps that can be used to design and conduct a bouncing-ball experiment.

Ask a question.

You might have a question about something you observe.

How high will the ball bounce on different surfaces?

State your hypothesis.

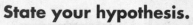

A **hypothesis** is a possible answer to your question. It often predicts an outcome of an experiment. Write it as an *If . . . then . . . because . . .* statement.

If I drop the ball, then it will bounce highest on the rubber mat, because the rubber mat is the most flexible.

Identify and control variables.

Variables are things that can change. For a fair test, choose just one variable to change. Keep the other variables the same.

In this experiment there are 3 types of variables. The *independent variable* is the thing that you change. In this experiment, the surface is the independent variable. The thing that you must measure or observe is the *dependent variable*. Here, the dependent variable is how high the ball bounces. *Controlled variables* are things you keep the same so they do not affect the dependent variable.

Test other surfaces. Bounce the ball off of wood, carpet, and a rubber mat.

4. Identify What are some of the controlled variables?

Temperature

Test your hypothesis.

Make a plan to test your hypothesis. Collect materials and tools. Then follow your plan. Each time you test a surface is called a trial. Repeat each trial three times.

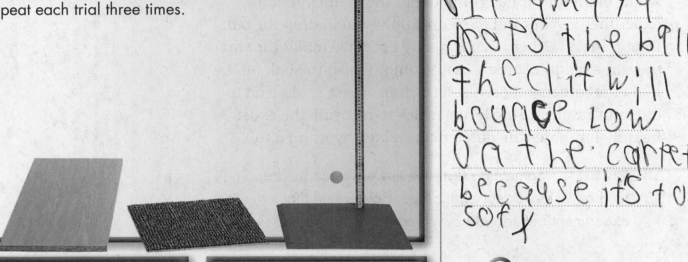

Collect and record your data.

Keep good records of what you do and find out. Use tables and pictures to help.

Interpret your data.

Organize your notes and records to make them clear. Make diagrams, charts, or graphs to help.

State your conclusion.

Your conclusion is a decision you make based on your data. Communicate what you found out. Tell whether your data supported your hypothesis.

The data did not support my hypothesis. The ball bounced highest when dropped onto the piece of wood.

Try it again.

Do the experiment a few more times. The results of one experiment might not be right. Be sure to do everything exactly the same each time.

5. Generate Write a new hypothesis about how high the ball will bounce on different surfaces.

If amaya drops the ball then it will bounce low on the carpet because its to soft

6. ◉ Text Features
Why are pictures shown with some of the steps?

evidence to show the evidence

7. Predict Tell how the outcome of the experiment might change when the experiment is repeated.

It will stay the same.

Creativity

Scientists have to be creative when designing experiments. They need to think of ways to control variables so trials are the same. They need to think of what might go wrong. Think about the bouncing ball experiment. What if the scientist only said to drop the ball from a table? Other scientists may not have tables that are the same height. Some scientists might push the ball off the table and others might just let it drop. These could lead to different results. Using a meterstick to measure the exact height eliminates the differences created by using a table.

8. CHALLENGE Sometimes tests like this are done by dropping the ball inside a clear plastic tube. How would that make the experiment better and how could it make it worse?

Observation and Evidence

Scientists make careful observations to find answers to their questions. Taking measurements is one way scientists can make observations. Scientists use evidence to decide whether their hypotheses are correct. Observations and facts gained from experiments are **evidence.**

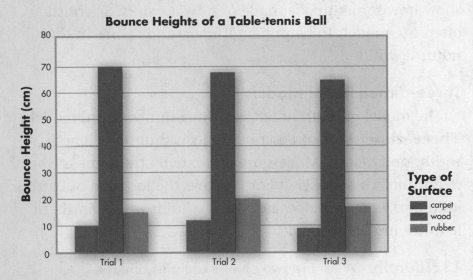

Bounce Heights of a Table-tennis Ball

Bounce Height (cm)

Trial 1   Trial 2   Trial 3

Type of Surface
- carpet
- wood
- rubber

Estimates and Measurements

Scientists often make estimates. They tell what they think an object's size, mass, or temperature will measure. Then they measure these factors in units. Scientists usually measure in metric units. The United States commonly uses non-metric units such as gallons, pounds, and inches.

Multiple Trials

A single trial may not give an accurate result. Because of this, scientists perform multiple trials during an experiment. When all the results are gathered together, patterns should develop. How many trials to perform depends on what you are trying to test. For example, the chart above shows results from three trials. Notice that all the heights in the trials are different. If you were testing the exact height a ball would bounce on a surface, you should complete several trials.

9. **Exemplify** What would you observe in the bouncing-ball experiment?

....

....

....

....

....

....

10. **Analyze** Do three trials give enough evidence to show which surface makes the ball bounce highest? Why or why not?

....

....

....

....

....

....

....

21

This is the largest moving model of Earth in the world.

Models

Sometimes scientists want to test things they cannot test on actual objects. For example, a scientist may want to know how strong winds affect an airplane. The scientist can test a model of the plane using a wind tunnel. Models are objects or ideas that represent other things. They may show how something is made or how it works. Scientists often use models to help them understand things in the natural world.

Three-dimensional models

The model of Earth at left is a three-dimensional model. **Three-dimensional** describes objects that have length, width, and height. Models are not exactly the same as the real thing. This model of Earth shows the location of Earth's land and water but does not show what is inside Earth, or features made by people.

11. Identify What are two other examples of three-dimensional models?

book peacil

Two-dimensional models

Some models are two-dimensional. **Two-dimensional** describes something that has length and width but not height. Two-dimensional models are flat. A map is an example of a two-dimensional model.

12. Produce Draw a two-dimensional model of your classroom.

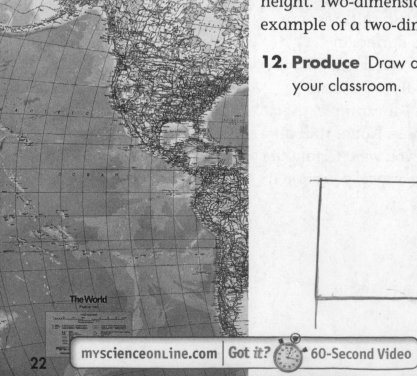

Explanations

After scientists design their experiments and run trials, they use evidence to explain the results. The explanation should answer the original question the experiment was designed to ask. The explanation will also tell whether the hypothesis was supported by data. An important thing to remember is that a hypothesis is a possible answer to the question. It is based on the best information you have at the time, but if your results do not support the hypothesis, an experiment is not a failure. It still gives information about the question.

At-Home Lab

Trial Testing
Test how high a table-tennis ball will bounce on concrete. Use the procedure from the bouncing-ball experiment. Record your data. Be sure to do multiple trials. Compare your data with others. Explain why the data might be different. Draw a conclusion.

13. Summarize What was the hypothesis in the bouncing-ball experiment? Did the data support the hypothesis?

See how high the ball will bounce is the hypothesis

Got it?

14. Summarize Name three methods scientists might use to investigate a question or problem.

observe, reserch, Expiriements,

15. UNLOCK THE BIG ? Why do you think evidence is important in science?

for people to know the scientist are telling the truth

⬛ **Stop!** I need help with

⏸ **Wait!** I have a question about

▶ **Go!** Now I know

How do scientists draw conclusions?

Envision It!

Tell what you think this scientist is writing down.

Explore It!

How can data help you draw a conclusion?

☑ **1.** Put the paper clips in a cup. Dip a magnet into the cup. Pull it out. Count the paper clips it picked up. **Record** your **data.**

☑ **2.** Repeat your trials 2 more times. Record. Make a bar graph

Explain Your Results

3. Communicate Compare the **records** of your **data** with the records made by other groups.

4. Draw a Conclusion Based on the data you recorded, how many paper clips is your magnet able to pick up? How did the data help you draw your conclusion?

Materials

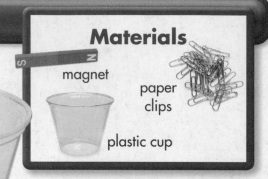

magnet

paper clips

plastic cup

Paper Clips Picked Up

Trial	Number
1	
2	
3	

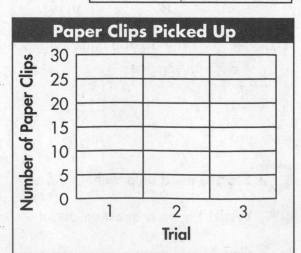

Paper Clips Picked Up

Number of Paper Clips — 30, 25, 20, 15, 10, 5, 0

Trial — 1, 2, 3

UNLOCK THE BIG ?

I will know how scientists keep records in order to share conclusions with other scientists.

Words to Know

procedure
inference

Record Procedures

The bouncing-ball experiment from the previous lesson identifies different variables to test the hypothesis. How can other scientists use the experiment to get their own results? How can you use the results to draw conclusions?

The scientist in the photo above is keeping records of underwater observations. Scientists must also carefully record how they performed experiments in procedures. A **procedure** is a set of step-by-step instructions for how to perform a test. When you write a procedure, be sure to be clear. This allows others to repeat the test to get similar results. When repeating an experiment, it is important to do a test exactly the same way each time.

1. **Analyze** What might happen if a procedure is not clearly written?

the scientist will not get the same result

Question: A table-tennis ball will bounce highest on which surface?

Hypothesis: If I drop the ball, then it will bounce highest on the rubber mat, because the rubber mat is the most flexible.

Materials: table-tennis ball, piece of wood, rubber mat, piece of carpet, meterstick

Procedure:
1. Place the piece of wood on the floor. Hold the meterstick upright on the wood.

2. Drop the table-tennis ball from a height of 1 meter onto the wood. Be careful not to push or throw the ball down.

3. Record how high the ball bounces.

4. Repeat Steps 1–3 using the rubber mat.

5. Repeat Steps 1–3 using the piece of carpet.

6. Repeat the entire experiment two more times.

Keep Records

By keeping detailed and accurate records of observations, scientists are able to share their information with others. The more scientists repeat an experiment and get the same results, the more they can rely on the data. Conclusions based on reliable data are more likely to continue to be useful in the future. For example, think of the diver on the previous page. If the records of the dive are accurate, scientists can look for more or different information on future dives.

Scientists continue to repeat an experiment until they are sure of the results. If scientists repeat an experiment and get different results, they look for reasons why the experiment was different. Good records and procedures can be helpful in finding those reasons.

Organize Your Data

Scientists keep accurate records of their experiments. Often they organize their data in a table. The table below contains important information about the bouncing-ball experiment. The title explains what was tested. The table names the materials used and gives the test results. The table also shows that the experiment was done three times.

2. ◉ **Text Features**
What information does the table give you?

....

....

3. Conclude Make a conclusion based on the data. Which surface caused the ball to bounce highest?

the ball bouced the highest on the wood

Bounce Heights of a Table-tennis Ball			
Material	Bounce Height (cm)		
	Trial 1	Trial 2	Trial 3
Carpet	10	12	9
Wood	70	68	65
Rubber	15	20	17

Presenting Data

There are many different formats for organizing and arranging your data. The table on the previous page is one format. Charts and graphs can also be helpful because they show information in a way that is easy to understand. However you format your data, it should be clearly labeled.

Bar graph

A bar graph uses rectangular bars to compare data. The bars may be vertical or horizontal. The bars often have different colors or shading for each variable.

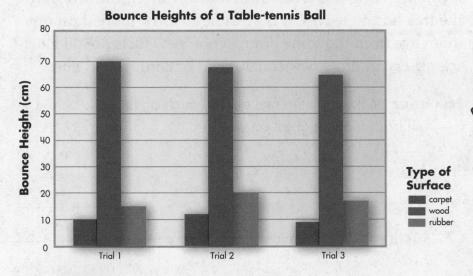

Bounce Heights of a Table-tennis Ball

Line graph

Line graphs connect points of data on a graph with straight lines. Line graphs are often used to show patterns of data over time. For example, a line graph could show the amount of rainfall a place gets over two weeks. A graph may use different colored lines to compare different data.

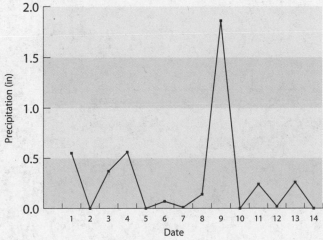

Daily Precipitation, Dallas-Ft. Worth Airport, October 2009

4. **Conclude** In the bar graph shown here, what would happen if the color key was missing?

5. **Express Data** Work with a partner to write a 1–2 sentence explanation of the data in the line graph. Read your explanation.

Evidence and Inferences

Scientists base their explanations on evidence. Evidence includes any information you have and observations that you make. An observation from an experiment is a piece of evidence. Facts you already have, or research you have done, are also evidence.

Scientists use evidence to make inferences. An **inference** is a conclusion drawn from data and observations. For example, the statement *The tree has no leaves on it* is an observation. *The tree lost its leaves because the season is fall* is an inference. It is a conclusion drawn from the fact that the tree has no leaves. It is possible to draw more than one inference from the same data. When new facts are added, scientists can draw new conclusions or confirm old ones.

8. Infer Someone noticed that a tree had no leaves and inferred that it lost its leaves because the season was fall. Write another reasonable inference based on this observation.

6. Infer Make an inference about which of the balls below will bounce the highest on wood.

....

....

7. Justify What evidence supports your inference?

....

....

fabric ball   golf ball   table-tennis ball

Reasonable Answers

Scientists attempt to develop reasonable answers to the questions they pose. To do this, they use evidence from their observations and experiments. For the bouncing-ball experiment, you would use evidence gathered by doing the procedure from the previous pages. A reasonable answer should not favor one opinion over another unless it is supported by evidence.

Compare Results

Scientists often compare their methods or procedures with those of their peers. They also compare their results. By comparing methods and results, scientists can work to find results that can be retested.

In the bouncing-ball experiment, one group can compare their results with another group. The scientists determine whether the results are similar or different. They try to explain why the results are similar or different. Scientists often do this to think of new questions or better ways to perform a test.

9. **Decide** Why is it important to compare results with others?

....

....

....

....

Lightning Lab

Observations and Inferences
Examine a coin. List everything you can about the coin that is factual. Next, make some inferences about the coin or the country that minted it. Compare your lists of facts and inferences with those of your classmates.

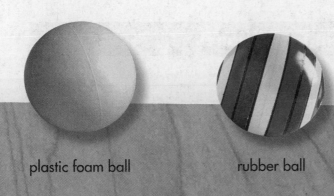

plastic foam ball   rubber ball

Go Further

Once an experiment is complete, scientists use what they learn. The results of an experiment can become part of the background research other scientists use for future experiments. An experiment may lead to new questions to test. Scientists may also think of better ways to do a test.

10. Formulate Suppose you wanted to get a more precise measurement of how high the ball would bounce on wood. How would you change the experiment?

Think back to the bouncing-ball experiment. The original question was how high a ball would bounce on different surfaces. The hypothesis was that a rubber surface would make the ball bounce higher. The conclusion was a wood surface made the ball bounce higher. The completed experiment might raise questions about how other surfaces would affect the ball. Or it may raise questions about the ball itself. Does the ball bounce differently if it is hot or cold? How might it bounce compared to other balls?

12. Predict This scientist is testing a pesticide on plants in a laboratory. When this experiment is complete, how might it lead to a new experiment?

11. Revise Suppose you wanted to perform three trials to test how high a ball bounced if it was at a cooler temperature. How might you organize your results? Complete the table below. (Circle) the independent variables in the completed table.

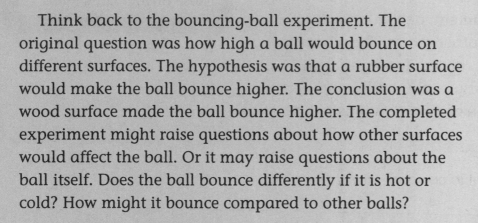

Bounce Heights at Different Temperatures			

myscienceonline.com | Got it? | 60-Second Video

Interpret Data

Three different students tried the experiment with the table-tennis ball. They tested materials to see which caused the ball to bounce highest. The chart shows their results.

Bounce Heights of a Table-tennis Ball

Material	Bounce Height (cm)		
	Student A	Student B	Student C
Carpet	7	12	6
Wood	70	73	65
Rubber	12	20	13

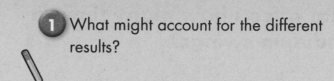

1 What might account for the different results?

....

....

....

2 What question were students trying to answer? What can they conclude?

....

....

....

Got it?

13. ◉ **Compare and Contrast** How is evidence different from an inference?

....

....

14. Evaluate Why is it important to do an experiment the same way each time?

....

■ **Stop!** I need help with ....

❚❚ **Wait!** I have a question about ....

▶ **Go!** Now I know ....

What affects how many times a pendulum swings?

Follow a Procedure

☑ **1.** Set up a pendulum system.

☑ **2. Identify variables** that might change how many times the pendulum swings in 15 seconds. Use the materials you have. Make a list with other groups.

....

....

....

....

☑ **3.** Choose a variable to investigate. Which variable did you choose?

....

....

....

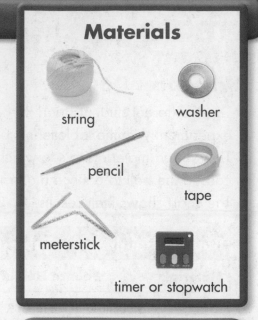

Materials

string

washer

pencil

tape

meterstick

timer or stopwatch

Inquiry Skill
Record your data on a chart. This can help you make **inferences** based on the data.

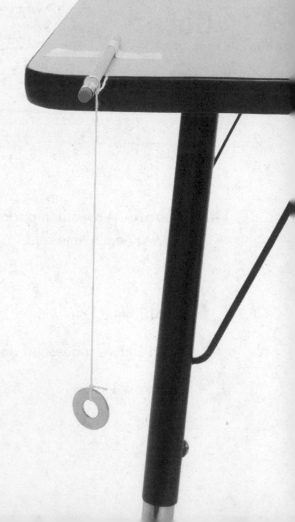

4. Swing the pendulum. **Measure** the number of swings in 15 seconds. **Record** on the chart.

5. Change the value of your variable. Repeat Step 4.

Observations of Pendulum Swings	
Variable: _____	Number of Swings in 15 seconds

Analyze and Conclude

6. Communicate Compare your results with other groups. Which variable had the greatest effect on the pendulum?

....

....

....

7. UNLOCK THE BIG ? **Infer** How did scientific methods help you during your investigation?

....

....

....

....

STEM

Healthcare Technology

Did you know your body has defense systems against germs? It does! These defenses include tears, saliva, skin, and blood. For example, the skin stops germs from entering the body. These defense systems help us resist germs and viruses in our environment.

What happens, though, if you get a cut? How can you help your body's defense systems? You could use a bandage to cover a cut! This helps your body defend itself. You could also get a shot to prevent infection! Bandages, needles, and shots are examples of healthcare technology. Doctors and nurses use this technology to help keep you safe from diseases.

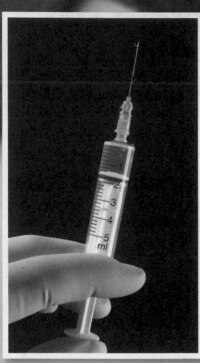

Vaccines help prevent the spread of viruses. One vaccine prevents the spread of diseases such as influenza, or the flu. A vaccine is a preparation of weakened germs that can keep people from getting sick.

Hypothesize How do bandages mimic the job of the skin?

Vocabulary Smart Cards

inquiry
investigation
tool
scientific methods
hypothesis
evidence
three-dimensional
two-dimensional
procedure
inference

Play a Game!

Cut out the Vocabulary Smart Cards.

Work with a partner. Choose a Vocabulary Smart Card.

Say as many words as you can think of that are related to that vocabulary word in some way.

Have your partner guess the word.

scientific methods

métodos científicos

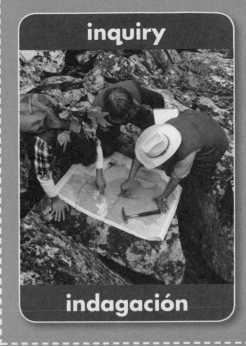

inquiry

indagación

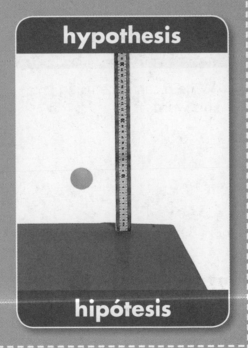

hypothesis

hipótesis

investigation

investigación

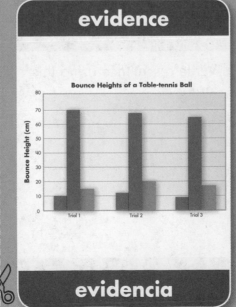

evidence

Bounce Heights of a Table-tennis Ball

Bounce Height (cm)

Trial 1   Trial 2   Trial 3

evidencia

tool

instrumento

the process of asking questions and searching for answers

Write a sentence using the verb form of this word.

....

....

....

proceso que consiste en preguntar y buscar respuestas

organized ways to answer questions and solve problems

Write two examples.

....

....

....

....

maneras organizadas de responder a preguntas y resolver problemas

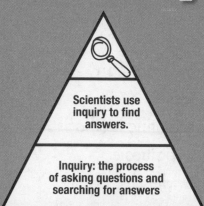

Scientists use inquiry to find answers.

Inquiry: the process of asking questions and searching for answers

Make a Word Pyramid!

Choose a vocabulary word and write the definition in the base of the pyramid. Write a sentence in the middle of the pyramid. Draw a picture of an example, or of something related, at the top.

a careful way of looking for something

Write three related words.

....

....

....

manera cuidadosa de buscar algo

a possible answer to a question

Write a sentence using this word.

....

....

....

....

respuesta posible a una pregunta

an object or device used to perform a task

Draw an example.

objeto o herramienta que se usa para hacer un trabajo

observations and facts gained from experiments

Write a sentence using this term.

....

....

....

observaciones y datos obtenidos de experimentos

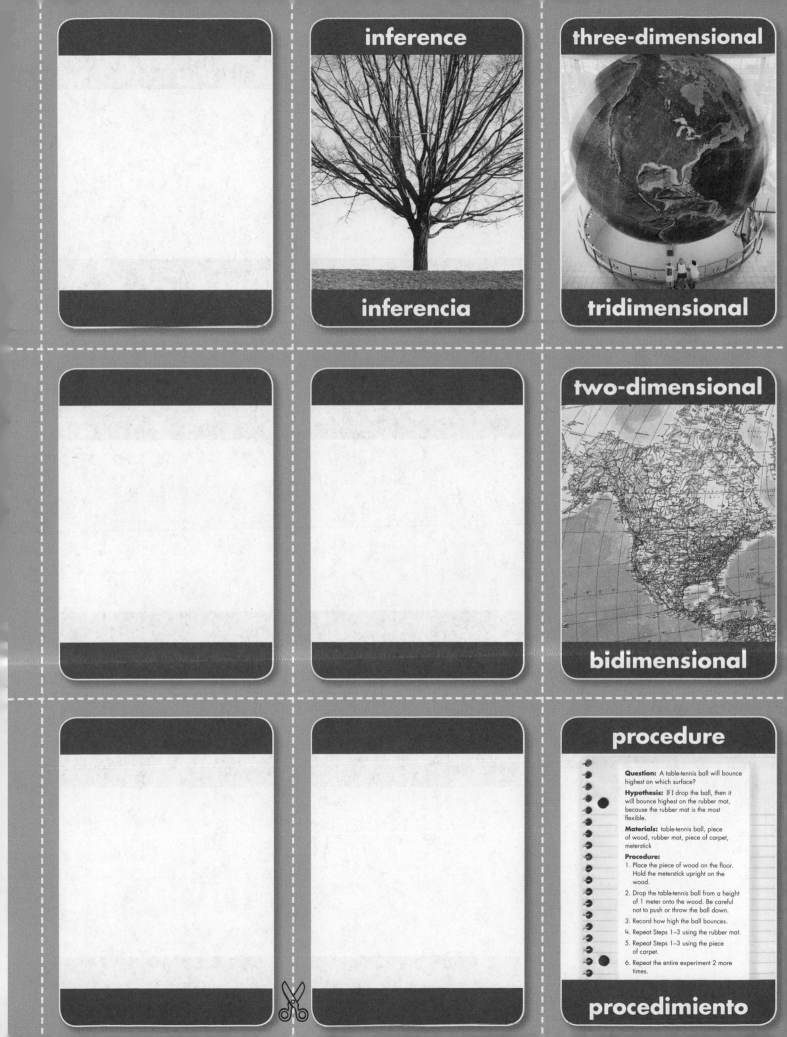

inference

inferencia

three-dimensional

tridimensional

two-dimensional

bidimensional

procedure

Question: A table-tennis ball will bounce highest on which surface?

Hypothesis: If I drop the ball, then it will bounce highest on the rubber mat, because the rubber mat is the most flexible.

Materials: table-tennis ball, piece of wood, rubber mat, piece of carpet, meterstick

Procedure:
1. Place the piece of wood on the floor. Hold the meterstick upright on the wood.
2. Drop the table-tennis ball from a height of 1 meter onto the wood. Be careful not to push or throw the ball down.
3. Record how high the ball bounces.
4. Repeat Steps 1–3 using the rubber mat.
5. Repeat Steps 1–3 using the piece of carpet.
6. Repeat the entire experiment 2 more times.

procedimiento

describes objects that have length, width, and height

Write three examples.

....
....
....
....

describe objetos que tienen largo, ancho y altura

---

a conclusion drawn from data and observations

Write a sentence using the verb form of this word.

....
....
....

conclusión que se saca de los datos y de las observaciones

---

describes something that has length and width, but not height

Draw an example.

describe algo que tiene largo y ancho, pero no tiene altura

....
....
....

....
....
....

---

a set of step-by-step instructions

Write three related words.

....
....
....
....

instrucciones paso por paso

....
....
....

....
....
....

Lesson 1

What questions do scientists ask?

- Scientists ask questions about the natural world.
- Scientists observe and do research while conducting investigations.
- Scientists develop hypotheses based on collected data.

Lesson 2

How do scientists use tools?

- A tool is an object or device used to perform a task.
- Scientists use many tools, including thermometers, microscopes, balances, and computers.

Lesson 3

How do scientists answer questions?

- Scientific methods are organized steps for doing an investigation.
- Evidence is used to develop reasonable answers to questions.
- Scientists compare their results with other scientists' results.

Lesson 4

How do scientists draw conclusions?

- Procedures are step-by-step instructions for how to perform tests.
- Scientists keep detailed and accurate records in order to share their findings with others.

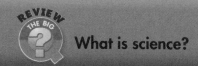
Lesson 1

What questions do scientists ask?

1. **Vocabulary** Inquiry is the process of
   A. doing work.
   B. asking questions.
   C. analyzing data.
   D. reporting results.

2. **Explain** How can scientists develop explanations about data?

   Text
   they use
   scieace tools.
   and do reserch

3. **Ask Questions** A team of scientists is studying the formation of islands in the Pacific Ocean. Provide a question that the team might ask.

   How did trees
   grow. How did
   sand grow.

   9lso to help ←
   other sientist
   do the expirement

Lesson 2

How do scientists use tools?

Measurement Long Ago

Long ago, people measured by using familiar objects. They used a forearm or a foot to measure length. For smaller measurements, they might have used the width of a man's thumb. They measured weight with stones or even with seeds from different plants.

4. **Text Features** What does the heading in the passage above tell you?

   It tells me what
   I will read about
   measurment Loca
   9g or

5. **Recognize** A graduated cylinder is used to measure
   A. temperature.
   B. mass.
   C. volume.
   D. weight.

6. **Explain** Why do scientists use tools to measure things and gather information?

   Leara about it
   to find a soluletion

Lesson 3

How do scientists answer questions?

7. **Summarize** What are some of the
organized steps that scientists use to
answer questions and solve problems?

Ask a question
identify and control
variables
collect and record
data figure out
what the data says
state there conclusion

8. **Evaluate** In an experiment, the thing
you are trying to measure or observe is
the

A. controlled variable.

B. dependent variable.

C. independent variable.

D. hypothesis.

Lesson 4

How do scientists draw conclusions?

9. **Write about It** Why do scientists keep
detailed and accurate records?

scientist keep
detailed acurate
to see if they
carl get the same
resuts

10. **APPLY THE BIG ?** **What is science?**

What does it mean to be
a scientist?

Benchmark Practice

Science,
Engineering,
and
Technology

Fill in the bubble next to the answer choice you think is correct
for each multiple-choice question.

1 Scientific knowledge is based on

- Ⓐ opinions.
- Ⓑ evidence.
- Ⓒ guesses.
- Ⓓ predictions.

2 What is a hypothesis?

- Ⓐ an observation
- Ⓑ a possible answer to a question
- Ⓒ a problem to be solved
- Ⓓ an accurate measurement

3 Which of these is not a measuring tool?

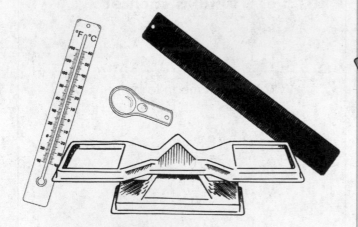

- Ⓐ a thermometer
- Ⓑ a pan balance
- Ⓒ a meterstick
- Ⓓ a hand lens

4 In a fair test, how many variables will change?

- Ⓐ 1
- Ⓑ 2
- Ⓒ 3
- Ⓓ 4

5 An inference is

- Ⓐ a question to be answered.
- Ⓑ a conclusion based on observations.
- Ⓒ a measurement that is not exact.
- Ⓓ the result of an experiment.

6 How might a three-dimensional model of a house be useful to the people constructing the house? Explain your answer.

....

....

....

....

....

....

....

Observing Plants

You can practice the skill of observation by carefully examining a plant. Go outside with an adult and a notebook. Bring a hand lens if you like. Find a plant that interests you. It can be in a garden, or it can be growing wild. Do not touch the plant. Observe the plant carefully. Draw the plant. Then write down observations about how it looks.

Illustrate Draw the plant.

Record observations about how it looks.

....

....

....

Use reference materials from your school media center to identify the plant. Write down the name of the plant and the title of the reference material you used.

....

....

What can you test in a wind tunnel?

Technology and Design

 Try It! How can you design a hovercraft?

Lesson 1 What is technology?

Lesson 2 What is the design process?

Investigate It! Which boat design will hold more cargo?

Scientists and engineers use wind tunnels to test how air moves around cars, planes, people, or other objects. The smoother the air flows around an object, the faster the object can travel and the less energy it will need to move.

 Predict What can a downhill skier learn from wind tunnel tests? Explain your answer.

....

....

....

THE BIG ? How does technology affect our lives?

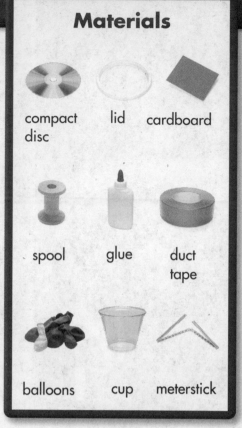

Materials

compact disc

lid

cardboard

spool

glue

duct tape

balloons

cup

meterstick

Inquiry ▸ Try It!

How can you design a hovercraft?

☑ **1. Design** a hovercraft. Use a spool for the nozzle. The nozzle will direct the airflow from the balloon to the body of the hovercraft.

☑ **2.** As part of the design, you will need to **choose materials.** Choose a balloon, a hovercraft body, and a way to attach the nozzle to the hovercraft body.

☐ **3.** Which materials will you use?

....

....

Inquiry Skill
You can **make and use a model** to test different designs you make.

☑ **4.** Build and test your hovercraft design.
Measure how far it travels. ....cm

☑ **5. Redesign** your hovercraft so it travels farther. **Communicate** your changes to others.

Explain Your Results

6. As a class, which combination of materials worked best?

....

....

7. **UNLOCK THE BIG ?** **Interpret Data** How did your **redesign** affect the distance the hovercraft traveled?

....

....

46

Cause and Effect

- A **cause** is why something happens.
- An **effect** is what happens.
- When you read, sometimes clue words such as ~~because~~ and ~~since~~ indicate a relationship of cause and effect.

Rubber Tires

Before the 1800s, wheels were made of wood and metal. A thin metal tire was wrapped around a wood rim. Riding in a vehicle with these rigid tires was very bumpy. Because of this, some inventors decided to use rubber to make tires. The flexibility of rubber made the ride less bumpy. Today, rubber tires are used on bikes, cars, tractors, and trucks.

Practice It!

Use the graphic organizer below to list one cause and one effect found in the example paragraph.

Cause

wooden tires was a very bubpy ride

Effect

some inventors decided to use rubber tires

What is technology?

Tell what problem this communications satellite might help solve.

MY PLANET DiARY

Ray Harroun's 1911 racecar

Side-view mirror

Rear-view camera in automobile

Connections

Sometimes adding older technology to something new can help solve problems. The first Indianapolis 500 automobile race was held in 1911. Racecars at the time carried two people. A mechanic would ride with the driver. The mechanic would fix the car and warn the driver about cars behind them.

Driver Ray Harroun was also an automobile designer. He designed a racecar with room for only one person. To see behind the car, Harroun attached a mirror above the steering wheel. It became the first known rear-view mirror on an automobile. Driving without a mechanic was risky, but it paid off. Harroun became the first Indy 500 winner.

Cars today are still built with rear-view and side-view mirrors. However, there is new technology to help drivers know what is around them. Some cars use video cameras so drivers can see behind them. Some cars have sensors in the bumpers. Sounds or computerized voices may signal the driver if a car is too close to a curb.

What other technologies can improve a car's safety?

seat belts gps system wipers Airbags breaks

UNLOCK THE BIG ?

I will know how technology solves problems and makes work easier.

Word to Know

technology

Scientific Discoveries

Scientific discoveries change our lives. The discovery of bacteria helped us develop modern medicine. Discoveries about how electricity works brought us telephones, computers, refrigerators, light bulbs, and many more devices. Scientific discoveries often lead to new technologies. **Technology** is the knowledge, processes, and products that solve problems and make work easier.

Just as scientific methods are used to answer scientific questions, people often use a process to design technology. This process involves identifying a problem, researching and testing possible solutions, and then redesigning if necessary.

This smartphone combines many technologies into one device. The icons on the screen show some of its functions.

1. **Identify** <u>Underline</u> the definition of technology.

2. ◉ **Cause and Effect** Write one cause and effect related to technology.

Cause	Effect
GPS from technology	No more maps.

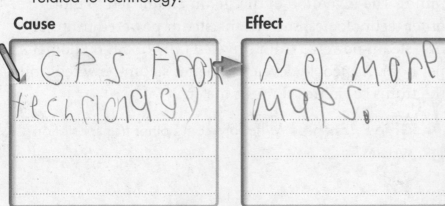

3. **Identify** What do you think people can do with a smartphone in addition to making phone calls?

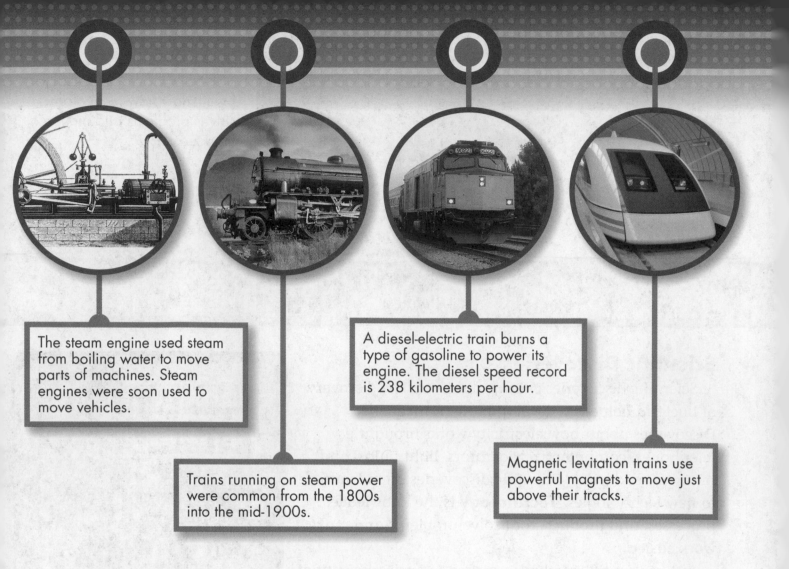

The steam engine used steam from boiling water to move parts of machines. Steam engines were soon used to move vehicles.

Trains running on steam power were common from the 1800s into the mid-1900s.

A diesel-electric train burns a type of gasoline to power its engine. The diesel speed record is 238 kilometers per hour.

Magnetic levitation trains use powerful magnets to move just above their tracks.

5. Predict Many large cities have problems with heavy traffic. What technology might be developed in the future to help solve this problem?

people getting supperpowers like teleporting or flying

Technology and Transportation Systems

Transportation systems move people and goods from place to place. Technology has made transportation systems faster and safer. Long trips that once took days or weeks may now take only hours.

During the 1700s, steam engines were being developed. They first were used to operate machines in factories and mines. The invention of the steam engine led to many other technologies, such as the steam-powered train. The first steam-powered train traveled only about 6 kilometers per hour. As people developed better steam-powered trains, the trains could travel much faster.

4. Give Examples What are some other transportation systems?

Steam trains had some disadvantages. Water was heated inside a boiler, changing the water to steam. As the water changed to steam, pressure would build up inside the boiler. Sometimes the heat inside the boiler would melt a hole in the steel. The sudden release of steam out of the hole would cause the boiler to explode.

Electric, diesel, and magnetic levitation trains have replaced steam-powered trains. These trains are safer since they do not have a boiler that could explode. These trains are also faster. Magnetic levitation trains can reach speeds of more than 500 kilometers per hour.

GPS device

GPS technology keeps track of this city bus's location.

Today's transportation systems often use computer technology. Computers keep systems running properly and on time. Global Positioning System (GPS) technology sends location data from satellites orbiting Earth. A driver using a GPS device can get directions to a destination. Some city bus systems now have GPS in their buses. People waiting for a bus can use cell phones to find out if their bus is running on time.

6. **Apply** What is another problem a GPS device might solve?

....

....

....

....

Kitchen Technology

Carefully examine a can opener. Draw a diagram of the can opener and identify its parts. Write about how you think the can opener works.

Everyday Technologies

You may be surprised at the technology you can find in your home or at school. Can openers, microwave ovens, refrigerators, windows, pens, computers, clocks, and microphones are all technologies.

Technology at Home

In the past, people would have to eat fresh fruits and vegetables soon after they bought them. As fruits and vegetables ripen, they release a gas that causes them to spoil. When they are kept cool, the spoiling process slows down. The invention of the refrigerator helped solve the problem of fruits and vegetables quickly spoiling. Today, new technologies are still being developed to keep food fresh. There are certain minerals that absorb the gas that causes fruits and vegetables to spoil. Special green food-storage bags are made with these minerals. Fruits and vegetables stored in these bags stay fresh even longer.

There are other technologies for heating food. You can have an entire meal ready in minutes using a microwave oven. Some new stoves use electromagnets instead of gas or electricity to produce heat. These new stoves are also more efficient. They use less energy than gas or electric stoves and can boil water in 90 seconds.

Green food-storage bag technology solves the problem of food quickly spoiling.

7. **Cause and Effect** How has the technology to keep food fresh affected how you eat?

cause Food going bad
Effect invented refrigera

computer

microwave oven

Technology at School

Many schools have public address systems so that announcements can be made to the entire school. These systems are a form of technology. The announcer speaks into a microphone where the sound is changed into electricity. The electricity travels through wires to speakers throughout the school. The speakers turn the electricity back into sound and you hear the announcement.

Many teachers have started using electronic white boards to teach. These white boards allow the students to learn lessons in a different way. Students can interact with the white board.

public address system

8. **Infer** How do you think an electronic white board could be used in your classroom?

....

....

electronic white board

Got it?

9. **Explain** How has train transportation changed over time?

....

....

....

10. **UNLOCK THE BIG ?** Identify one technology you use everyday. How does it affect your life?

....

....

⬛ **Stop!** I need help with ....

⏸ **Wait!** I have a question about ....

▶ **Go!** Now I know ....

What is the design process?

Why do you think these aircraft have different designs?

 **Explore It!**

How can the design of a model help you learn about the real thing?

☑ **1.** Make 2 paper planes (**models**) with wings of different shapes but the same size (area). Plane A has wide, short wings. Plane B has long, narrow wings.

☑ **2.** Make a plan to test how far each plane flies. Test each plane 3 times. **Record** your **data.**

Explain Your Results

3. Draw a Conclusion How might the shape of a plane's wings affect how far it flies?

....

....

4. Communicate Based on what you learned, discuss the shape of wings on passenger planes.

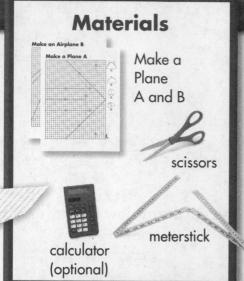

Materials

Make a Plane A and B

scissors

calculator (optional)

meterstick

Effect of Wing Shape on Distance Traveled		
Trial	Distance Traveled (meters)	
	Plane A (wide, short wings)	Plane B (long, narrow wings)
1		
2		
3		
Average		

myscienceonline.com | **Explore It!** Animation

Words to Know

design process
prototype

Design Process

People often have problems that can be solved with a new product or an improved process. For example, people have always looked for faster ways to travel from one place to another.

Orville and Wilbur Wright had a dream to design the world's first piloted and powered flying machine. Other inventors had created gliders. A glider is a kind of aircraft that can sail from a high place to a lower one without a motor. Early gliders were difficult to control. After many experiments, Orville and Wilbur invented a way to control flight. On December 17, 1903, their motorized airplane, the *Flyer,* flew for 12 seconds.

The way the Wright brothers designed the airplane can show how the design process is used. The **design process** is a set of steps for developing products and processes that solve problems.

1. **Identify** **Underline** the definition of the design process.

2. **Predict** Why is it important to use the design process when developing a new product?

The steps give a person a easy way of developing a new product

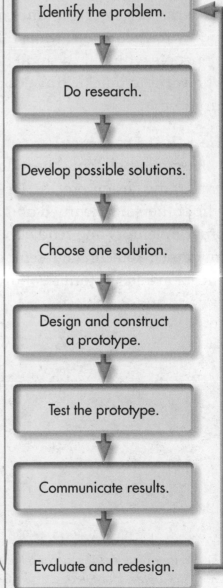

Identify the problem.

Do research.

Develop possible solutions.

Choose one solution.

Design and construct a prototype.

Test the prototype.

Communicate results.

Evaluate and redesign.

Steps of the Design Process

Many people, such as engineers and scientists, use the design process when forming a solution to a problem. They may use different steps or use them in a different order. However, the goal of finding a solution to a problem remains the same.

Step 1: Identify the problem.

The first step in the design process is to identify the problem. One of the problems the Wright brothers noticed was that aircraft could not turn easily.

When you identify the problem, it is also important to identify who will benefit from your solution. If they could control how the airplane turned, then it could be used by almost anyone who wanted to learn how to fly. Modern passenger airplanes are designed to be used by highly trained pilots, while other airplanes can be used by people with only a small amount of training. People who want to quickly travel long distances benefit from the airplane.

Step 2: Do research.

Researching what others have learned is an important part of the design process. Orville and Wilbur researched what others had learned about flight. They talked to other inventors and read about the experiments of other inventors. You can do research by using the Internet, encyclopedias, informational books, and by interviewing experts on the subject.

3. Identify Name a problem that can be solved by a new design. Who would use your design?

hacking proof phone

4. Infer Why do you think research is important?

to know what you're doing

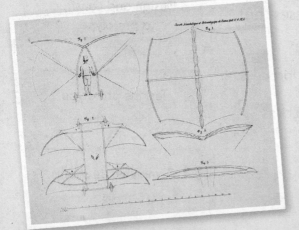

The Wright brothers researched the work of Sir George Cayley. Here is one of Sir Cayley's diagrams.

This picture shows one of Otto Lilienthal's gliding experiments. His work was also part of the Wrights' research.

myscienceonline.com | THE BIG ? | I Will Know...

Step 3: Develop possible solutions.

The next step is to think of one or more solutions to the problem. Wilbur decided to make airplane wings that could be twisted. The wings could then be moved to turn the plane. Orville and Wilbur called twisting the wings of the plane "wing-warping."

It is important to measure the size and weight and identify the shape of each part of your design. How much each part weighs can affect how your design works. Drawing or building a model of your solution helps you determine which solution is best.

Math and science will help you develop possible solutions to your design problem. The Wright brothers made careful measurements and calculations to perfect the design of the airplane. Knowledge of scientific principles related to motion helped them develop solutions.

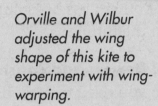

Orville and Wilbur adjusted the wing shape of this kite to experiment with wing-warping.

5. **Compare** Look at the captions and images on this page. How has adjusting an aircraft's wing-shape changed?

modern planes do not use wing warping they use ailedons

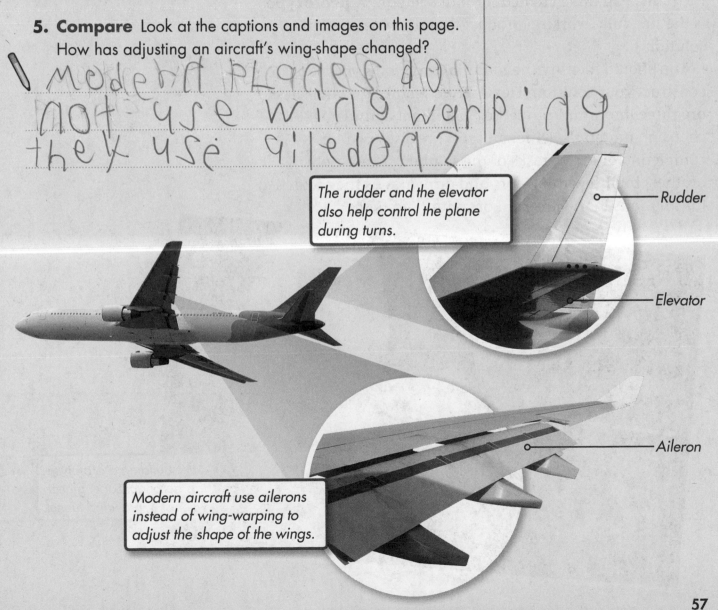

The rudder and the elevator also help control the plane during turns.

Rudder

Elevator

Aileron

Modern aircraft use ailerons instead of wing-warping to adjust the shape of the wings.

Step 4: Choose one solution.

In the design process, several factors can influence the solution that you choose. The solution must solve the problem you identified. The solution must also be affordable. If your solution costs too much, you may not be able to sell it. The amount of time you have can also affect which solution you choose. Safety is another factor to consider when choosing a solution.

When choosing a solution, engineers have to make trade-offs. If a plane design is fast, but not safe, a safer design should be chosen. You should save all the plans you have for other possible solutions because you may need them in the future.

Step 5: Design and construct a prototype.

Next, you need to carefully construct a prototype using the plans you have created for that solution. A **prototype** is the first fully working product that uses your design solution.

You should identify the materials and tools you need to construct your solution. Flexibility, strength, and hardness are three important properties you might consider when choosing materials. Different tools are also used for completing different tasks of the solution. The Wright brothers built several gliders and airplanes as they searched for solutions to the problem of controlling flight.

6. ⊙ **Cause and Effect Underline** the factors that may affect which solution you choose to build.

7. **Explain** What materials do you think the Wright brothers used to construct the wings of their plane? Why?

cloth, metal

After building a prototype, this aeronautical engineer will test it in a wind tunnel.

58

Step 6: Test the prototype.

The product needs to be carefully tested to see if it works safely and solves the problem it was designed for. Tests should use careful measurements. Recording the results of the tests you do will help you make adjustments to your design. After the tests, you should evaluate whether or not your product solved the problem.

Orville and Wilbur tested their gliders and planes. They observed how well the plane was controlled and made changes to their design to improve control during turns.

The Wright brothers used this glider to test their ideas.

8. **Infer** Why do you think it is important to record your measurements and observations?

 to Know if you need to make big or small

Do the math!

Elapsed Time

The Wrights measured the elapsed time from take-off to landing for each flight. Elapsed time is the amount of time that passes from the start time to the end time. A flight departs at 7:00 A.M. and arrives at 11:20 A.M. How long is the flight?

Find the starting time.

Count the hours.   Count the minutes.

The flight lasted 4 hours, 20 minutes.

Find the elapsed time for each flight.

1. Departure Time: 9:00 A.M.
   Arrival Time: 10:45 A.M.

2. Departure Time: 1:30 P.M.
   Arrival Time: 3:55 P.M.

3. Departure Time: 11:00 A.M.
   Arrival Time: 2:15 P.M.

Go Green

Pollution

Pollution is a common problem related to technology. Research different kinds of pollution an airplane may produce. Think of different ways the pollution can be reduced. Write a plan. Share your plan with your class.

Step 7: Communicate results.

Many times, a team of people work together to design a solution to a problem. It is important to document and communicate with your team members the solution and the data, or evidence, you collect. There are many ways to document and communicate this information. Tables and graphs can help you communicate data. Labeled diagrams, graphic organizers, and lists are also helpful in communicating your solution to others. The procedure for building the solution and for the tests performed on it should be written carefully.

Other team members should be able to use your procedures, observations, and diagrams to do their own investigations. After you have communicated your results to others, they may help you find solutions to problems with your product.

Solving one problem may create new problems. You should think of ways your solution will affect society. The invention of the airplane made travel much quicker. This benefits the lives of many people. Some inventions can have harmful effects. Noise pollution is a common problem related to airplane technology.

9. **Identify** (Circle) two things you need to communicate to others about your product.

10. **Explain** Tell why diagrams can be an effective way to communicate information.

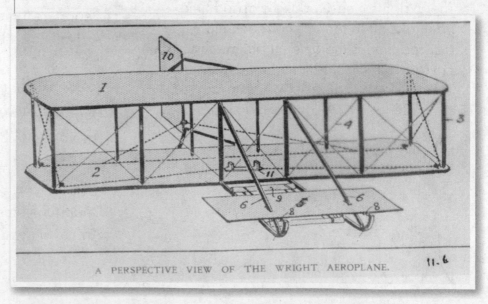

A PERSPECTIVE VIEW OF THE WRIGHT AEROPLANE.

This diagram was used to communicate information about the design of the Wright brothers' invention to the U.S. Patent Office.

myscienceonline.com | Got it? | 60-Second Video

Step 8: Evaluate and redesign.

After testing your prototype, you should evaluate how well it solves the problem. You may need to redesign your product. Orville and Wilbur redesigned their airplane many times. Since then, airplanes have been redesigned many times by many other people. Modern airplanes have many different designs because they have different purposes. Planes travel faster and farther today than the planes the Wright brothers made.

Redesigning your product will help solve some of the problems that you discovered as you tested it. The new solution should go through the design process again.

This modern jet solves the problem of turning in a different way.

11. Contrast Explain one way this modern airplane is different from the Wright brothers' first successful airplane.

better protection And confert

Got it?

12. Identify What are the steps in the design process?

13. Judge Why do you think it is important to communicate your solution to others?

⬛ **Stop!** I need help with

⏸ **Wait!** I have a question about

▶ **Go!** Now I know

Which boat design will hold more cargo?

Follow a Procedure

☑ **1. Make a Model**

Make a boat out of clay.

Make a boat of the same size and shape out of foil.

Pennies are the cargo your boat will hold.

☑ **2.** Place each boat in water.

Record your **observations.**

☑ **3. Predict** which boat will hold more pennies.

Record your prediction.

☑ **4.** Dry off the clay boat. Place it back in the water.

Place a penny in the boat.

Keep adding pennies until the boat sinks.

Record your **data.**

☑ **5.** Repeat Step 4 with the foil boat.

Materials

clay

heavy-duty
aluminum foil

pennies

plastic tub of water

Inquiry Skill

Making a model can help you make inferences about objects and events that are too large to test.

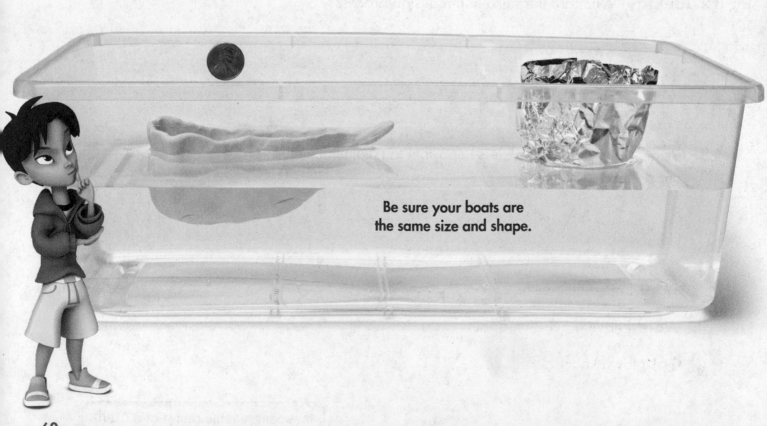

Be sure your boats are
the same size and shape.

Observations of Boats With and Without Cargo		
Boat	Without Cargo	With Cargo
Clay		
Foil		

Analyze and Conclude

6. Which boat floated better without cargo?

....

....

7. How many pennies did each boat hold?
Did your **observations** support your **predictions**?

....

....

8. Infer Compare your boat **design** with those of other groups.
What inferences can you make about boat design based on this activity?

....

....

9. UNLOCK THE BIG **?** How can physical **models** help engineers design
boats and ships?

....

....

....

STEM

Scientists use submersibles similar to this one to explore the bottom of the ocean.

Submersibles

Scientists and engineers have worked together to develop and build new technologies to explore the oceans. A submersible, a type of small submarine, is an example of this kind of technology. As the ocean becomes deeper, its pressure increases. The increased pressure makes exploring the ocean difficult and unsafe. Scientists needed a vehicle that was strong enough to withstand the pressure. Engineers designed submersibles with strong glass and metals to protect humans from the high pressure of the deep ocean.

Using submersibles, scientists have discovered new, unusual animals. One unusual animal was the dumbo octopus. This species of octopus can live far below the surface of the ocean. Some can live more than 5,500 meters below sea level. Scientists can use a submersible to safely explore the habitat of the dumbo octopus. Submersibles are an example of science, engineering, and technology working together!

dumbo octopus

Determine Why is it important for scientists and engineers to work together to design new submersibles?

Vocabulary Smart Cards

technology
design process
prototype

Play a Game!

Cut out the Vocabulary Smart Cards.

Work with a partner. Choose a Vocabulary Smart Card. Do not let your partner see your card.

Draw a picture to show what the term means. Have your partner guess the term. Take turns drawing and guessing.

technology

tecnología

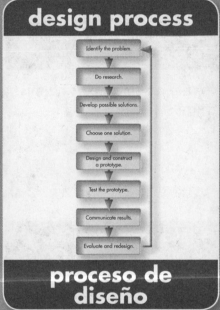

design process

proceso de diseño

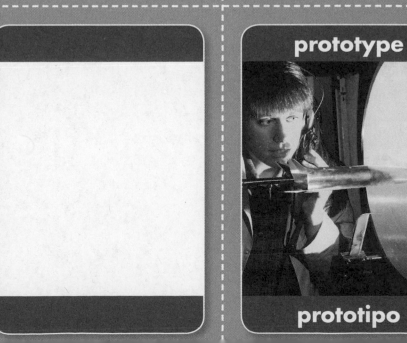

prototype

prototipo

the knowledge, processes, and products that solve problems and make work easier

Write two examples.

....

....

el conocimiento, los procesos y los productos con que se resuelven los problemas y se facilita el trabajo

---

a set of steps for developing products and processes that solve problems

Write a sentence using this term.

....

....

serie de pasos para desarrollar productos y procesos que resuelven problemas

---

first fully working product that uses a design solution

What is the prefix in this word and what does it mean?

....

....

el primer producto que demuestra una solución de diseño

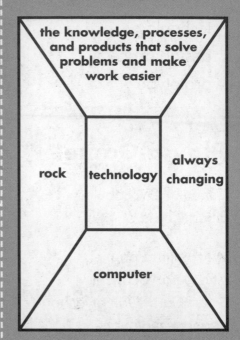

the knowledge, processes, and products that solve problems and make work easier

rock | technology | always changing

computer

Make a Word Square!

Choose a vocabulary term and write it in the center of the square. Fill in the other spaces with a definition, a characteristic, an example, and something that is not an example.

Lesson 1

What is technology?

- Technology can help solve problems and make work easier.
- Transportation technologies help move people and products quickly and safely from place to place.

Lesson 2

What is the design process?

- The design process is a set of steps for developing products and processes that solve problems.
- A prototype is the first fully working product that uses your solution.

Lesson 1

What is technology?

1. Infer Why is technology important?

It helps with problems.

2. Write About It Explain how trains have changed over time.

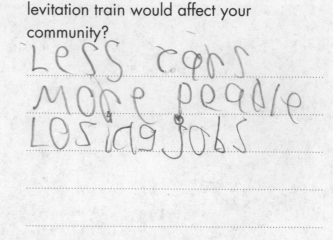

3. **Do the math!** Suppose a car travels 70 kilometers per hour. How far will the car travel in 3 hours and 30 minutes?

4. Predict How do you think a magnetic levitation train would affect your community?

Less cars
more people
losing jobs

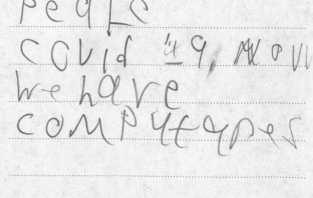

5. ◉ **Cause and Effect** Explain how technology affects your school.

peple
could 49, Akou
we have
computers

Lesson 2

What is the design process?

6. Vocabulary Which of the following is NOT a step in the design process?
A. Do research.
B. Construct a prototype.
C. Identify and control variables.
D. Redesign.

7. Explain How might cost affect which prototype you choose to build?

If the cost is to high people will not buy it.

8. Infer Why do you think engineers build prototypes of their designs?

If the phototype does not work the real thing will not work

9. Identify What are two steps in the design process that the Wright brothers used when building their plane?

they built a prototype, they identified the problem

10. **APPLY THE BIG ?** **How does technology affect our lives?**

Choose a transportation technology and explain how it affects your life.

Chapter 2
Benchmark Practice

Science,
Engineering,
and
Technology

Fill in the bubble next to the answer choice you think is correct for each multiple-choice question.

1 What is a prototype?

Ⓐ a procedure for building a solution
Ⓑ the first fully working product that uses a design solution
Ⓒ a final solution
Ⓓ a set of steps that solve problems

2 Some cars have a Global Positioning System (GPS). A GPS uses data from _____ to provide information about a car's location.

Ⓐ engineers
Ⓑ public address systems
Ⓒ microwaves
Ⓓ satellites

3 The knowledge, processes, and products that solve problems and make work easier are called

Ⓐ discoveries.
Ⓑ technology.
Ⓒ science.
Ⓓ computers.

4 What is the last step in the design process?

Ⓐ Communicate results.
Ⓑ Choose one solution.
Ⓒ Evaluate and redesign.
Ⓓ Test the prototype.

5 Explain how an engineer might use the design process to build a bridge.

....
....
....
....
....
....
....
....
....
....
....
....
....

Green Transportation

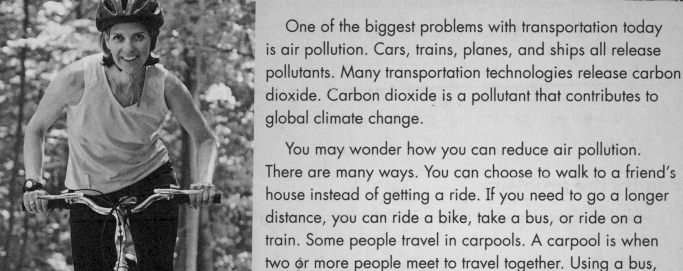

Go Green!

One of the biggest problems with transportation today is air pollution. Cars, trains, planes, and ships all release pollutants. Many transportation technologies release carbon dioxide. Carbon dioxide is a pollutant that contributes to global climate change.

You may wonder how you can reduce air pollution. There are many ways. You can choose to walk to a friend's house instead of getting a ride. If you need to go a longer distance, you can ride a bike, take a bus, or ride on a train. Some people travel in carpools. A carpool is when two or more people meet to travel together. Using a bus, train, or carpool helps to reduce the number of cars on the road. Fewer cars mean less pollution.

Some technologies help to reduce the amount of pollution cars produce. Hybrid cars can run on electricity and gasoline. This reduces the amount of pollution they produce. Cars today have catalytic converters. This technology changes some of the toxic gases given off by an engine to less harmful gases.

REVIEW THE BIG ?

What is a positive effect of transportation technology?

....

....

What is a negative effect of transportation technology?

....

What design will carry cargo best?

Cargo must be moved from one place to another and delivered on time. Different transportation systems may be used to move the cargo. Many times cargo of different weights and shapes must be moved on trains and trucks. The cargo must be arranged and secured in the vehicle so nothing shifts or falls off. The way the cargo is loaded onto the truck is a design.

You need to design a way to load a group of objects on a cart. Your cargo is a metric ruler, a wooden block, 15 cm of tape, 4 unsharpened pencils, 4 table-tennis balls, 4 large rubber bands, 100 cm of string, a half-full bottle of water, $\frac{1}{2}$ stick of clay, and an inflated balloon. After the cart is loaded you will test your loading design by pulling it through a course your teacher has provided.

Identify the problem.

☑ **1.** Identify the problems you need to address in your **design.**

....

....

....

72

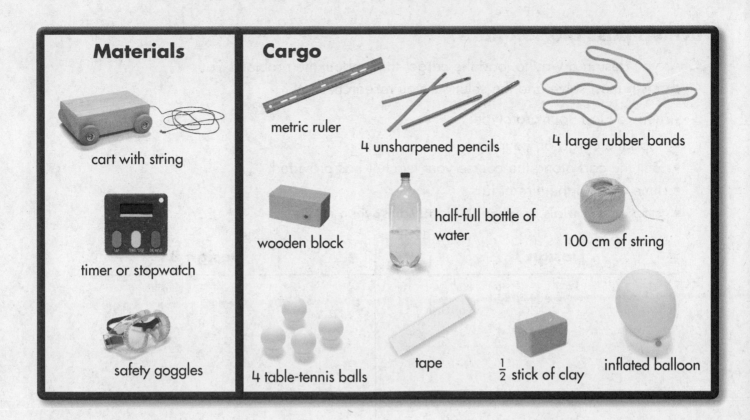

Materials	Cargo
cart with string	metric ruler
timer or stopwatch	4 unsharpened pencils
safety goggles	4 large rubber bands
	wooden block
	half-full bottle of water
	100 cm of string
	4 table-tennis balls
	tape
	$\frac{1}{2}$ stick of clay
	inflated balloon

Do research.

☑ **2.** Consider the problems you have identified. Research **design** solutions
others have used that address those problems. Brainstorm ideas with others.
List three examples of solutions others have used or suggested.

Develop possible solutions.

3. As you design a way to load the cargo, think about the problems your **design** must solve and the solutions you researched.

When you test your prototype:

- load the cargo on your cart.
- pull the cart along the course your teacher has provided.
- time each of the three trials.
- stop after 3 trials or when the load spills when moving.

Design A	Design B

Choose one solution.

4. Choose one **design** to build and **test.** Tell which design you chose. Explain why you chose that design.

....

....

....

....

Design and construct a prototype.

☑ **5.** Draw the **design** you will use to make a prototype.
Explain why you chose that design.

☑ **6.** Tell how to load the cart.

Test the prototype.

7. Test your **design** on the course. Use the timer to record the time it takes to complete one lap of the course.

Prototype Testing Results		
Trial	**Time (seconds)**	**Notes**
1		
2		
3		

Communicate results.

8. What elements of your **design** worked in your prototype? Use your **test** results and your **observations** to support your **conclusions.**

....

....

....

....

9. What elements of your design could be improved?

....

....

....

....

Evaluate and redesign.

☑ **10.** Evaluate what did and did not work in your prototype.
Use what you learned from testing to **redesign** your prototype.
Write or draw your design changes.

Conduct a Survey

Choose a question to ask each of your classmates. You might ask them what their favorite fruit is or how many pets they have. Collect all the answers. Graph the results of your survey.

Write a Report

Choose one kind of transportation system. You may choose airplanes, cars, trucks, or boats. Research how that transportation system has changed society. Write a report about what you learn. Identify the books or other sources in which you found your information.

Design a Package

Suppose you want to send fresh flowers to a friend. Design a package that will keep the flowers fresh. The flowers and stems should not bend or break. Make sure the flowers can get the light and water that they need.

Using Scientific Methods

1. Ask a question.
2. State your hypothesis.
3. Identify and control variables.
4. Test your hypothesis.
5. Collect and record your data.
6. Interpret your data.
7. State your conclusion.
8. Try it again.

Life Science

Where is this coconut going?

Plants and Animals

 Try It! How can flower parts be classified?

Lesson 1 How are plants and animals classified?

Lesson 2 How do plants reproduce?

Lesson 3 How do plants make food?

Lesson 4 What are adaptations?

Lesson 5 What plant and animal characteristics are inherited?

Lesson 6 How do animals respond to the environment?

Investigate It! What is inside an owl pellet?

You might not recognize it from the grocery store, but this floating seed is a coconut! Coconut seeds are hollow in the center and have thick shells, called husks. Coconuts can float across the water until they wash up on a shore. Then the seed can grow into a new coconut tree.

 Predict How do a coconut's hollow center and thick husk help it travel?

....

....

THE BIG ? What do living organisms need to survive?

How can flower parts be classified?

Flowering plants make seeds to reproduce.

☐ **1.** Carefully separate the different parts of 3 types of flowers. **Observe** how the parts are alike and different.

☐ **2.** Use the yarn circles to help **classify** the parts into groups. Label each group. **Record** the names of the groups.

petal

Materials

3 flowers

6 labels

hand lens

yarn circles

Inquiry Skill

Botanists make close observations of plant parts. Their observations show similarities and differences that they use to **classify** plants.

Explain Your Results

3. **Observe** how other students **classified** their flower parts. Discuss with other groups. Tell another way you could have classified the flower parts.

Text Features

Text features, such as headings, pictures, and captions, give you clues about what you will read.

Headings tell what the content that follows is about.

A **picture** shows something you will read about.

A **caption** tells specific information about the picture.

Parts of a Flower

Flowers are the organs that make seeds in flowering plants. Most flowers have four main parts. They are different shapes and sizes on different flowers. The part that you can see easily is the petal. Petals are often colorful. They protect the parts of the flower that make seeds. They attract bees, butterflies, birds, and other living things.

The wide green leaves below the petals are sepals. **Sepals** are the leaflike parts that cover and protect the flower bud before the flower opens.

The female part of the flower is the **pistil**. The pistil extends into the flower and contains the ovary, where egg cells are produced. The **stamen** is the male part of the flower. Stamens surround the pistil and produce pollen. The pollen contains sperm cells. Sperm cells in pollen combine with egg cells to make seeds.

2. ⊙ **Text Feature Underline** the part of each sentence that explains the word highlighted in yellow.

3. **Infer** Which part of a flower might you be able to see before the flower is ready to bloom?

4. **Identify Outline** the female part of the flower. **Draw** a rectangle around the male part of the flower.

These are the top parts of the pistil.

anther

The smaller stalks around the pistil are stamens. At the tips of the stamens are the anthers. The anthers make tiny grains of pollen.

The petals are often the most colorful part of the flower.

As the bud opens and the flower spreads its petals, the sepals are pushed apart.

94

myscienceonline.com ⊙ I Will Know... 95

picture of a pencil

yellow highlight

technology bar

Practice It!

Find the text features in the textbook pages shown above. Write a clue that each one gives you about the content.

Text feature	Clue

Lesson 1

How are plants and animals classified?

Which picture do you think shows a plant? Which shows an animal? Label each picture with your choice.

Inquiry **Explore It!**

What are some ways you can classify animals?

☐ **1.** Look at the Animal Cards.

☐ **2.** Think of a way to **classify** the animals. **Record** your system.

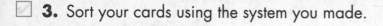

☐ **3.** Sort your cards using the system you made.

Explain Your Results

4. What systems did other groups use to **classify** the animals?

5. Interpret Data How were the different systems useful?

Materials

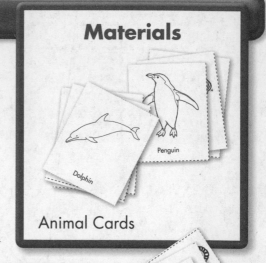

Animal Cards

myscienceonline.com | **Explore It!** Animation

Words to Know

classify
vertebrates
invertebrates

Classifying Organisms

Scientists sort all living things, such as plants and animals, into different groups. To arrange or sort objects or living things according to their properties or characteristics is to **classify.**

Scientists ask questions about the organism they want to classify. They look closely at its appearance. They think about where it lives and how it gets its food. All organisms in the same group have some common characteristics. The smallest two groups are genus and species. A genus is a group of closely related living things. Black-footed cats and house cats are classified in the *Felis* genus. They share characteristics such as sharp claws and hunting behaviors. A species is a group of similar organisms that can mate and produce offspring that can also produce offspring. All house cats are classified in the same species.

The species name of the house cat is domesticus.

The species name of the black-footed cat is nigripes.

1. ◉ **Text Features** In the graphic organizer, write the content clues that the text features give you.

Text feature	Clue
Picture	two different cats
Caption	scientific names of cats

2. **Apply** The word *domesticus* is Latin for "of the house." What does this name tell you about the animal?

House cat

Classifying Plants

Scientists use several characteristics to classify plants. Two of these characteristics are how plants transport nutrients and how they reproduce.

Water and Nutrient Transportation

Some plants have tubelike structures that connect their leaves, stems, and roots. These structures transport water and nutrients to all parts of the plant. They also add support to the stems and leaves. The added support helps the plant grow larger. Plants with tubelike structures are called vascular plants. Ferns, wildflowers, and many other plants are classified as vascular plants. Plants that pass water and nutrients from cell to cell are called nonvascular plants. Mosses are classified as nonvascular plants.

3. **CHALLENGE** Why do mosses grow low to the ground?

because it is nonvascular plant.

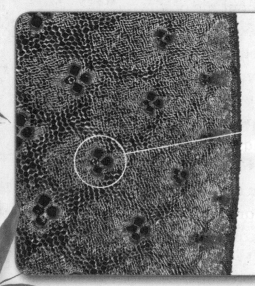

Tubelike structure
If you look at a very thin slice of bamboo stem with a microscope, you can see the tubelike structures.

4. **Observe** Tell what you notice about the bamboo's tubelike structures.

5. **Explain** How do the bamboo leaves at the top of the plant get the water they need from the bamboo roots?

bamboo

myscienceonline.com | **I Will Know...**

Reproduction

Plants have different ways of reproducing. Plants with flowers or cones produce seeds. A seed has many cells. It has a young plant and stored food inside a protective covering. Other plants produce spores. Each spore is one cell surrounded by a protective cell wall. A spore needs a moist, shady place where it can get nutrients and begin to grow.

Flowers and Seeds

Flowering plants are vascular plants. Daffodils are flowering plants. They produce seeds.

6. Exemplify List three other types of flowering plants.

Dandalions, roses, sunflowers

daffodils

Cones and Seeds

Plants with cones are vascular plants called conifers. The long-leaf pine and red cedar are conifers. They make seeds and have cones instead of flowers.

pine cones

Vascular Plants with Spores

Some vascular plants form spores. Fern spores form in cases on the underside of leaves. They look like brown dots or streaks.

ferns

Nonvascular Plants with Spores

Mosses are nonvascular plants. They make spores. Their spores form in cases at the tips of short stalks. Each spore case holds hundreds of spores.

7. Conclude Why do you think a moss produces many spores?

....

moss

Classifying Animals

Like plants, animals are classified based on their similarities and differences. One way scientists classify animals is by physical characteristics. Some animals have backbones while others do not have backbones.

Animals with Backbones

Animals that have backbones are called **vertebrates.** There are five groups of vertebrates. These groups are fish, amphibians, reptiles, birds, and mammals.

Fish

Fish are usually covered with scales. They all live in water. Fish breathe mostly with gills. They are cold-blooded, so their body temperature depends on the temperature of their surroundings. Most fish lay eggs.

red drum fish

southern dusky salamander

southern crawfish frog

Amphibians

Amphibians are covered with a smooth skin. They can live both on land and in the water. They breathe with lungs or gills or both. They are cold-blooded. Amphibians hatch from eggs.

8. Classify A southern crawfish frog has lungs and hatches from an egg. Is this frog a fish or an amphibian? Explain.

Aq Phibed

pine snake

Reptiles

Reptiles are covered with scales. Most reptiles live on land. Some can live in water. They have lungs and breathe air. Reptiles are cold-blooded. Most reptiles lay eggs.

Birds

Birds are covered with feathers. They usually live on land, but many birds spend much of their time on water. Birds have lungs and breathe air. They are warm-blooded, which means that their body controls their temperature. All birds lay eggs.

painted bunting

bobcat

Mammals

All mammals have hair or fur. Most mammals live on land, but some live in water. They have lungs and breathe air. Mammals are warm-blooded. Most mammals do not lay eggs. They make milk to feed their young.

9. **Analyze** An animal lives in the water, has scales, is cold-blooded, and lays eggs. What else do you need to know to classify its vertebrate group?

where they Live?
How they breathe?

Animals Without Backbones

Animals without backbones are called **invertebrates.** Most animals on Earth are invertebrates. Arthropods are the largest group of invertebrates. Insects, spiders, crabs, and shrimp are arthropods. Their legs and bodies are divided into sections. Their bodies are covered by a hard, lightweight outer skin, or exoskeleton. The exoskeleton protects their soft bodies. Other invertebrates, such as worms, have no protection for their soft bodies. Others, such as snails and clams, have a soft body inside a hard shell.

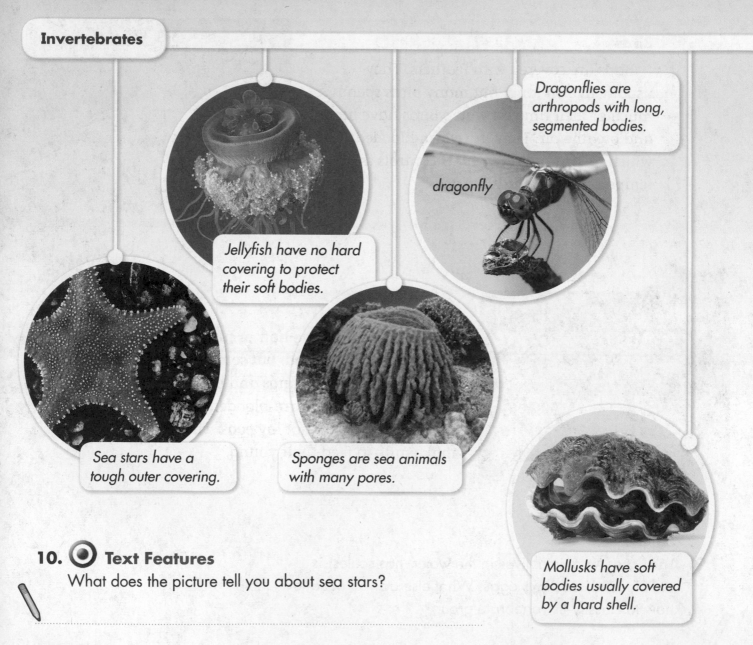

Invertebrates

Jellyfish have no hard covering to protect their soft bodies.

Dragonflies are arthropods with long, segmented bodies.

dragonfly

Sea stars have a tough outer covering.

Sponges are sea animals with many pores.

Mollusks have soft bodies usually covered by a hard shell.

10. ◉ Text Features

What does the picture tell you about sea stars?

....

....

....

myscienceonLine.com | Got it? ⏱ 60-Second Video

Like all arthropods, spiders have an exoskelton and jointed legs.

spider

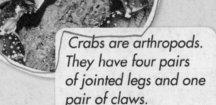

Crabs are arthropods. They have four pairs of jointed legs and one pair of claws.

Earthworms have soft bodies made of segments.

11. Recognize (Circle) the animals on these pages that are arthropods.

Got it?

12. Classify A cedar tree is a vascular plant. It produces cones. What kind of plant is it?

conifers

13. Apply Suppose you find an animal you have never seen before. What are some questions you might ask to help you classify it?

....

....

⬛ **Stop!** I need help with ....

⏸ **Wait!** I have a question about ....

▶ **Go!** Now I know ....

How do plants reproduce?

Envision It!

Tell what you think will happen when these seeds blow away.

my planet diary

FunFact

You walk by a potted plant and you think, Yuck! Something around here does not smell good! It would never occur to you that the smell is coming from the potted plant's pretty flowers. After all, some of the best scents come from flowers like the rose or the lily. But some flowers have a terrible smell!

The carrion plant gets its name because its flowers smell like carrion, which is decaying meat. This smell attracts lots of flies, which carry the plant's pollen from flower to stinky flower.

Some flowers only release their fragrance at night. What could be a reason?

....

....

In spite of their smell, carrion plants are popular in gardens!

UNLOCK THE BIG ?

I will know structures that help plants survive and reproduce.

Words to Know

sepal	pollination
pistil	fertilization
stamen	germinate

Plants That Make Seeds

An important function of plants is to reproduce, or make more of the same kind of plant. Scientists often classify plants by how they reproduce. In nature, most plants make seeds that can grow into new plants. Other plants reproduce by forming tiny cells that can grow into new plants. These cells are called spores. Ferns and mosses are examples of plants that use spores to reproduce.

The plants that make seeds are classified again by the parts they use to produce seeds. Some plants, such as pine trees, grow cones to make seeds. Other plants make seeds by growing flowers. In this lesson, you will learn how flowering plants reproduce.

The hard pit in an avocado is actually an avocado seed. Roots and stems produced by the seed will grow into a tree.

1. **Compare** How is the way an avocado reproduces different from the way a fern reproduces?

....

....

....

Spore cases are on the underside of fern leaves. Each case contains tiny spores that may grow into a fern.

Parts of a Flower

Flowers are the organs that make seeds in flowering plants. Most flowers have four main parts. They are different shapes and sizes on different flowers. The part that you can see easily is the petal. Petals are often colorful. They protect the parts of the flower that make seeds. They attract bees, butterflies, birds, and other living things.

The wide green leaves below the petals are sepals. **Sepals** are the leaflike parts that cover and protect the flower bud before the flower opens.

The female part of the flower is the **pistil.** The pistil extends into the flower and contains the ovary, where egg cells are produced. The **stamen** is the male part of the flower. Stamens surround the pistil and produce pollen. The pollen contains sperm cells. Sperm cells in pollen combine with egg cells to make seeds.

2. ◉ **Text Feature Underline** the part of each sentence that explains the word highlighted in yellow.

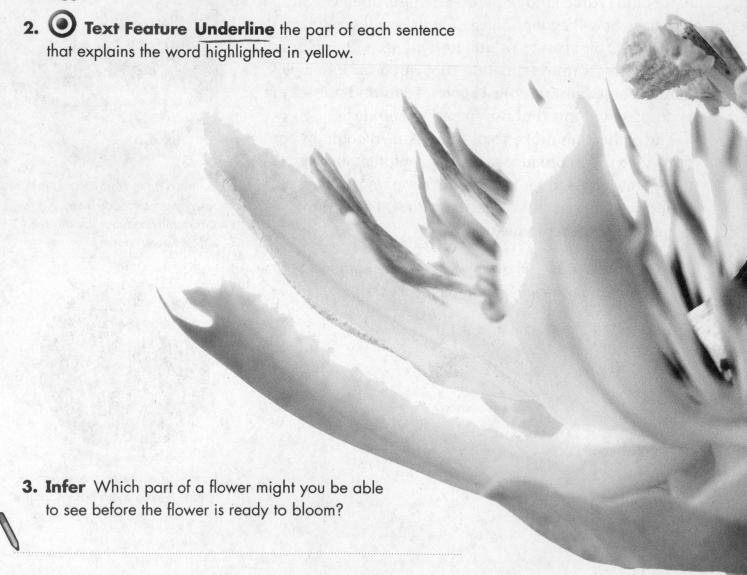

3. **Infer** Which part of a flower might you be able to see before the flower is ready to bloom?

4. Identify Outline the female part of the flower. **Draw** a rectangle around the male part of the flower.

These are the top parts of the pistil.

anther

The smaller stalks around the pistil are stamens. At the tips of the stamens are the anthers. The anthers make tiny grains of pollen.

The petals are often the most colorful part of the flower.

As the bud opens and the flower spreads its petals, the sepals are pushed apart.

Pollen on the Move

In order for seeds to form, pollen has to get from a stamen to a pistil. Sometimes animals may help play a part in moving pollen.

pollen

Flowers make a sweet liquid called nectar. This is a tasty food for bats, bees, butterflies, and birds. Scent and color guide animals to the flower. As an animal feeds, pollen from the stamens rubs off onto its body. The pollen may then rub off onto the pistil of the next flower the animal visits. This movement of pollen from stamen to pistil is called **pollination.**

5. **Analyze** Look at the photos of the bees on these pages. How do a bee's features help pollinate plants?

....

....

Most trees and grasses rely on wind for pollination. These plants do not attract animals. They do not have sweet smells or big flowers with colorful petals. However, they produce huge amounts of pollen. The wind will carry at least a few pollen grains to the pistil of another plant.

6. **Infer** Some people are allergic to pollen. Why do you think their allergies are worse on windy days?

....

....

....

After Pollination

Once a pollen grain lands on a pistil, a thin tube grows down through the pistil. This pollen tube reaches the thick bottom part of the pistil called the ovary. Sperm cells from the pollen travel down the pollen tube to the egg cells. The sperm cell and egg cell combine in a process called **fertilization.**

The flower changes after fertilization. The petals and stamens dry up and fall off. The fertilized egg inside the ovary develops into a seed. The ovary grows into a fruit, which protects the seed or seeds. When the fruit is ripe, the seeds are ready to grow into new plants.

7. **Explain** How are the seeds in this apple protected?

....

....

....

Dandelion seeds spread with the wind—or by a person blowing on them.

The wing-shaped fruits of maple trees twirl through the air like propellers.

Seeds on the Move

Suppose that all the seeds on a tree fell to the ground nearby. Many of the seeds would start to grow. But the parent tree would take up most of the living space and resources that the seeds would need to grow properly. They would grow much better if they were scattered farther from the parent tree. That is why plants have adaptations that help them scatter their seeds. This scattering of plant seeds is also called seed dispersal. Some seeds are built to spread with the wind. Some can float. Some have tiny hooks that stick to an animal's fur or a person's clothes. Some animals, such as squirrels, gather and bury nuts and seeds to be eaten later. Some of those nuts and seeds will grow.

A seed that falls to the ground contains a small, young plant. Each seed needs water, oxygen, and the right temperature to **germinate**, or start to grow. Food stored in the seed gives the young plant enough energy to germinate. The pictures below show a germinating plant.

8. **Underline** a reason why seeds may not grow well near the parent tree.

9. ◉ **Text Features** How do the photographs and captions help you understand how seeds move?

....

....

leaf

seed coat

stem

root

myscienceonline.com | Got it? 60-Second Video

Life Cycle of a Plant

A plant's life cycle includes all of the changes the plant goes through from fertilization to death. When a seed has the right conditions, it sprouts. The young roots grow downward because of gravity. The new stem looks like it is reaching for the sunlight as it pushes up through the seed coat. The seedling grows into an adult plant. The plant gets larger. Flowers start to grow. The color of the flowers is one of the traits that the plant gets from its parents.

Flowers that are pollinated produce fertilized eggs that develop into seeds. Fruit grows around the seeds. In time, the fruit and seeds separate from the parent plant. The new seeds germinate, and the cycle begins again.

10. Paraphrase Explain in your own words what a plant's life cycle is.

....

....

After fertilization, an apple tree's flowers develop into seeds. Apples grow around the seeds.

Got it?

11. **Identify** What are the functions of the pistil and stamen in flowering plants?

....

....

....

12. Infer Why is reproduction important to the survival of a plant species?

....

....

Stop! I need help with ....

Wait! I have a question about ....

Go! Now I know ....

Lesson 3

How do plants make food?

Tell what plant parts you can see in this photo.

Inquiry **Explore It!**

How can plants react to light?

☑ **1.** Set a shoebox on one end, as shown in the picture. The hole in the box's other end should be on the left. Place a sprouted bean plant on the left side of the box.

☑ **2.** Tape an index card inside the box. The hole in the index card should be on the right.

☑ **3.** Cover the box. Place the box in bright light.

☑ **4.** **Predict** what may happen. **Observe** the plant every day for 5 days.

Explain Your Results

5. Discuss how the plant's growth changed.

6. **Infer** You observed how the stem grew. What is one function of this plant structure?

Materials

shoebox (with hole) and lid

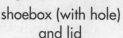

tape

cup with sprouted bean seed

index card with hole

Water your plant as needed. Do not overwater.

myscienceonline.com | **Explore It!** Animation

I will know the roles of roots, leaves, and stems in making food.

Words to Know

photosynthesis
chlorophyll

Needs of Plants

Suppose you are taking care of plants in a garden. You make sure that they get plenty of sunlight and water. Sunlight and water are two things that plants need to live, grow, and reproduce. Plants also need carbon dioxide from the air and nutrients from the soil.

The amounts of sunlight and water that plants need can be different. Some plants need different amounts of sunlight. For example, petunias and irises are flowering plants. Petunias need direct sunlight to grow well. However, irises can grow well in partly shaded areas that receive indirect sunlight. Some plants need only a little water. For example, a cactus is able to grow in the desert where little rain falls.

1. **Infer** How might you be able to tell if a plant in a garden needs more water?

....

....

2. **Apply** These children are caring for plants in a garden. What kinds of information do they need to know about the plants?

....

....

....

....

How Plants Make Food

Unlike animals, plants make their own food. Most plants have three special parts: roots, leaves, and stems. Each part plays a role in making food for a plant. Most plants make food in their leaves. Plants must take in a gas called carbon dioxide, water, nutrients, and sunlight to make food.

Photosynthesis

The food plants make is sugar. The process in which plants make sugar is called **photosynthesis.** In photosynthesis, plants use carbon dioxide that their leaves absorb from the air, and water and nutrients that their roots absorb from the soil. The water and the nutrients travel through tubes in the stems to the leaves. The plants use sunlight energy to change these ingredients into food that the plant can use. Oxygen, the waste product of photosynthesis, passes into the air through the openings in leaves. Tubes in the stem carry sugar to other parts of the plant. The stems, roots, and leaves of a plant all store extra sugar.

3. [CHALLENGE] Why do you think it is helpful for the widest part of a leaf to face the sky?

4. ◉ **Text Features** What content clues does the picture give you?

Leaves absorb energy from sunlight and take in carbon dioxide.

Stems hold the leaves up to the sunlight. Water moves through stems to the leaves.

Roots take in the water and nutrients needed to make food.

Chlorophyll

Plant cells contain tiny structures called chloroplasts. Photosynthesis usually takes place in the chloroplasts of leaf cells. When you look at a chloroplast through a microscope, you see stacks of dark green disks connected by threadlike materials.

Chloroplasts contain chlorophyll. **Chlorophyll** is the substance in plants that makes their parts green and captures energy from sunlight. Plants use this energy and nutrients from the soil during photosynthesis to change water and carbon dioxide into sugar and oxygen.

5. **Underline** the sentence that tells where photosynthesis usually takes place.

6. Mark an ✗ on a tubelike structure in the diagram that brings water to the cells for photosynthesis.

Cross Section of a Leaf

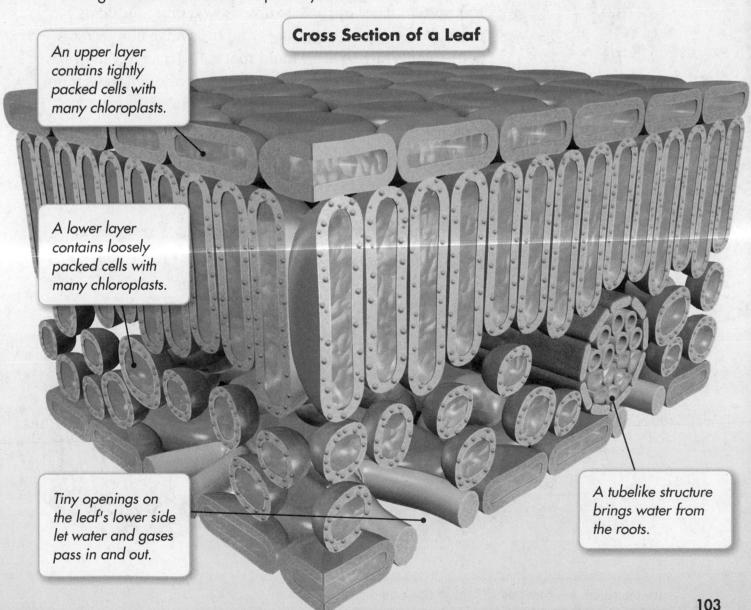

An upper layer contains tightly packed cells with many chloroplasts.

A lower layer contains loosely packed cells with many chloroplasts.

Tiny openings on the leaf's lower side let water and gases pass in and out.

A tubelike structure brings water from the roots.

Ash trees have an opposite leaf pattern.

Leaves, Stems, and Roots

The shape and positioning of leaves helps them catch the sunlight they need to make food. Most leaves are flat on top to catch as much sunlight as possible. Leaves are usually spread out along stems in ways that catch the most sunlight. Some leaves grow opposite each other, like a mirror image. Some leaves grow in a staggered, zig-zag pattern. Some leaves grow in a circle around the same point on the stem.

Stems also grow toward light. The woody stems of trees and bushes are hard and rigid. A waxy covering protects the stems and prevents them from drying out. The stems of many other plants are soft and flexible. These stems are usually green and carry out photosynthesis just like leaves do.

Roots grow away from the stem in search of water and nutrients. Gravity causes roots to grow down. In some plants the roots spread out in many directions, forming a fibrous root system. They are able to absorb water and nutrients from a large area. Most grasses and trees have fibrous roots. Some plants have a large main root called a *taproot*. It grows straight down. The taproot absorbs water and nutrients from the soil. As it stores food for the plant, it grows thicker. Carrots and radishes are taproots.

Grape vines have a zig-zag leaf pattern.

7. **Analyze** Why do you think there are different kinds of leaves, stems, and roots?

....

....

Clover has a circle leaf pattern.

taproots

fibrous roots

myscienceonline.com | Got it? | 60-Second Video

Plants Without Roots

Some plants do not have true underground roots. Yet they are able to get what they need to make their own food. These air plants, as they are called, absorb moisture directly from the air. They take the nutrients they need from dust in the air. Spanish moss is an air plant that grows in many parts of the southern United States.

8. Mark an ✗ on the Spanish moss in the picture.

9. **Infer** The leaves of Spanish moss are long and thin. They are covered with cuplike scales. How might the structure of the leaves help the plant survive?

....

....

Spanish moss wraps its scaly stems around tree branches.

Got it?

10. **Explain** How do water and nutrients get from the soil into a plant's leaves?

....

....

11. **Summarize** What is the function of leaves in a plant's ability to make food?

....

....

⏹ **Stop!** I need help with ....

⏸ **Wait!** I have a question about ....

▶ **Go!** Now I know ....

Lesson 4
What are adaptations?

bald eagle

Tell how you think the feet of each bird shown above help it survive in its habitat.

Inquiry Explore It!

How can some fish float?

Some fish have swim bladders that help them float. Inherited behaviors allow a fish to use its swim bladder to help get food and stay safe.

Materials

tape

balloon

straw

plastic tub of water

plastic bottle

☑ **1.** Tape the mouth of a balloon around one end of a straw. Put the balloon inside a bottle.

☑ **2.** Put the bottle in a tub of water. Tip the bottle until all the air escapes. **Observe** what happens. **Record.**

☑ **3.** Blow into the straw to inflate the balloon. Observe. Record.

bottle = model of fish

Explain Your Results

4. Think about your **model. Infer** how a fish uses its swim bladder to help get food and stay safe.

balloon = model of swim bladder

myscienceonline.com | **Explore It!** Animation

mallard duck

I will know how physical features and behaviors help organisms interact with their environments.

Word to Know

adaptation

Adaptations

Animals and plants inherit characteristics from their parents. These special features and behaviors help them survive. An **adaptation** is a physical feature or behavior that helps an organism survive in its environment. An environment is everything that surrounds a living thing. Organisms with useful adaptations for their environment are more likely than other organisms to get the resources they need to survive. If they survive, they are more likely to reproduce and pass their adaptations to their young.

Plants and animals in different areas often have different adaptations. A plant or animal adapted to one ecosystem may not survive in a different ecosystem. Hares that live in snowy environments have different adaptations from hares that live in a desert. So, a hare from a snowy environment might not survive in a desert.

snowshoe hare

2. **Explain** How do you think the snowshoe hare in the picture is adapted to live in an environment that has a lot of snow?

....

....

....

....

....

....

1. ⊙ **Text Features** Complete the chart below to identify some text features on this page.

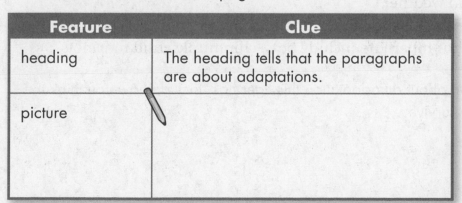

Feature	Clue
heading	The heading tells that the paragraphs are about adaptations.
picture	

Animal Adaptations

Animals have many adaptations that help them survive in their environments. Some adaptations, such as sharp beaks, teeth, or claws, may help them get food. Other adaptations, such as stingers, quills, smelly sprays, or bitter-tasting flesh, protect some animals from being eaten by predators. Bright colors, like those of the monarch butterfly, may warn predators that the animal is poisonous.

Some adaptations for moving help an animal protect itself. For example, fins enable a fish to swim away from its enemies. Birds' wings help them quickly move if they need to get away from predators or cold weather.

Hibernation, or a state of rest, is a behavior that helps some animals survive low temperatures. Some animals that hibernate include bats, chipmunks, and marmots.

3. **Describe** Write a caption about an adaptation this tiger has. Include how you think the adaptation helps the tiger survive.

....

....

4. Classify Read about the animals on this page. (Circle) the names of the animals with adaptations for getting food. **Underline** the names of the animals with adaptations for protection.

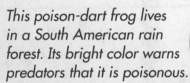

The porcupine lives in grasslands and other areas. Its quills are very sharp. The quills protect the porcupine against predators.

This poison-dart frog lives in a South American rain forest. Its bright color warns predators that it is poisonous.

This flying gecko lives in the jungle forest. It has flaps of skin that help it to glide away from predators.

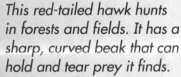

This red-tailed hawk hunts in forests and fields. It has a sharp, curved beak that can hold and tear prey it finds.

Chameleons live in deserts and tropical areas. Their long tongues stretch to catch insects.

5. Observe and Compare Look at the animals on these pages. Describe to a partner how each is adapted to its environment. Tell how their physical characteristics are alike.

Plant Adaptations

Like animals, plants have many adaptations that help them survive in their environments. Some adaptations, such as cactus thorns, protect plants from harm. Other adaptations help plants reproduce. These adaptations may help plants pollinate or spread their seeds.

Adaptations such as harmful oils and thorns may protect a plant from being eaten. Other adaptations allow plants to survive in extreme conditions. For example, sundew plants that live in nutrient-poor soil have a sticky substance that attracts insects. These insects provide nutrients to the plant.

6. **Apply** The hairs on a stinging nettle release a chemical that irritates skin. Explain how this adaptation might help the plant.

....

....

This burdock bush has seeds with spikes that stick to furry animals that brush against them.

Cactus plants live in deserts where there is little rain. They have tiny needle-like leaves and a thick waxy coating on their stem that keeps them from drying out.

Some flowering plants depend on insects or other animals to pollinate their flowers. This is how they make new plants. The flower of a bee orchid looks like a bee. This adaptation helps the orchid attract insects.

bee orchid

7. **Illustrate** Draw another plant you know. Describe an adaptation the plant has and how it helps the plant.

Got it?

8. **Describe** How is a cactus adapted to its habitat?

9. **Analyze** How is a duck adapted to help it survive in its environment?

■ **Stop!** I need help with

❚❚ **Wait!** I have a question about

▶ **Go!** Now I know

What plant and animal characteristics are inherited?

Envision It!

Tell why you think peacocks have inherited showy tails.

Inquiry Explore It!

How can some characteristics be affected by the environment?

Many characteristics are inherited. Some are affected by the environment. *A Cards* show living things as they often appear. *B Cards* show how the living things may appear depending on the environment. *C Cards* tell what factors affected the living things.

☑ **1. Observe** the living thing on an *A Card*. Match it with a *B Card*.

☑ **2.** Find the matching *C Card*.

☑ **3.** Repeat for each *A Card*. Compare your matches with others. Explain any differences.

Materials
Environmental Effect Cards

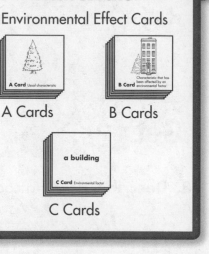

A Cards   B Cards

C Cards

A Card Usual characteristic

B Card Characteristic that has been affected by an environmental factor

a building

C Card Environmental factor

Explain Your Results

4. Communicate Pick an *A Card*. Explain how the characteristic was affected by the environment.

myscienceonline.com | **Explore It!** Animation

UNLOCK THE BIG Q

I will know that plants and animals inherit characteristics that may help them survive and reproduce.

Words to Know

characteristics
inherit
advantage

Characteristics of Living Things

In the middle of the nineteenth century, a monk named Gregor Mendel was hard at work in his garden. He noticed that his pea plants were not all exactly alike. All of the pea plants had stems, leaves, flowers, pods, and peas. But they also had some differences in characteristics. **Characteristics** are the qualities an organism has. Some of the plants were tall while others were short. Some had purple flowers while others had white ones. The pods might be green or yellow. The peas themselves might be smooth or wrinkled.

pea plant

The pea plants were like their parents because of characteristics passed on to them. But Mendel found that the offspring did not always look exactly like their parents. Sometimes they received different characteristics. Some offspring even had different characteristics than other plants with the same parents. Mendel asked himself why. Many years later, his work became the basis for the scientific study of heredity, or the passing of characteristics from parents to offspring.

1. **Underline** the different characteristics Mendel's pea plants showed.

2. **Infer** What characteristics will all pea plants have?

_____

_____

The general coat pattern is shared by zebras of the same kind. The pattern of each individual zebra is different.

Inherited Characteristics

Animals and plants inherit their characteristics from their parents and look very much like them. In science, to **inherit** is to receive characteristics from an organism's parents. Animals and plants will pass these traits on to their own offspring.

Plants

The prickly pear cactus has sharp spines. Look at its paddle-shaped pads. These are flattened stems that act like leaves. They have a waxy coating to help the plant hold in moisture. Notice that the pads have two kinds of sharp spines. Some spines are long. Other spines are short but break off easily. The cactus looks the way it does because it has inherited these traits.

3. Conclude What characteristic helps the prickly pear cactus survive in a dry environment?

....

....

....

Animals

You are not likely to mistake a zebra for any other animal. They look like horses, but they are not horses. Zebras have black and white stripes. Their manes are short and stand up on their necks. These are inherited characteristics. They are shared by all zebras.

4. Analyze How is a zebra's pattern like a fingerprint?

....

....

....

5. Text Features Find five text features on these pages. Tell a partner the clues they give you.

Did you look twice at the fish in the photo? Something does not look quite right. The peacock flounder has both eyes on one side of its body! This flat fish is unusual in another way too. The peacock flounder can change its color and pattern to match its background. This allows it to surprise the animals it eats as they swim by. It also hides itself from animals that would eat it. This fish looks and acts the way it does because it has inherited these traits.

6. ⊙ **Summarize** List three characteristics that the peacock flounder inherited.

....

....

....

Human Beings

People also inherit many characteristics from their parents. A person's parents may be very tall, and so that person may grow to be very tall also. However, this is not always the case. Sometimes a child may grow up to be taller or shorter than his or her parents. Height is not the only inherited characteristic. Some characteristics, such as hair and eye color, are also inherited.

7. **Give an Example**
Write a characteristic you may have inherited from your parents.

....

....

Parents, Offspring, and Advantages

You know that baby animals look somewhat like their parents. Cats give birth to kittens, and lions give birth to lion cubs. Sometimes, offspring from the same parents can look different from each other. They may have different characteristics than other organisms of the same type. It may be easier or more difficult for the offspring with different characteristics to compete. Competition occurs when two or more living things need the same resources in order to survive.

8. CHALLENGE Trees get energy from sunlight. How might competition affect the height of a tree?

....

....

....

One example that shows competition is in giraffes. Male giraffes use their long necks to fight with other males. The winner of the fight is more attractive to the female giraffe. This male reproduces. The longer and stronger a male giraffe's neck is, the better chance he has to pass these characteristics on to offspring. Over time, giraffes inherit longer and stronger necks.

9. **Infer** How did giraffes' necks get so long?

....

....

....

....

male giraffes competing

In England, peppered moths used to survive by using their light color as camouflage on the lichens growing on trees. As coal use increased in England, the lichens began to die off. Birds that eat peppered moths could see them more easily against the dark color of the trees. Moths that inherited a darker color could blend in better against the trees. These moths survived and had offspring who were also darker in color. Over time, the common color of the peppered moth shifted from light to dark. The darker color gave those individual organisms an advantage over the lighter colored moths. An **advantage** is a characteristic that can help an individual compete.

10. **Summarize** Describe how the dark moths' coloring gives them an advantage over the light-colored moths.

....

....

Got it?

11. **Apply** What is one characteristic that might give a hawk an advantage over other hawks?

....

....

12. **UNLOCK THE BIG ?** Think about what you learned in this lesson. Describe why offspring usually look like their parents.

....

....

⬛ **Stop!** I need help with ....

⏸ **Wait!** I have a question about ....

▶ **Go!** Now I know ....

How do animals respond to the environment?

Envision It!

Tell how these monkeys are responding to their environment.

my planet diary

//// MISCONCEPTION ////

Have you ever heard that bats cannot see? A common misconception about bats is that they are blind. Some bats use something called echolocation to locate prey, such as insects. Echolocation uses sound energy. Bats make a sound and then hear the echo as it bounces off an object, such as a delicious mosquito. Then the bat knows how far away and in what direction the insect is flying. Because bats can find prey in the dark, many people have assumed they were blind. But all types of bats have eyes that can see. They can see only in black, white, and shades of gray.

How can some bats get information from their environments?

....

....

myscienceonline.com | my planet diary

I will know how animals respond to their environments and get what they need.

Words to Know

stimulus
instinct

Animal Behaviors

Have you ever tried to touch a turtle? If so, you may have seen a typical behavior of turtles. When a turtle feels threatened, it may pull its head inside its shell. This behavior protects the turtle from other animals.

Behaviors are the ways that animals act. Every behavior is caused by a stimulus. A **stimulus** is something that causes a reaction in a living thing. Some behaviors are responses to stimuli in the environment. When a turtle pulls its head inside its shell, it is reacting to something it has heard, seen, or smelled in its environment. Other behaviors are responses to stimuli inside an animal. For example, hunger is a stimulus that causes animals to look for food and eat.

1. **Apply** Give an example of a stimulus that might cause a turtle to pull its head into its shell.

   ....

   ....

   ....

The box turtle is hiding in its shell.

Animal Instincts

Animals inherit physical characteristics, such as wings or fur, from their parents. They can also inherit behaviors. An **instinct** is a behavior that is inherited. Instincts help animals meet their needs and respond to stimuli in their environments.

Sea stars, for example, have an important instinct that helps them respond to changes in temperature. Sea stars live along the coast. During low tide, the water gets shallower in these areas. There is less water for sunlight to pass through, so the ocean floor gets warmer. Sea stars prepare for the warmer temperatures of low tide by sucking in cold water during high tide. The cooler water inside the animal keeps it from getting too hot.

2. Paraphrase Explain in your own words what an instinct is.

sea star

Do the math!

Division

Animals often travel great distances. Some geese travel from Hudson Bay in Canada to central Wisconsin. The distance is about 1,400 km. About how many hours of flying would it take geese to migrate on this route if they fly 50 km per hour? To find out, divide the distance by the speed:

$$\frac{1400 \text{ km}}{50 \text{ km/hr}} = 28 \text{ hours}$$

Use the formula to solve these problems.

1 A peregrine falcon travels from Maine to Argentina. The distance is about 8,100 km. About how many hours of flying would the falcon's trip be if it flew at 45 km/hr?

2 A flock of pelicans travels from Washington to California's Channel Islands. The distance is about 1,469 km. About how many hours of flying would it take the pelicans to migrate at 43 km/hr?

Examples of Instinctive Behaviors

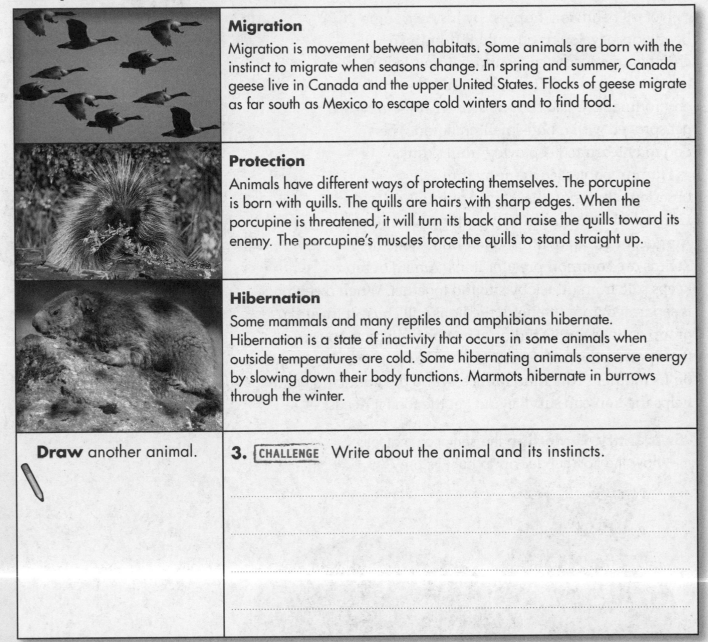

Migration

Migration is movement between habitats. Some animals are born with the instinct to migrate when seasons change. In spring and summer, Canada geese live in Canada and the upper United States. Flocks of geese migrate as far south as Mexico to escape cold winters and to find food.

Protection

Animals have different ways of protecting themselves. The porcupine is born with quills. The quills are hairs with sharp edges. When the porcupine is threatened, it will turn its back and raise the quills toward its enemy. The porcupine's muscles force the quills to stand straight up.

Hibernation

Some mammals and many reptiles and amphibians hibernate. Hibernation is a state of inactivity that occurs in some animals when outside temperatures are cold. Some hibernating animals conserve energy by slowing down their body functions. Marmots hibernate in burrows through the winter.

Draw another animal.

3. CHALLENGE Write about the animal and its instincts.

....

....

....

....

4. ● **Text Features** Tell why a chart is a good way to organize the information on this page.

At-Home Lab

Migrating Animals
Identify an animal in your area that migrates. Describe the path of the animal's migration.

Learned Behavior

Not all behaviors happen by instinct. Some behaviors develop as a result of training or changes in experience. Young animals learn many things as they interact with the environment. A dog that attacks a skunk may get sprayed with a bad-smelling liquid. The dog may learn to keep away from skunks.

Human babies learn many things by observing their parents. Young animals do too. Lion cubs learn to hunt by watching older lions. A pride, or group of lions, often hunts together. Zebras are common prey for lions. A herd of zebras keeps safe from attack by staying together. When a zebra is separated from the herd, the lions will chase it toward a group of lions that is hiding. The lions will then pounce on their prey. A lion cub learns to pounce on its prey by pouncing on its mother's twitching tail. Learning the pouncing behavior helps the lion cub survive and get the food it needs.

5. Identify Underline the sentence that tells how the lion cub learns to hunt its prey.

6. Exemplify Name two behaviors that a human baby might learn from her parents.

....

....

....

....

mYscienceonLine.com | Got it? 60-Second Video

Learning and Instinct Combined

Some behaviors are partly instinctive and partly learned. The white-crowned sparrow inherits the ability to recognize the song its species sings. But knowing how to sing the song is not inherited. Sparrows must learn the song from their parents. Scientists have found that young sparrows that are separated from their parents never learn to sing the complete song.

Humans inherit the ability to learn much more than animals can learn. For example, humans inherit the ability to learn language. But we are not born knowing English, Spanish, or Chinese. We must learn the words used in our language.

7. ⦿ **Draw Conclusions** If this adult sparrow cannot complete its song, what can you conclude?

....

....

Got it?

8. **Identify** **Underline** the behavior that is a response to a stimulus in the environment.

   A thirsty elephant looks for water.

   A fish moves to deeper water as the temperature of a lake changes.

9. **Classify** Humans sometimes build fires to keep warm. Is this an instinctive behavior or a learned behavior? Explain how you know.

....

....

⬛ **Stop!** I need help with ....

⏸ **Wait!** I have a question about ....

▶ **Go!** Now I know ....

What is inside an owl pellet?

Follow a Procedure

☑ **1.** Place an owl pellet on a sheet of paper. **Measure** its length.

☑ **2.** **Observe** the pellet. Separate the contents of the pellet.

Materials

safety goggles

owl pellet

wooden probe

forceps

hand lens

sheet of paper   metric ruler

Inquiry Skill
You **infer** when you explain your observations.

Be careful! **Wear safety goggles. Wash your hands when finished.**

3. Fill in the chart to **classify** the contents of the pellet.

4. **Record** your observations below.

Owl Pellet Observations					
	Pellet Length	**Skulls**	**Other Bones**	**Teeth**	**Fur or Feathers?** (describe)
Pellet contents					

Analyze and Conclude

5. Draw a Conclusion   What can you **infer** about the diet of the owl?

....

....

....

....

....

6. UNLOCK THE BIG **?**   How does examining an owl pellet help you learn about the ecosystem of an owl?

....

....

....

....

....

Wildlife Biologist

If you like animals, you might like to be a wildlife biologist. Wildlife biologists study animals and their habitats. They want to know how the animals live and how they behave.

At the International Crane Foundation (ICF) near Baraboo, Wisconsin, biologists study cranes in captivity and in the wild. With the information the biologists gather, they hope to increase the number of these endangered birds.

One important job the biologists have is to teach cranes raised in captivity to migrate. Cranes raised in captivity do not learn migration routes from their parents. So biologists teach the cranes how to migrate. Biologists fly small aircraft and train the cranes to follow them.

If you think wildlife biology is for you, plan to take science classes in high school. You might volunteer to work with animals in a local habitat. You will need a college degree in biology or a related science.

APPLY THE BIG ? How does a captive environment affect the cranes' ability to survive?

Vocabulary Smart Cards

- classify
- vertebrates
- invertebrates
- sepal
- pistil
- stamen
- pollination
- fertilization
- germinate
- photosynthesis
- chlorophyll
- adaptation
- characteristics
- inherit
- advantage
- stimulus
- instinct

Play a Game!

Cut out the Vocabulary Smart Cards.

Work with a partner. Choose a Vocabulary Smart Card. Say as many words as you can think of that describe that vocabulary word. Have your partner guess the word.

sepal

sépalo

classify

clasificar

pistil

pistilo

vertebrates

vertebrados

stamen

estambre

invertebrates

invertebrados

to arrange or sort objects or living things according to their properties or characteristics

What is the noun form of this word?

....

....

ordenar o agrupar objetos o seres vivos según sus propiedades o características

---

one of the leaflike parts that cover and protect the flower bud

Draw an example.

una de las partes en forma de hoja que cubren y protegen el botón de las flores

---

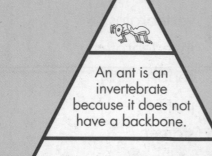

An ant is an invertebrate because it does not have a backbone.

invertebrates: animals without backbones

---

animals that have backbones

Draw an example.

animales que tienen columna vertebral

---

a female structure in plants that produces egg cells

Draw an example.

estructura femenina de las plantas donde se producen los óvulos

---

Make a Word Pyramid!

Choose a vocabulary word and write the definition in the base of the pyramid. Write a sentence in the middle of the pyramid. Draw a picture of an example, or of something related, at the top.

---

animals without backbones

Write an example.

....

....

....

animales que no tienen columna vertebral

---

male structure in plants that makes pollen

Write a sentence using this word.

....

....

....

estructura masculina de las plantas que produce el polen

characteristics  **rasgos**	**photosynthesis**  **fotosíntesis**	**pollination**  **polinización**
inherit  **heredar**	**chlorophyll** 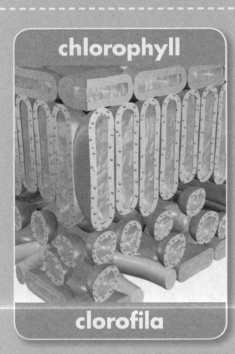 **clorofila**	**fertilization**  **fertilización**
advantage  **ventaja**	**adaptation**  **adaptación**	**germinate**  **germinar**

the movement of pollen from stamen to pistil

What is the verb form of this word?

....

....

....

proceso por el cual el polen se mueve del estambre al pistilo

---

the process in which plants make sugar

Write a sentence using this word.

....

....

....

proceso en el cual las plantas producen azúcar

---

the qualities an organism has

Write an example.

....

....

....

....

cualidades que tiene un organismo

---

the process in which a sperm cell and an egg cell combine

What is the verb form of this word?

....

....

....

proceso por el cual se unen un óvulo y un espermatozoide

---

the substance in plants that makes their parts green and captures energy from sunlight

Write a sentence using this word.

....

....

....

sustancia que se encuentra en las plantas y que da color verde a sus partes y capta energía de la luz solar

---

to receive characteristics from an organism's parents

Write an example.

....

....

....

....

recibir rasgos de los padres de un organismo

---

to start to grow

Draw an example.

empezar a crecer

---

a physical feature or behavior that helps an organism survive in its environment

Write an example.

....

....

....

rasgo físico o forma de conducta que ayuda a un organismo a sobrevivir en su medio ambiente

---

a characteristic that can help an individual compete

Write a synonym for this word.

....

....

....

característica que le permite a un individuo competir

stimulus

estímulo

instinct

instinto

something that causes a
reaction in a living thing

Write an example.

....

....

....

....

algo que provoca una
reacción en un ser vivo

a behavior that is inherited

Write a sentence using this
word.

....

....

....

....

conducta que se hereda

Study Guide

 REVIEW THE BIG ? **What do living organisms need to survive?**

 Life Science

Lesson 1

How are plants and animals classified?

- Scientists classify plants and animals into groups.
- Vertebrates are animals that have a backbone.
- Invertebrates are animals without a backbone.

Lesson 2

How do plants reproduce?

- Plant seeds form when pollen cells fertilize egg cells in the pistil.
- Seeds begin to germinate, or grow, when they have the water, oxygen, and temperature they need.

Lesson 3

How do plants make food?

- Plants make sugar through a process called photosynthesis.
- Chlorophyll is a green substance in plants that captures energy from sunlight for photosynthesis.

Lesson 4

What are adaptations?

- Adaptations help organisms survive in their environments.
- Some adaptations help animals get food or protect themselves.
- Some adaptations help plants survive or reproduce.

Lesson 5

What plant and animal characteristics are inherited?

- Organisms inherit some characteristics from their parents.
- Some characteristics may give an individual an advantage over other individuals.

Lesson 6

How do animals respond to the environment?

- Animal behaviors are a response to stimuli in the environment or stimuli within the animal.
- Animals inherit instinctive behaviors. Other behaviors are learned.

Chapter Review

What do living organisms need to survive?

Lesson 1

How are plants and animals classified?

1. Summarize What are two characteristics scientists might use to classify a plant?

....

....

....

....

....

....

Lesson 2

How do plants reproduce?

2. Vocabulary The part of a flower that makes pollen is a(n)
   A. pistil.
   B. stamen.
   C. sepal.
   D. ovary.

Lesson 3

How do plants make food?

3. Describe What are the roles of a plant's roots, stems, and leaves in the process of making food?

....

....

....

....

....

....

....

Lesson 4

What are adaptations?

4. Explain How do the wings of an eagle help the eagle survive?

....

....

....

....

....

....

....

Lesson 5

What plant and animal characteristics are inherited?

5. ⊙**Text Features** How does this photograph of peppered moths help you understand how the color a moth inherits can give it an advantage?

....

....

....

....

....

6. **Explain** What does it mean to inherit a characteristic?

....

....

7. **Give an Example** Write one characteristic that humans may inherit.

....

Lesson 6

How do animals respond to the environment?

8. **Write About It** How is an instinct different from a learned behavior?

....

....

....

....

....

9. **APPLY THE BIG ?** **What do living organisms need to survive?**

Think about a newly born crocodile. After the crocodile has hatched, how does it compare to its parents? What does it need to survive?

....

....

....

....

....

Benchmark Practice

Fill in the bubble next to the answer choice you think is correct
for each multiple-choice question.

1 Scientists classify insects, spiders, and
crabs as

Ⓐ vertebrates.

Ⓑ reptiles.

Ⓒ arthropods.

Ⓓ mollusks.

2 Something that causes a reaction in a
living thing is called a(n)

Ⓐ stimulus.

Ⓑ behavior.

Ⓒ instinct.

Ⓓ inherited characteristic.

3 Plants are green because they contain

Ⓐ sugar.

Ⓑ oxygen.

Ⓒ nutrients.

Ⓓ chlorophyll.

4 Giraffes with longer necks have an
advantage in

Ⓐ competition.

Ⓑ adaptation.

Ⓒ nutrition.

Ⓓ protection.

5 Which adaptation might help protect
a plant from being eaten?

Ⓐ a flower that looks like a bee

Ⓑ a waxy coating

Ⓒ a substance that attracts insects

Ⓓ a thorny stem

6 This diagram shows the parts of a
flower. Describe the role of each part in
reproduction.

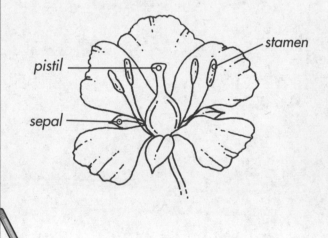

STEM

Plant Engineering

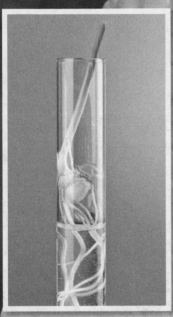

Some corn we eat today is a result of selective breeding and genetic engineering.

For centuries, people selectively bred plants with traits valuable to humans. People still selectively breed plants. What is selective breeding? It is when a few organisms with desired traits serve as parents of offspring. When scientists and farmers selectively breed plants, they want to make better plants. Genetic engineering is another way to change plants. Genetic engineering is the changing of the structure of an organism's genes to change inherited traits.

Why do companies change the genes of a plant? They change the genes of a plant for many reasons. For example, the genes of some corn are altered to resist insects that kill corn plants. Genetic engineering may also cause problems. Seeds of plants with newly changed genes may spread to other areas and affect ecosystems.

Predict How could seeds with changed genes help NASA scientists prepare for human life on the moon or Mars?

....

....

What do armadillos eat?

Ecosystems

Try It! How can you estimate how many animals live in an ecosystem?

Investigate It! How do earthworms meet their needs in a model of an ecosystem?

Nine-banded armadillos live in brush, woods, scrub, and grasslands. The armadillo is a medium-sized, insect-eating mammal.

Predict What things do you think an armadillo needs to survive?

_____

_____

_____

THE BIG ? How do living things interact with their environments?

How can you estimate how many animals live in an ecosystem?

Scientists can figure out how many animals live in a large area by counting how many animals there are in small parts of the area and then **estimating.** The more small parts that they check, the better their estimate usually is.

☑ **1.** Scatter two handfuls of cereal on a checkerboard. Guess how many pieces are on the board.

....

☑ **2.** Work with a partner. Determine a way to **estimate** the total number of pieces on the board.

Write your estimate. ....
Hint: Start with a small area.

☑ **3.** Count all the pieces of cereal on the board. ....

Explain Your Results

4. Which was easiest: guessing, **estimating,** or counting?

....

Which was most accurate? ....

5. Infer How do you think you could make your estimate more accurate?

....

6. **UNLOCK THE BIG ?** **Infer** Why do you think scientists might want to know how many animals live in an ecosystem?

....

....

....

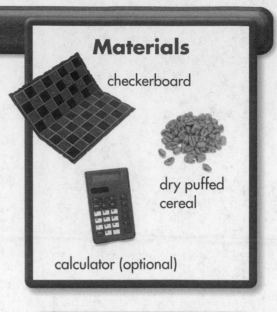

Materials

checkerboard

dry puffed cereal

calculator (optional)

Inquiry Skill Sometimes you can use math to help you make a good **estimate.**

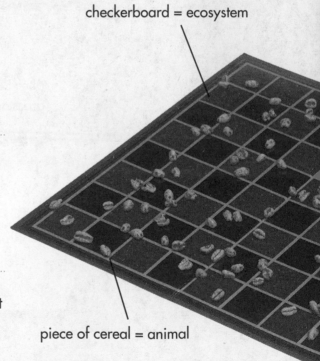

checkerboard = ecosystem

piece of cereal = animal

⊙ Main Idea and Details

- The **main idea** is the most important idea in a reading selection.
- Supporting **details** tell more about the main idea.

The Desert Ecosystem

Plants can live in a hot, dry desert. Long roots that grow close to the surface allow a cactus to take in as much rainwater as possible during a single storm. The roots of a large saguaro cactus may grow to 15 meters in length. The stem of a cactus expands to fill with the rainwater it collects.

Practice It!

Complete the graphic organizer below to show the main idea and details in the example paragraph.

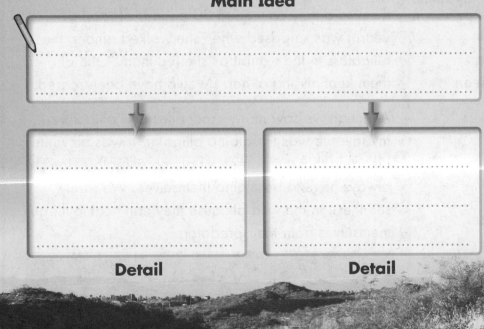

Main Idea

Detail

Detail

What are ecosystems?

Tell how the organisms in this picture interact.

my PLaneT DiaRY

Let's Blog!

by Emma
Middleburg, FL

Write a response to Emma's blog. Talk about an animal you have seen or read about.

Today we went to the Alligator Farm in St. Augustine. We saw American alligators. One alligator was an albino. Did you know they feed them rodents called Cavia? The worker that fed them said they only need 80 pounds of food a year. I was surprised when she walked among the alligators in the exhibit as she fed them. One of them kept hissing at her. I would have been scared.

Although we saw many crocodiles and alligators, my favorite was the albino alligator. It was all white. I learned that the parents of albino alligators don't always have to be albino themselves. We rarely see these in the wild because they can't camouflage themselves from their predators.

It was an exciting day and a great way to spend the afternoon learning.

UNLOCK
THE BIG
?

I will know the parts of ecosystems and some examples of ecosystems. I will know how specific structures of organisms help them live in their habitats.

Words to Know

ecosystem   population
habitat

Parts of an Ecosystem

An **ecosystem** is all the living and nonliving things in an environment and the many ways they interact. An ecosystem may be large like the ocean or small like a park. Animals and plants are living parts of an ecosystem. These organisms interact with each other and with the nonliving parts of the system. The nonliving parts of an ecosystem include air, water, soil, sunlight, and landforms.

1. ◉ **Main Idea and Details** Complete the graphic organizer below. Write details about ecosystems.

2. **Infer** The seahorse interacts with its ocean ecosystem by holding on to the coral. Why do you think the seahorse holds on to the coral?

....

....

....

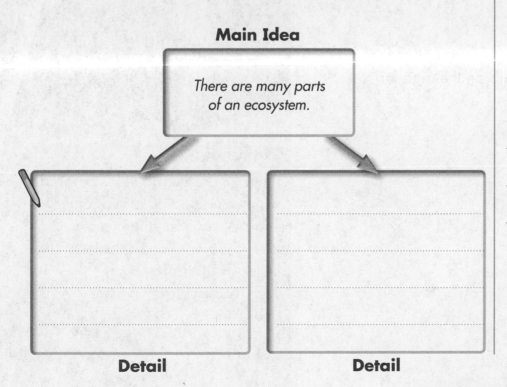

Main Idea

There are many parts of an ecosystem.

Detail

Detail

Kinds of Ecosystems

There are several different ecosystems in North America, such as tundra, rain forest, desert, grassland, and forest. Many factors, such as climate and soil, make ecosystems different. Some ecosystems are cold and dry, while others are warm and wet. Some ecosystems have sandy soil while others have fertile soil. The kinds of plants and animals that live in an area depend on the climate and soil. Organisms can survive only in environments in which their needs are met. In any environment, some kinds of plants and animals survive better than others.

For example, you may think that nothing can live in a desert ecosystem, but deserts have many organisms living there. Cacti and lizards live in deserts. Sandy soil is used as a hiding place for the desert horned lizard. The lizard can quickly become invisible by throwing sand over its body.

3. ◎ **Main Idea and Details** Read the first paragraph again. **Underline** the main idea. (Circle) the details.

4. [CHALLENGE] How might a grassland change if very little precipitation falls on the area for several years?

....

....

....

....

....

....

Wetlands

In wetlands, the ground is covered with water for at least part of the year. Water lilies and cypress trees grow in some wetlands. Different kinds of animals, such as insects, raccoons, and alligators, live in wetlands too.

raccoon

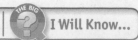

myscienceonline.com | ? THE BIG | I Will Know...

Tundra

1 A tundra is a cold region. The ground beneath the surface is frozen all year. Some grasses can grow, but trees cannot. Arctic foxes, caribou, and other animals thrive in these areas.

caribou

Rain Forests

2 Not all rain forests are tropical. The mild and rainy climate of the Pacific Northwest supports temperate rain forests. They are home to organisms such as spotted owls, banana slugs, and Douglas fir trees.

northern spotted owl

Desert

3 The driest ecosystem is a desert. Some plants and animals have adapted to the limited water supply. Cacti, coyotes, and lizards are desert organisms.

Grassland

4 Grasslands, as their name suggests, are covered with grasses. They receive a medium amount of rain. Grasshoppers, prairie chickens, and bison are animals that live in grasslands in North America.

grasshopper

desert horned lizard

Living Things Within Their Ecosystems

Habitat

The area or place where an organism lives in an ecosystem is its **habitat.** You can think of a habitat as an "address." The habitat of the lion is open grassland with shrubs, trees, and water. A habitat contains all the living and nonliving things that an organism needs to survive.

Population

Look at the picture on this page. It shows a savannah ecosystem in Africa. A savannah is a kind of grassland. There are many populations found in this savannah. A **population** is all the members of one species that live within an area of an ecosystem. For example, the wildebeests that live in the African plains form a population. A population may be large or small.

5. **Apply** Find another population in the picture and draw an ✗ on each member of that population.

6. **Identify** Write the names of two other populations that you think could be part of the ecosystem shown here.

....

....

giraffe

a habitat within a savannah ecosystem

wildebeest

zebra

Structures for Survival

Many organisms such as the platypus have special structures that help them survive in their habitats. These structures may include wings that allow them to fly, webbed feet that help them swim, and fur that keeps them warm. Different organisms in an ecosystem may have similar structures that help them live there. For example, many organisms that live in the ocean have fins that help them move easily through water.

7. **Infer** What kind of ecosystem might this animal live in? Explain how you know.

....

....

Got it?

8. **Identify** What kind of habitat do you think an animal with long, thick fur would most likely live in?

....

....

9. **Explain** What structures might monkeys have that help them to live in trees?

....

....

Stop! I need help with ....

Wait! I have a question about ....

Go! Now I know ....

How do living things get energy?

Envision It!

Sun   Energy

Animals get energy from the food they eat.

Inquiry **Explore It!**

What do yeast use for energy?

Yeast are tiny living things. They cannot make their own food.

☐ **1.** Put $\frac{1}{2}$ spoonful of yeast in a cup. Fill the cup half full with warm water. Stir. **Observe** for 10 minutes.

☐ **2.** Add 1 spoonful of sugar. Stir. Observe for 10 minutes.

Materials

plastic cup

yeast

warm water

spoon

sugar

Explain Your Results

3. Compare what you **observed** before and after adding the sugar.

....

....

4. Infer What did the yeast use for energy? Cite your evidence.

....

....

myscienceonline.com | **Explore It!** Animation

Energy → → Energy

Chipmunk

Draw what the chipmunk gets energy from and what gets energy from the chipmunk.

I will know that animals get energy from the plants and animals they eat. I will know the consequences of the removal of one component in a balanced ecosystem.

Words to Know

producer   carnivore
consumer   omnivore
herbivore   decomposer

Producers

All living things in an ecosystem need water, nutrients, growing space, and temperatures that allow them to grow and reproduce. Above all, they need energy to survive. But where does this energy come from? It comes mainly from sunlight. The sun's energy enters the ecosystem and flows through all living things. It changes form as it moves through the ecosystem.

The energy flow starts in plants. During a process called photosynthesis, green plants use energy from sunlight to change carbon dioxide and water into food and oxygen. Plants use energy from the food they make to grow and live. Plants are called **producers** because they make, or produce, their own food. In almost all ecosystems, green plants are the only producers.

1. **Locate Underline** the main source of energy in an ecosystem.

2. **Infer** Write a sentence that describes how energy flows into the vegetables.

....

....

....

....

....

Some of the energy in plants is stored in their roots.

mys012enceonline.com | **Envision It!**

3. **Infer** What kind of consumer is a rabbit?

4. **Word Structure**

The suffix *-vore* means "eating." What do you think a spongivore like the hawksbill turtle eats?

At-Home Lab

For the Birds!
Make a bird feeder. Work with an adult. Hollow out half of an orange. Make 3 small, equally spaced holes 1 cm from the edge. Put a different string through each hole and tie the string to make a loop. Hang the 3 loops on a branch. Fill the orange with bird seed. Observe for several days. Record the number and types of birds you see.

Consumers

Can you make your own food like a plant? No, and neither can any other animal. Animals get energy by eating, or consuming, plants or other animals. Living things that eat other living things are called **consumers.**

The sun's energy stored in plants flows into the animals that eat the plants. **Herbivores** are animals that eat plants. Each herbivore uses some energy to live and grow. Some energy is released as heat, but some energy is stored in its body. The unused, stored energy is transferred when the herbivore is eaten.

Animals that get food by eating other animals are **carnivores.** The carnivore uses some of the transferred energy to live and grow. The unused energy is stored in the carnivore's body. When the carnivore is eaten, whatever stored energy is left is passed on. Some animals, called **omnivores,** eat plants and other animals.

The red-bellied woodpecker is an omnivore. It eats beetles, grasshoppers, acorns, fruits, and seeds. Red-bellied woodpeckers search for insects in trees.

myscienceonline.com |  I Will Know...

5. Identify Write words to fill in the diagram.
Use words that describe each kind of consumer.

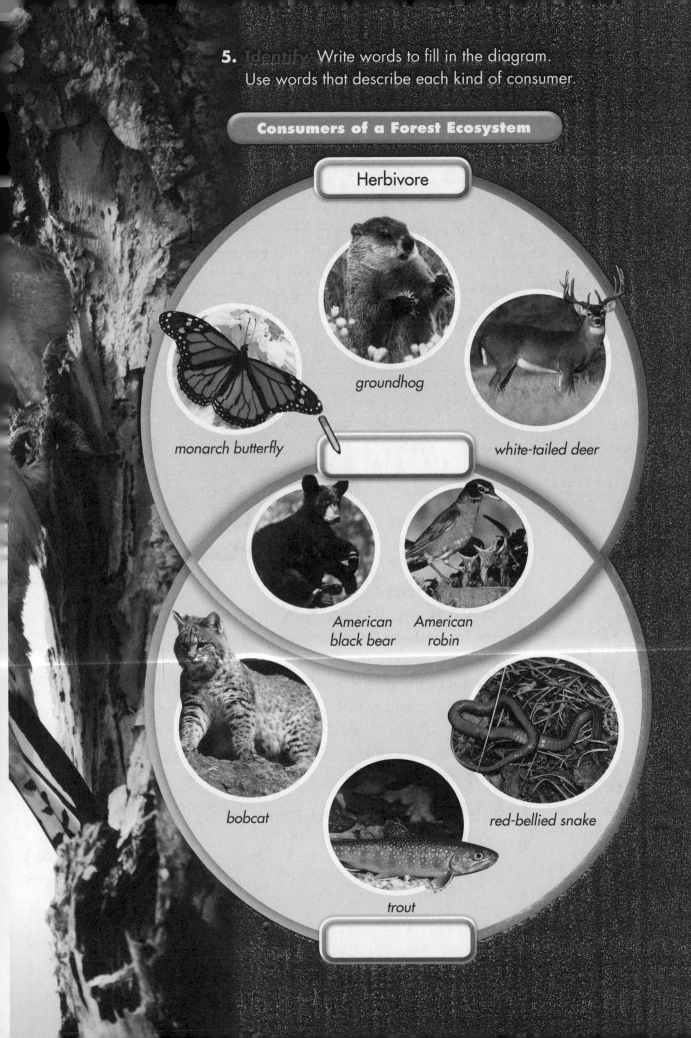

Consumers of a Forest Ecosystem

Herbivore

monarch butterfly

groundhog

white-tailed deer

American black bear

American robin

bobcat

trout

red-bellied snake

Read a Graph

A rabbit is a kind of consumer. Scientists sometimes conduct studies on how rabbit populations change over time. The graph shows how the size of one rabbit population changed over a 10-year period.

Consumer Populations

1. What was the size of the population in year 9?
   A. 200,000   C. 600,000
   B. 400,000   D. 850,000

2. Draw a dot on the graph for the year when the population of rabbits was about 700,000.

7. Draw The common wood louse is a decomposer found in gardens. It is only 1.5 cm long. Draw a 1.5-cm line to show the actual length of the wood louse.

Decomposers

When plants and animals die or leave wastes, what happens to their unused energy? Other organisms such as some earthworms, fungi, and bacteria break down the dead material or the waste. The unused energy is transferred to them. Organisms that break down plant and animal waste and remains are called **decomposers.** In this way, energy flows from the sun to producers, to consumers, and to decomposers.

6. CHALLENGE In what ways are producers, consumers, and decomposers alike and different?

....

....

....

Removal of One Component

A change in a living or nonliving part of an ecosystem upsets the balance in the ecosystem. For example, the materials that decomposers break down become nutrients in the soil that plants need. If a group of decomposers dies out in an ecosystem, the nutrients they would have put in the soil are not available for plants to use. The plants might weaken or die. Then there might be fewer plants for herbivores to eat.

8. **Predict** How might this chipmunk be affected if the decomposers in this ecosystem decrease a lot?

chipmunk

fungus

....

....

....

....

Got it?

9. **Describe** How might a carnivore be affected if an herbivore were removed from a balanced ecosystem?

....

....

10. **UNLOCK THE BIG ?** Think about what you learned in this lesson. How do living things interact in their environments?

....

....

⬛ **Stop!** I need help with ....

⏸ **Wait!** I have a question about ....

▶ **Go!** Now I know ....

Lesson 3

What are food chains and food webs?

Draw and label producers and consumers found in an ecosystem near your school.

Inquiry **Explore It!**

How do food webs show connections?

☐ **1.** Choose a card. Hold it so it can be seen. Stand in a circle with your group. Look for organisms that your organism eats or that eat you. Toss the ball of yarn to one of them, but hold onto the end of the yarn.

☑ **2.** Take turns until everyone is connected. You have made a **model** of a food web.

☑ **3.** Lay down the yarn and the cards. Using the names of the organisms, draw your food web in the space to the right.

Materials

Food Web Cards   yarn

Explain Your Results

4. Interpret Data Look at your food web. Explain the relationships the web shows. Give examples.

....

....

....

myscienceonline.com | **Explore It!** Animation

Tell how you think they get food.

UNLOCK THE BIG ?

I will know how energy flows in a food chain and a food web. I will know how some organisms compete for the same resources.

Words to Know

food chain   food web

Energy Pyramids

In an ecosystem, energy flows from the sun to producers, to herbivores, carnivores, and decomposers. However, most of the energy within an organism that is consumed does not reach the next organism.

An energy pyramid is a diagram that shows the amount of energy that flows from producers to consumers. The base of the energy pyramid is widest. This shows the energy in the producers. Producers have the greatest amount of energy in an ecosystem. Notice that the pyramid becomes narrower at the upper levels. This shows that less energy flows upward from the lower levels to the higher ones.

mountain lion

deer

ferns

1. **Explain** Why is an animal's food and energy traced back to plants and the sun?

....

....

....

....

2. **Infer** Some energy cannot flow upward in the pyramid because most of the energy has changed. For example, energy is used to warm the organism's body. What other ways might animals use energy?

....

Food Chains

The energy stored by producers can be transferred along a food chain. A **food chain** is the transfer of energy from one organism to another by eating and being eaten.

A food chain always begins with energy from sunlight. Producers are the next link in the chain. Sunlight is absorbed by the green parts of plants. In a process called photosynthesis, plants use carbon dioxide, water, and sunlight to make food.

When animals eat plants, both energy and matter are passed to other living things. The flow of energy through the chain happens in one direction. In a diagram of a food chain, arrows show the flow of energy. Arrows point from the "eaten" to the "eater."

energy from the sun

ferns

deer

3. **Arrange** Write a number below each picture to show the flow of energy in the food chain.

mouse

owl

ferns

myscienceonline.com | THE BIG ? | I Will Know...

In a forest ecosystem, a food chain might consist of the sun, plants, a deer, and a mountain lion. Mountain lions are predators. Predators get the energy they need by hunting and killing prey. Deer are prey for the mountain lion. The mountain lion uses the food energy that was stored in plants and passed to the deer.

Decomposers such as fungi and bacteria are at each level of a food chain. They get what they need from dead organisms and other waste. Decomposers return matter to the soil, air, and water. Producers can then reuse this matter.

4. **Discuss** Tell why decomposers, such as the banana slug, are important in a food chain.

The banana slug is a decomposer. It gets its energy from leaves, animal waste, and dead plant materials. Then, it recycles what it eats into the soil.

mountain lion

energy from the sun

At-Home Lab

Decomposers Delight
Sprinkle yeast on a banana slice. Put it in a resealable bag. Close tightly. Observe every day for 1 week. Record your observations.

Food Webs

An ecosystem has many food chains. The same food source can be part of more than one food chain. As a result, one food chain often overlaps other food chains. Many food chains combine to form a food web. A **food web** is a system of overlapping food chains in which the flow of energy branches out in many directions.

In any ecosystem, producers and consumers can be eaten by more than one kind of organism. Some predators eat more than one prey. In a forest ecosystem, owls compete for food with mountain lions. Both populations hunt rabbits, mice, and squirrels.

All living things are connected in some way. A change in one part of a food web can affect all parts. All living things depend on other living things for what they need to survive. Anything that affects the size of a population of organisms also affects the food web. Disease, storms, pollution, and hunting are events that can affect a food web.

5. **Show** Circle a producer on this food web. Draw an X on three consumers. Trace with your finger the flow of energy from the sun as it is transferred along the food chain through producers to the consumers.

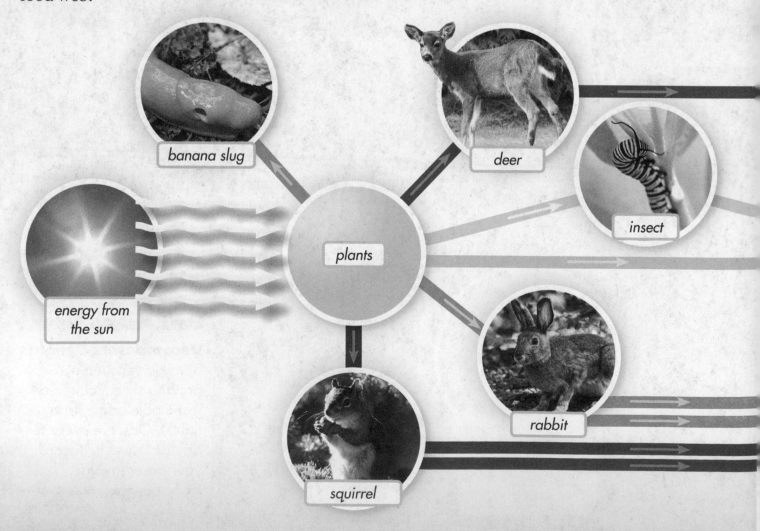

banana slug

deer

insect

energy from the sun

plants

rabbit

squirrel

6. [CHALLENGE] Which animal is both a predator and a prey?

....

....

7. Identify For what same resource do the mountain lion and the owl compete?

....

....

8. Explain Give an example of how changing one part of a food web to the left can change other parts of the web.

....

....

....

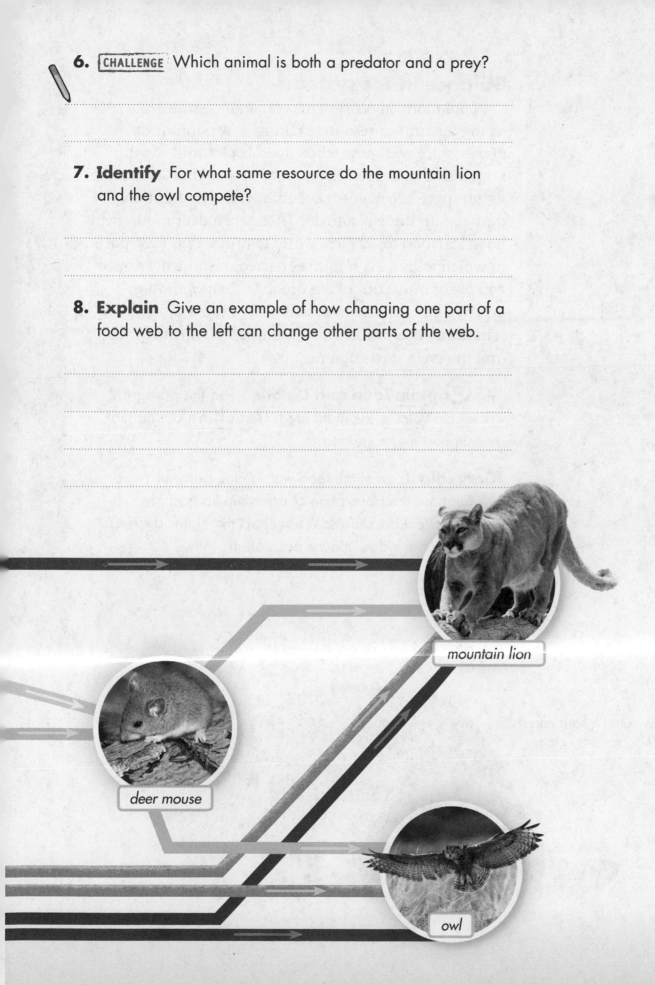

mountain lion

deer mouse

owl

Balance in Ecosystems

Populations in ecosystems can change naturally as the amount of resources changes. A population of deer mice will grow where food is plentiful. As the population increases, more food, more water, and more living space are needed. Eventually, the population may use up these resources. Then, each deer mouse will have less food to eat, less water to drink, and less space in which to live. As resources decrease, some deer mice will die or move out of the area. As the population decreases, more resources will be available to the remaining deer mice. The population begins to grow, and the cycle starts again.

9. **Main Idea and Details** Read the paragraph again. Circle the main idea. **Underline** details that support the main idea.

10. **Predict** Look at the food web on the previous page. Suppose the population of mountain lions in an ecosystem decreases. What effect might this decrease have on the deer mouse population? Why?

....

....

Mountain lions often hunt for prey alone.

11. **Design** Think about an ecosystem near where you live. Draw and label the living and nonliving parts in that ecosystem in the space provided.

Got it?

12. **Explain** What is one result of organisms competing for the same resources in an ecosystem?

13. **Describe** How is a food web different than a food chain?

Stop! I need help with ....

Wait! I have a question about ....

Go! Now I know ....

How do living things affect the environment?

Envision It!

Tell how humans have affected this deer's environment.

Inquiry ▸ Explore It!

What happens when one part of an ecosystem is removed?

In this model of an ecosystem, you will find out what can happen to animals when a resource decreases.

☑ **1. Make a Model** Lay out blue paper squares. Lay two red squares of paper to overlap each blue square.

☑ **2.** Roll the dot cube. Remove that number of water holes.

☑ **3.** Roll the cube five times. After each roll, match animals with water holes.

☑ **4.** No more than two animals can be at a water hole. Remove extra animals. **Record** information on the Water Holes and Animals Chart.

Explain Your Results

5. Infer What might happen to animals when there is a long drought?

....

....

Materials

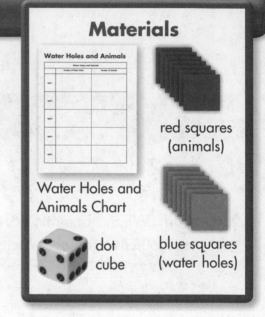

Water Holes and Animals Chart

red squares (animals)

dot cube

blue squares (water holes)

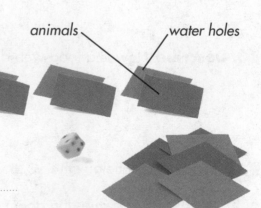

animals   water holes

I will know the effect of a sudden change of one group of organisms on another group.

Word to Know

competition

Changes to the Environment

The environment is like a balance. One side holds what lives in the environment. The other side holds resources that the environment provides. If the environment provides enough resources to support life, the balance is level.

Change often tips the balance. For example, tree seeds may sprout on a log and start to grow. The young trees need light and space to grow. The young trees are in competition. **Competition** occurs when two or more living things need the same resources in order to survive. Some trees get enough light. As their branches grow, they shade nearby plants. The environment changes. Other young trees may not get enough light to survive.

1. **Identify** In the paragraphs on this page **underline** what young trees are competing for against other living things.

2. **Examine** How can the fallen tree in this picture change a forest habitat?

....

....

....

....

....

....

....

Plants Cause Change

Changes can help some living things and harm others. For example, a plant called purple loosestrife was brought to the United States. No animals eat this plant. It is spreading to new places. That is great for the loosestrife! However, there is less space for other plants to grow. Some kinds of plants are completely pushed out of the environment.

A plant called kudzu was originally brought to the United States from Japan. At first, kudzu was thought to be beneficial to the environment. Kudzu was used in gardens for its beauty and in many open spaces as a cover over soil to prevent erosion. The plant, however, grows very well in the southeastern United States. Because the vines grow so well, they destroy forests by blocking trees' sunlight.

3. **Summarize** How has kudzu both helped and harmed habitats?

....

....

....

....

....

....

kudzu

Animals Cause Change

Some animals change the environment to improve their habitat. Beavers, for example, need deep water. If the stream where they live is too shallow, the beavers build a pond. They cut down trees with their teeth. They use the wood to build a dam across the stream. The blocked water forms a pond behind the dam.

The change helps plants and animals that need to live in still water. Also, the trees the beavers cut down no longer shade the ground below. Small plants and shrubs that benefit from direct sunlight grow in their place.

The change harms plants and animals whose homes are flooded. Trees needed to make the dam are lost. The pond also takes homes away from plants and animals that prefer the flowing water of streams.

4. Conclude This habitat was once a grassy meadow. How has this beaver dam changed it?

....

....

....

....

A beaver can cut down over 200 trees per year!

A beaver can add over 5 feet of length to its dam per day.

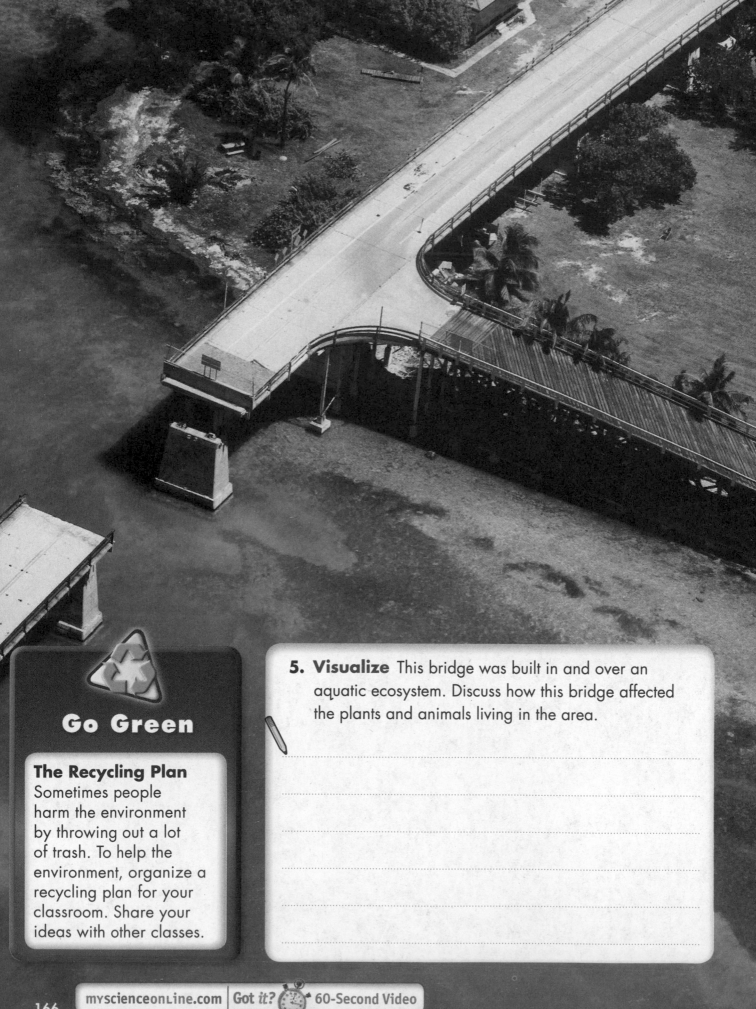

Go Green

The Recycling Plan
Sometimes people harm the environment by throwing out a lot of trash. To help the environment, organize a recycling plan for your classroom. Share your ideas with other classes.

5. Visualize This bridge was built in and over an aquatic ecosystem. Discuss how this bridge affected the plants and animals living in the area.

myscienceonline.com | Got it? 60-Second Video

Humans Cause Sudden Change

People often change the environment to meet their needs. Some changes people make cause sudden changes in the environment. When they build a new group of homes, they may cut down a small forest in days to make room for houses. Some people may build birdhouses in their backyards. This provides shelter and food for certain kinds of birds in the area. But most birds and other animals must move away to find new homes all of a sudden.

Some people use chemicals to kill organisms such as beetles and other insects that eat crops or plants around their homes. These chemicals quickly decrease the number of these organisms. Birds that feed on these organisms might have less to eat and may move away or die.

6. **Explain** How did this birdhouse affect the environment?

....

....

Got it?

7. **Describe** How do beavers and humans modify their environments?

....

8. **UNLOCK THE BIG ?** Think about what you learned in this lesson. Are changes to the environment always harmful?

....

....

....

⬛ **Stop!** I need help with ....

⏸ **Wait!** I have a question about ....

▶ **Go!** Now I know ....

What are fossils?

Compare the tracks. **Tell** what you can conclude about the animals that made them.

my planet diary DISCOVERY

Woolly mammoths disappeared from Earth about 10,000 years ago. Scientists have learned about mammoths by studying their bones and other remains. In 2007, however, scientists got an amazing opportunity to learn what mammoths were like.

That year, reindeer herders in northern Russia discovered the frozen body of a baby mammoth. The mammoth had been frozen underground for about 40,000 years. Except for missing toenails and hair, the month-old mammoth was in nearly perfect condition. Even the food in its stomach was preserved!

What do you think scientists might learn by studying the baby mammoth?

....

....

....

The baby mammoth has been named Lyuba.

 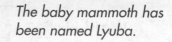

I will know that a fossil is the remains or mark of a living thing from long ago. I will know the ways a fossil can form.

Words to Know

fossil
extinct

Fossil Clues

Some plants and animals that lived millions of years ago have left clues about their lives. A line of footprints preserved in rock can show how an animal walked. The skeleton of a small animal can help scientists understand what the animal looked like.

Skeletons and footprints are examples of fossils. A **fossil** is the remains or mark of an animal or plant that lived long ago. Scientists can study fossils to learn about species that are extinct. An **extinct** species no longer exists. More than one million species currently live on Earth, but many more have become extinct. In fact, most types of organisms that have lived on Earth no longer exist.

1. ⦿ **Main Idea and Details** Read the first paragraph again. **Underline** the main idea.

2. **Explain** Read the caption below. What is one thing scientists might learn by examining a trilobite fossil?

....

....

....

Trilobites are now extinct. These animals had hard shells and lived in the sea hundreds of millions of years ago.

How Fossils Form

Fossils form in different ways. Most fossils form when a plant or animal dies and becomes buried under layers of sediments. Sediments are bits of rock, sand, shell, and other material. Over time, the sediments harden into rock and preserve the shape of the buried plant or animal. The diagram below shows this process.

Usually only the hard parts of animals, such as bones and shells, become fossils. The soft parts decay or may be eaten by other animals. Once the remains of an animal are buried, different things can happen. Sometimes the buried remains break down and disappear, leaving an empty space in the sedimentary rock. A space in rock in the shape of a living thing is called a *mold fossil*. Later, minerals from the surrounding rock might fill the mold fossil. Over time, these minerals harden into the shape of the mold. This type of fossil is called a *cast fossil*. Dinosaur "bones" that come from cast fossils are not bones at all! They are hardened minerals.

3. Fill in the Blanks Complete the captions in the diagram below. Fill in each blank with the correct word.

Most fossils are found within sedimentary rock, or rock that forms in layers.

An animal dies and sinks to the bottom of a lake or shallow sea. The _____ parts of its body decay.

Sand, mud, and other _____ settle on top of the animal's remains.

4. **Identify** Draw an ✗ on the mold fossils. (Circle) the cast fossil.

5. **Infer** Many dinosaurs once roamed Earth, but fossils do not exist for all of them. Look at the diagram. What might be some reasons why not all dinosaurs left fossils?

....

....

....

These are Ammonite fossils.

More layers of sediments form. The sediments harden into .... *, preserving the shape of the animal's parts.*

Over time the rock layers above the fossil wear away. The fossil appears at or near Earth's surface.

This fly has been preserved in amber.

The skull of this saber-toothed cat was preserved in a tar pit.

Other Types of Fossils

Casts and molds are called *body fossils* because they are formed from the body parts of living things. There are several other types of body fossils. Sometimes, the whole body of an animal may be preserved in a fossil. For example, insects can become trapped in sticky tree sap. The sap surrounds the insect and hardens over time. The hardened sap is called amber. Amber preserves all of an insect's remains—both the hard parts and the soft parts.

Parts of an animal's body, such as teeth or bones, make up another type of body fossil. The bones of some animals were preserved in tar pits. Tar pits are oily pools that exist on Earth's surface. Animals that fell into tar pits became trapped. The soft parts of their bodies broke down, but their bones remained. Fossils of these animals are actual bone and not hardened minerals.

7. **Contrast** How are the fossils of the saber-toothed cat different from cast fossils?

6. CHALLENGE What do you think scientists can learn from an insect preserved in amber?

Trace Fossils

Most fossils show what the parts of a plant or animal looked like. *Trace fossils* give clues about a living thing's activities. Footprints, or tracks, are a kind of trace fossil. Preserved burrows, nests, and eggshells are also trace fossils. Studying trace fossils can help scientists answer questions about where an animal lived, what it ate, and how fast it moved.

8. Identify Draw an ✗ on the photo of a trace fossil.

Got it?

9. Infer Explain how a mold fossil of a footprint would form.

....

....

10. Conclude Suppose you are a scientist studying saber-toothed cats. Would you be more excited to find cast fossils or fossils from a tar pit? Explain your answer.

....

....

 Stop! I need help with ....

Wait! I have a question about ....

 Go! Now I know ....

What can fossils tell us?

Tell what clues this fossil gives about what this dinosaur ate.

MY PLANET DIARY

//// MISCONCEPTION ////

Dinosaurs were a group of reptiles that lived on Earth for about 150 million years. That period has been called the Age of the Dinosaurs. A common misconception is that all of the large reptiles alive at that time were dinosaurs. In fact, Earth was home to many other kinds of reptiles during the Age of the Dinosaurs.

Pterosaurs, for example, were a group of flying reptiles. They did not have feathers, but flew on wings made of skin. The largest pterosaur had wings measuring more than 30 feet from tip to tip!

Pterodactyls are sometimes called "flying dinosaurs." In fact, the pterodactyl was a kind of pterosaur.

Pterosaurs and dinosaurs shared a common ancestor. But scientists have used fossils to identify important differences between the two. Dinosaurs, for example, had a different hip structure than pterosaurs. Like dinosaurs, pterosaurs became extinct about 65 million years ago.

Write one way in which dinosaurs and pterosaurs were alike and one way in which they were different.

....

....

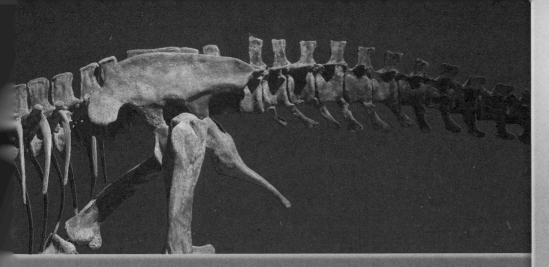

I will know how scientists use fossils to learn about the past.

Word to Know

paleontologist

Windows to the Past

Scientists study fossils to learn about plants, animals, and environments of the past. A scientist who studies fossils is called a **paleontologist.**

Some fossils show us what extinct organisms looked like and how they lived. For example, paleontologists have found skulls from dinosaurs called sauropods. Sauropods were a group of dinosaurs that had small heads, long necks, and enormous bodies. They ate plants and may have used their long necks to reach tall trees.

Because of their size, these dinosaurs needed huge amounts of food. However, their small heads meant that they could only take small bites. How did they get enough to eat? Paleontologists studied the dinosaurs' skulls and the shape of their teeth. They concluded that some sauropods may have swallowed their food without chewing it. Doing this allowed the dinosaurs to get food to their stomachs more quickly and take more bites.

This illustration shows what one kind of sauropod may have looked like.

1. **Recall** What did paleontologists conclude about sauropods by studying their skulls and teeth?

....

....

....

....

....

paleontologist

myscienceonline.com | Envision It!

Fossils and Living Organisms

One way paleontologists learn about extinct plants and animals is by comparing them with plants and animals that exist today. For example, fossils show that some dinosaurs called hadrosaurs had large, hollow crests on their heads. Paleontologists have different ideas about the purposes of these crests. One idea came from comparing hadrosaurs to birds called peacocks. Male peacocks have large, brightly colored tails. They use their tails to attract mates. Paleontologists hypothesize that hadrosaurs may have used their crests in the same way.

Fossils can also show how plants and animals have changed over time. Many living things today are related to plants and animals of the past. Fossils show that some extinct plant species looked a lot like modern plants. For example, compare the pictures of the horsetail fossil and the modern horsetail plant. Some horsetail plants of the past grew to the size of trees. Modern horsetail plants are much smaller. This suggests that the plants changed slowly over time.

This illustration shows what one kind of hadrosaur might have looked like.

3. **Hypothesize** What is another possible use of the hadrosaur's hollow crest?

....

....

....

....

....

2. **Compare** Tell how the horsetail fossil and the modern horsetail plant are alike.

Then

Now

myscienceonline.com | THE BIG ? | I Will Know...

Fossils and the Environment

Fossils also show that Earth's environment has changed. For example, scientists in Kansas have found the remains of sea animals called ammonites. Ammonites are related to modern squids, but they died out 65 million years ago. In South Dakota, scientists have discovered fossils of giant sea turtles. These turtles lived about 70 million years ago but are now extinct. What do these discoveries tell us? They show that areas of present-day states such as Kansas and South Dakota were once covered with water!

4. **Describe** How has the environment of Kansas changed?

....

....

5. ◉ **Main Idea and Details** What details support the idea that Earth's environment has changed?

....

....

....

....

Then

Now

ammonite

Geologic Time Scale

Present

Cenozoic Era
In the last 65 million years, dogs, cats, and humans appeared.

65 million years ago

Mesozoic Era
The Mesozoic Era, also called the Age of the Dinosaurs, was the time of hadrosaurs and Tyrannosaurus rex. Most dinosaurs became extinct at the end of this period.

248 million years ago

Paleozoic Era
Fish, simple plants, insects, and early land animals lived during this time.

544 million years ago

Precambrian
Some rocks from the late Precambrian time have fossils of jellyfish.

Fossil Age

Scientists determine the age of fossils in two ways. Many fossils are located within layers of rock. Older layers of rock are under newer layers of rock. Scientists can conclude that fossils found in deeper or lower layers are older than those found in layers above.

Scientists can also determine the age of fossils by examining how quickly certain materials in the fossils change. These materials change at steady rates after a plant or animal dies. Scientists can measure these materials in a fossil to determine how long ago the organism died.

Geologic Time Scale

Scientists have used information about the ages of fossils and rocks to make a timeline of the history of Earth. This timeline is called the geologic time scale. When they draw the scale, scientists place the earliest time span at the bottom. They put the most recent time span at the top. This matches the way rock layers of different ages are arranged. The time scale helps scientists show when different animals, including the dinosaurs, existed.

6. **Infer** What era are the sea turtle fossils of South Dakota from?

7. ◎ **Draw Conclusions** Suppose that you found two different fossils in two different layers of rock. How could you tell which fossil was older?

Scientists divide Earth's history into time spans of millions of years. These time spans are labeled on the geologic time scale.

myscienceonline.com | Got it? ⏱ 60-Second Video

Fossil Fuels

Did you know that fuels such as coal and oil are a kind of fossil? Most of these "fossil fuels" come from the remains of organisms that lived millions of years ago. It took millions of years for the remains to become coal or oil. At power plants, fossil fuels are used to produce the electricity that powers homes and businesses.

8. [CHALLENGE] What might happen if people use up all the fossil fuels currently available? Explain your answer.

....

....

....

....

Go Green

Fossil Fuel Use
With a partner, list three things you and your classmates can do to reduce electricity use and conserve fossil fuels. Share your list with the class.

Got it?

9. ◉ **Draw Conclusions** A scientist finds the fossil of a sea creature on top of a mountain range. What can the scientist conclude about the land around the fossil?

....

10. **Summarize** What can paleontologists learn from studying fossils?

....

....

....

☐ **Stop!** I need help with ....

❚❚ **Wait!** I have a question about ....

▶ **Go!** Now I know ....

How do earthworms meet their needs in a model of an ecosystem?

Follow a Procedure

☑ **1.** Obtain an earthworm bottle from your teacher. Use a spoon to add a thin layer of sand. Add 6 worms.

 Be careful! Earthworms are living organisms. Handle with care.

Materials

spoon

safety goggles

foil

earthworm bottle

plastic cup with sand

black paper

rubber band

6 earthworms

masking tape

☑ **2.** Tape black paper around the bottle. Cover the top with foil fastened with a rubber band. Wait 24 hours.

Inquiry Skill

Scientists make careful observations and record data accurately. They use their data to help make **inferences.**

3. Remove the paper and foil. **Observe** the sand, dirt, and earthworms. **Record** your observations.

	Earthworm Observations
Day	**Observations**
Day 1 (24 hours after making ecosystem)	
Day 2	
Day 3	
Day 4	

4. Replace the paper and the foil. Observe daily for 3 more days. Record your observations.

Be careful! **Wash your hands when finished.**

Analyze and Conclude

5. Explain your **observations.**

....

....

....

6. Infer Do the earthworms get what they need from the ecosystem? Tell how you know.

....

....

7. UNLOCK THE BIG **?** What does the model ecosystem show about how living things interact in their environments?

....

....

Rachel Carson

In the 1950s, people used a chemical called DDT to poison harmful insects. Farmers sprayed it on their fields. In cities and towns, it was used on the plants in parks.

Rachel Carson was a scientist and a writer. She began to notice that every spring there were fewer and fewer songbirds. She wondered what was happening to the bird populations. After making careful observations, Carson learned that DDT was building up on land and in lakes and streams. The chemical had entered the food chains and webs of many ecosystems.

Carson wanted to warn as many people as possible about the dangers of using DDT. In 1962, she wrote a book titled *Silent Spring*. Because of her book, laws forbidding the use of DDT were passed. Society has been more aware of the delicate balance of ecosystems ever since.

 How do you think the interaction of DDT in the environment affected the birds?

....

....

....

....

Vocabulary Smart Cards

ecosystem
habitat
population
producer
consumer
herbivore
carnivore
omnivore
decomposer
food chain
food web
competition
fossil
extinct
paleontologist

Play a Game!

Cut out the Vocabulary Smart Cards.

Work with a partner. Choose a Vocabulary Smart Card.

Say as many words as you can think of that describe that vocabulary word.

Have your partner guess the word.

producer

productor

ecosystem

ecosistema

consumer

consumidor

habitat

hábitat

herbivore

herbívoro

population

población

all the living and nonliving things in an environment and the many ways they interact

What is the prefix for this word and what does it mean?

....

todos los seres vivos y las cosas sin vida que hay en un medio ambiente y las múltiples interacciones entre ellos

---

living thing that makes its own food

Write three related words.

....

....

....

....

ser vivo que genera su propio alimento

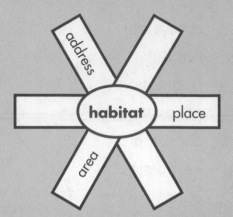

Choose a vocabulary word and write it in the center of the Word Wheel graphic organizer. Write synonyms or related words on the wheel spokes.

---

area or place where an organism lives in an ecosystem

Use a dictionary. Find as many synonyms for this word as you can.

....

....

área o lugar de un ecosistema donde vive un organismo

---

living thing that eats other living things

Write what the verb form of this word means.

....

....

....

....

ser vivo que se alimenta de otros seres vivos

---

all the members of one species that live within an area of an ecosystem

Write another definition for this word.

....

....

todos los miembros de una especie que viven en un área de un ecosistema

---

animal that eats plants

Draw an example.

animal que come plantas

fossil

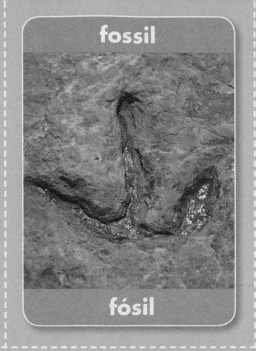

fósil

food chain

cadena alimentaria

carnivore

carnívoro

extinct

extinto

food web

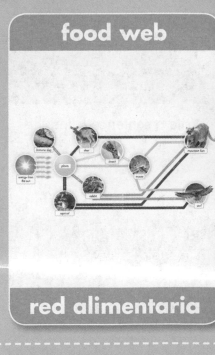

red alimentaria

omnivore

omnívoro

paleontologist

paleontólogo

competition

competencia

decomposer

descomponedor

animal that gets food by eating other animals

Write three examples.

....

....

....

....

animal que se alimenta al comerse otros animales

---

the transfer of energy from one organism to another by eating and being eaten

Draw an example.

transmisión de energía de un organismo a otro al comerlo o al ser comido

---

remains or mark of an animal or plant that lived long ago

Draw an example.

restos o marca de un ser vivo que existió hace mucho tiempo

---

animal that eats plants and other animals

What is the prefix of this word and what does it mean?

....

....

....

animal que come plantas y otros animales

---

system of overlapping food chains in which the flow of energy branches out in many directions

Write a sentence using this term.

....

sistema de cadenas alimentarias que se sobreponen, en el cual la energía fluye en muchas direcciones

---

no longer existing as a species

Write a sentence using the word.

....

....

....

....

ya no existe más como especie

---

organism that breaks down plant and animal waste and remains

What is the suffix of this word and what does it mean?

....

....

organismo que destruye residuos y desechos de animales y vegetales

---

occurs when two or more living things need the same resources in order to survive

Write a sentence using the verb form of this word.

....

....

situación en la que dos o más seres vivos necesitan los mismos recursos para sobrevivir

---

a scientist who studies fossils

What is the suffix of this word and what does it mean?

....

....

....

científico que estudia los fósiles

Chapter 4
Study Guide

REVIEW THE BIG ? How do living things interact with their environments?

Life Science

Lesson 1

What are ecosystems?

- An ecosystem is all the living and nonliving things in an environment.
- There are many ecosystems including desert, tundra, and forest.
- Special structures help many organisms survive in their habitats.

Lesson 2

How do living things get energy?

- Some living things eat plants, animals, or both to get energy.
- The removal of one part of an ecosystem can affect the balance of the energy in the ecosystem.

Lesson 3

What are food chains and food webs?

- In an ecosystem, energy flows from producers to consumers.
- Food chains show how energy is transferred.
- A food web is a system of overlapping food chains.

Lesson 4

How do living things affect the environment?

- Living things compete with each other for food and space.
- Some animals change the environment to improve their habitat.
- Changes in the environment help some living things and harm others.

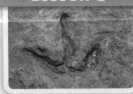

Lesson 5

What are fossils?

- A fossil is the remains or mark of an animal or plant that lived long ago.
- Most fossils form when a plant or animal dies and becomes buried under layers of sediments.

Lesson 6

What can fossils tell us?

- Paleontologists study fossils to learn about extinct organisms.
- Fossils can show how plants, animals, and Earth's environment have changed over time.

Chapter Review

REVIEW THE BIG ? How do living things interact with their environments?

Lesson 1

What are ecosystems?

1. **Vocabulary** A group of organisms of the same kind living in an area is a(n)_____.
   A. community.
   B. population.
   C. ecosystem.
   D. habitat.

2. **Explain** How do the fins of a sunfish help it survive in water?

....

....

3. **Define** What makes up an ecosystem?

....

....

....

....

....

Lesson 2

How do living things get energy?

4. ◉ **Main Idea and Details** (Circle) the main idea and **underline** the details in the following paragraph.

   Decomposers have an important role in food webs. They break down and recycle waste and dead organisms. Decomposers recycle the minerals and nutrients that are found in the waste and dead material. These nutrients become available to plants.

Lesson 3

What are food chains and food webs?

Do the math!

5. In most food chains, $\frac{9}{10}$ of the energy that an animal gets from its food is used by the animal. What fraction of the food energy is not used?

....

6. **Infer** Can there be an ecosystem that has only carnivores? Why or why not?

....

....

....

Lesson 4

How do living things affect the environment?

7. Communicate People build roads in new areas. How does this activity affect the living things in that environment?

....
....
....
....

Lesson 5

What are fossils?

8. Explain Tell how this mold fossil of an ammonite may have formed.

....
....
....
....

Lesson 6

What can fossils tell us?

9. Conclude Horseshoe crabs are called "living fossils" because they have changed little in 300 million years. How do paleontologists know this?

horseshoe crab

10. APPLY THE BIG **?** **How do living things interact with their environments?**

Think about an ecosystem near where you live. How do the organisms there interact?

....
....
....
....

Fill in the bubble next to the answer choice you think is correct
for each multiple-choice question.

1 What is the main source of energy in
an ecosystem?

Ⓐ predators
Ⓑ water
Ⓒ sunlight
Ⓓ plants

2 Which of these things might trees
compete for in an environment?

Ⓐ ecosystems
Ⓑ consumers
Ⓒ populations
Ⓓ resources

3 In a simple food chain, a frog eats
insects and a snake eats the frog. The
primary role of the frog in the food
chain is

Ⓐ to be a source of energy.
Ⓑ to find a space to live.
Ⓒ to start a new species.
Ⓓ to make an ecosystem.

4 What might a paleontologist conclude
about a dinosaur that left fossil
footprints of webbed feet?

Ⓐ The dinosaur ran fast.
Ⓑ The dinosaur ate plants.
Ⓒ The dinosaur was large.
Ⓓ The dinosaur could swim.

5 The diagram below shows different
consumers in different ecosystems.

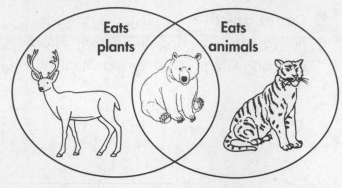

Eats
plants

Eats
animals

Suppose the populations of these
consumers are removed from their
ecosystems. How might this change
affect the ecosystem of each consumer?

....

....

....

....

....

....

....

....

....

....

Denver Zoo

You can visit a zoo to learn about many types of animals. Animals that live in different habitats in the wild can all be seen in one place. At the Denver Zoo, you can see Komodo dragons in the Tropical Discovery exhibit. You might see a rhinoceros at the Pachyderm Habitat. These animals live far apart in nature, but you can see them in one day at the zoo!

Animals must find their own food in the wild. At the zoo, zookeepers give the animals the food they need. This food includes fruits, vegetables, meats, fish, and insects. A zoo needs many types of food because it has herbivores, carnivores, and omnivores to feed.

Suppose a zoo gets a new type of animal. What might the zookeepers need to know about the animal?

....

....

Materials

small plastic tub

2 sponges

water

plastic spoon

plastic cup of sand

10 mealworms and food

Inquiry Skill

Experiments have a **variable** you change and a variable you observe.

Do mealworms prefer damp or dry places?

A mealworm can sense whether the environment is damp or dry. Sometimes conditions change. You will **experiment** to find out how the environment affects mealworms' behavior.

Ask a question.

Do mealworms prefer to live in a damp place or a dry place?

State a hypothesis.

1. Write a **hypothesis** by circling one choice and finishing the sentence.
   If mealworms can move to a damp place or a dry place, then they will move to a place that is (a) *damp* or (b) *dry* because

....

....

....

Identify and control variables.

2. In this experiment you will observe where the mealworms move. You must change only one variable. Everything else must remain the same. What should stay the same? List two examples.

....

....

3. Tell the one change you will make.

....

....

....

....

Design your test.

☑ **4.** Draw how you will set up your test.

☑ **5.** List your steps in the order you will do them.

Do your test.

☑ **6.** Follow the steps you wrote.

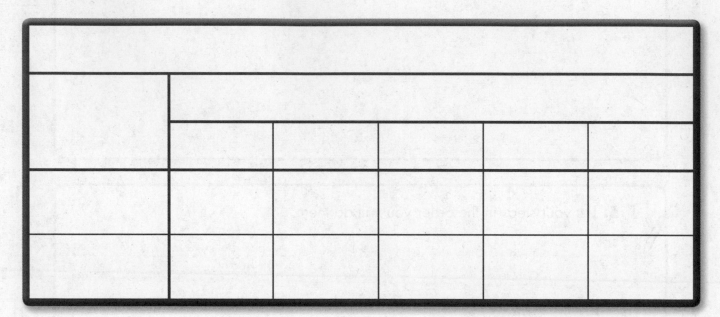 **Be careful!** They are alive! Handle with care!
Wash your hands after handling mealworms.

☑ **7.** Make sure to **record** your **observations** in the table.

Collect and record your data.

☑ **8.** Fill in the chart.

Check to see if your data are reasonable. You started with 10 mealworms. Each day add up the total number of mealworms. Make sure the total is 10.

Work Like a Scientist

Scientists work with other scientists. Compare your observations with other groups. Seek reasons that might explain any differences.

Interpret your data.

☑ **9.** Use your data to make bar graphs.

☑ **10.** Compare what you see in the 2 graphs.

....

....

....

....

State your conclusion.

11. Communicate your conclusion. Compare your hypothesis with your results. Share your results with others.

....

....

....

Technology Tools

Your teacher may want you to use a computer (with the right software) or a graphing calculator to help collect, organize, analyze, and present your data. These tools can help you make tables, charts, and graphs.

Build a Model of an Ecosystem

Choose one type of ecosystem you have read about. Use a cardboard box, clay, construction paper, foam, or other materials to build a model of your ecosystem. Include labeled models of living and nonliving things. Write about the adaptations of the plants and animals in your ecosystem.

Write a Biography

Choose an animal found in your state, and write a biography for the animal. Be sure to include these things:

- the type of animal
- the animal's ecosystem and habitat
- the adaptations that help the animal survive in its environment
- ways the animal responds to changes in its environment

Make a Presentation

Like beavers, humans build dams that change the flow of rivers. Research some dams in your state to find out more about how dams change environments. Find or draw pictures of one dam to show in a presentation to your class. Write captions for the pictures, explaining how the dam affects the environment. Share your findings in your presentation.

Using Scientific Methods

1. Ask a question.
2. State your hypothesis.
3. Identify and control variables.
4. Test your hypothesis.
5. Collect and record your data.
6. Interpret your data.
7. State your conclusion.
8. Try it again.

Earth Science

How can magma form steps?

Earth's Resources

 Try It!   How can rocks and minerals be classified?

Investigate It!   How does the steepness of a stream affect how fast it flows?

Giant's Causeway is a formation of about 40,000 stone pillars in Northern Ireland. The tops of the pillars form a path of stepping stones to the sea. Cooling magma from an ancient volcano formed Giant's Causeway between 50 and 60 million years ago.

 Predict   What forces might have shaped this formation?

....

....

THE BIG ?   How do Earth's resources change?

How can rocks and minerals be classified?

Minerals are the building blocks for rocks.

☑ **1. Observe** the rocks and minerals.

☑ **2. Classify** the rocks and minerals into groups.
Use texture, color, and hardness.
Draw a picture and label the groups.

☑ **3.** Sort the rocks and minerals in other ways.

Materials

rocks and minerals

hand lens

Inquiry Skill
Observing objects carefully can help you **classify** them.

This group of rocks and minerals is
....

This group of rocks and minerals is
....

This group of rocks and minerals is
....

This group of rocks and minerals is
....

Explain Your Results

4. List the property or properties you used to help **classify** the rocks and minerals.

....

....

Draw Conclusions

- A **conclusion** is a decision you reach after you think about observations and data that you know or have gathered.
- The conclusion should make sense and be supported by the facts.

Quartz

Amethyst is the purple form of the mineral quartz. Citrines are also quartz, but they range in color from yellow to orange. A green form of quartz is known as prasiolite. Pure quartz, called rock crystal, is clear and colorless. All of these forms of quartz are used in rings, necklaces, and other jewelry.

Practice It!

Complete the graphic organizer. Read the three facts about quartz from the paragraph above. Then write a conclusion.

Facts	Conclusion
Amethyst is purple quartz.	
Citrine is yellow or orange quartz.	
Pure quartz is clear and colorless.	

Lesson 1

How are minerals classified?

One of these minerals is gold. Write which one you think is gold and which is "fool's gold."

my planet diary

//// **MISCONCEPTION** ////

You may have seen or heard people talk about minerals in food. Does that mean you are eating rocks? No! In this case, the word mineral refers to small amounts of chemicals, called elements, that are found in the foods you eat. These elements also make up certain minerals that are found in rocks in Earth's crust.

For example, iron helps your blood cells carry oxygen throughout your body. Foods containing iron include red meat and leafy green vegetables. Iron is also found in many minerals. But the iron in food is in a different form than the iron in minerals. You would not be able to digest the iron in a mineral.

How do you think iron and other minerals get into vegetables?

....

....

....

....

....

Words to Know

mineral   streak

luster   cleavage

hardness

Mineral Crystals

The salt you sprinkle on your food is a mineral. The metal fork you use when you eat is made from minerals. The ceramic plate you put food on is made from minerals. **Minerals** are natural, nonliving solid crystals that make up rocks. Scientists have identified more than 4,000 kinds of minerals. But most of Earth's rocks are made up of only a small number of them. These are often called the "rock-forming" minerals.

All around the world, each mineral has the same chemical composition. A grain of the mineral quartz from a beach in Australia has the same chemicals in it as a chunk of quartz chipped from a mountain in California.

Pure quartz is clear. Different impurities give quartz its color.

1. **Analyze** What is the relationship between minerals and rocks?

....

....

2. ⊙ **Compare and Contrast** How are the two examples of quartz described above alike? How are they different?

....

....

....

Mohs Scale for Hardness

| 10 diamond | 9 corundum | 8 topaz | 7 quartz | 6 feldspar |

Properties of Minerals

Most rocks are made of different combinations of minerals. Each type of rock always has a similar combination of minerals. Granite always contains quartz and feldspar crystals. Some rocks have only one or two minerals. White marble is made only of the mineral calcite.

How can you tell minerals apart? Scientists identify minerals by testing their properties. These include color, luster, hardness, streak, cleavage, and crystal shape.

Color and Luster

It is easy to see the color of a mineral. But the same mineral can be different colors. So color alone is usually not enough to identify a mineral. Scientists must look at other properties, such as luster. **Luster** is the way the surface of a mineral reflects light. A glassy luster is shiny, like glass. A metallic luster looks like polished metal. A soft shine can be described as a waxy, silky, or pearly luster. Some minerals have a greasy or a dull, chalky luster.

3. **Classify** Look at the Mohs Scale for Hardness at the top of these pages. Write adjectives on the scale describing the luster of the mineral samples shown in the scale.

Satin spar gypsum has a silky luster.

Calcite has a pearly luster. It can be colorless, white, or other pale colors.

Galena has a metallic luster.

myscienceonline.com **THE BIG ?** I Will Know...

softest

| 5 apatite | 4 fluorite | 3 calcite | 2 gypsum | 1 talc |

Hardness

Scientists may also measure a mineral's hardness. **Hardness** is how easily the surface of a mineral can be scratched. The Mohs Scale shown above ranks minerals by hardness. Talc is the softest mineral. It has a hardness of 1. Diamonds are the hardest minerals.

A mineral can scratch other minerals with lower Mohs rankings. For example, fluorite has a hardness of 4. It can scratch all minerals with a hardness of less than 4, such as gypsum.

Streak

The same mineral can be different colors. But all samples of a certain mineral will leave the same streak. **Streak** is the color of the powder that a mineral leaves when it is scratched across a special plate. Some minerals, such as gold, leave streaks that match their colors. But sometimes the streak is a different color than the mineral itself. For example, hematite can be silver or red. But its streak is always red.

4. **Analyze** Look again at the *Envision It!* at the start of this lesson. What could you do to help tell the difference between gold and fool's gold?

....

....

....

....

....

Cinnabar has a bright red streak.

Pyrite, or fool's gold, has a green-black streak.

Orpiment has a pale yellow streak.

Lightning Lab

Texture and Effervescence

Work with an adult. Find 8 rocks. Classify them by texture. Then put a few drops of vinegar on each. Observe if bubbles form. Classify the rock based on effervescence.

Shape and Cleavage

Each mineral has crystals that are a particular shape. These crystal shapes can be helpful when trying to identify a mineral crystal. Crystals are classified by these shapes and the angles that they form. For example, fluorite has cube-shaped crystals. Corundum crystals look more like hexagons. The shape of a mineral is not always easy to see. Scientists must sometimes use magnifiers or microscopes to see a crystal's shape.

Most minerals will break in definite patterns. Minerals that break along smooth, flat surfaces have **cleavage.** For example, mica has perfect cleavage. It breaks into thin, shiny layers that are flat and smooth. Some minerals do not have any cleavage. Quartz often breaks into pieces with smooth surfaces that look like the inside of a seashell. Still other minerals splinter, like pieces of wood.

5. [CHALLENGE] Draw the three directions of cleavage on the halite sample below.

Mica breaks into thin flakes that are flat and smooth.

Magnetite crystals often form shapes called octahedrons.

6. **Classify** If you have a small mineral sample, why might testing for cleavage be one of the last things you do?

....

....

....

....

....

Halite has cleavage in three directions. Halite is the mineral form of table salt.

Other Mineral Properties

There are many other ways to identify certain minerals. Two minerals, pyrrhotite and magnetite, are attracted by magnets. Sometimes magnetite can actually be a magnet. Some minerals, such as gold, silver, and copper, can be shaped or cut. Scientists can use chemical tests to identify some minerals. For example, if you drop vinegar on calcite, bubbling will occur.

You can use other senses to identify minerals. Not all minerals feel the same when you touch them. Some minerals can be identified by their smell or taste.

7. **Draw Conclusions** Which of your senses might you use most often when identifying minerals?

The magnetite in this lodestone attracts objects that contain iron.

Got it?

8. **UNLOCK THE BIG ?** **Explain** How can minerals be classified?

9. **Infer** Which property might you test by rubbing one mineral directly against another?

⬜ **Stop!** I need help with

⏸ **Wait!** I have a question about

▶ **Go!** Now I know

How are rocks classified?

Tell what you think will happen to this lava when it hits the water.

Inquiry Explore It!

What can you learn from rock layers?

☑ **1. Make a model** of rock layers. Fill a small cup with sand. Slowly pour the sand into a large cup.

☑ **2.** Put a paper clip in the sand so it touches the side of the cup. The paper clip represents a fossil animal.

☑ **3.** Slowly add layers of other materials to the cup. To make a model of more fossil animals, put a rubber band and crayon piece in two of the layers.

Explain Your Results

4. Infer Suppose you found 2 fossils in 2 different layers of rock. Would the older one be in the upper or lower layer of rock? Explain.

....

....

....

....

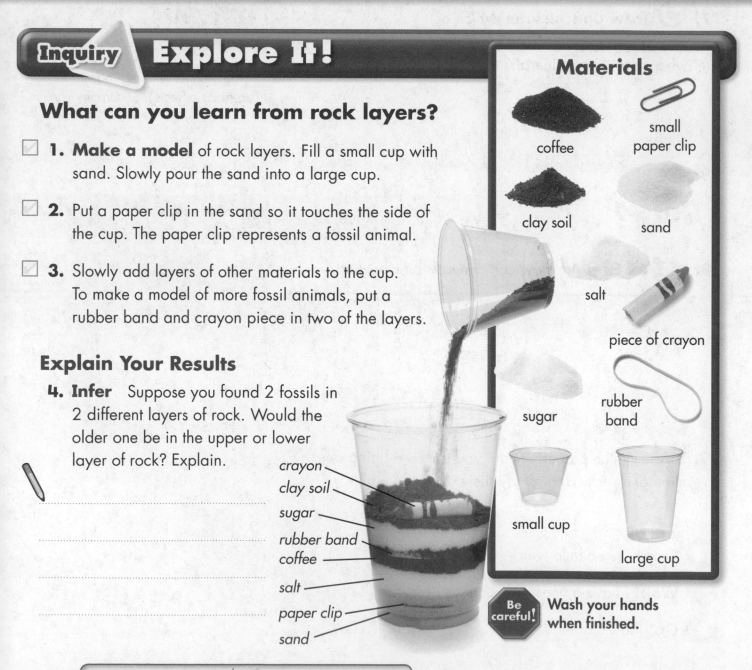

Materials

coffee

small paper clip

clay soil

sand

salt

piece of crayon

sugar

rubber band

small cup

large cup

crayon
clay soil
sugar
rubber band
coffee
salt
paper clip
sand

Be careful! Wash your hands when finished.

myscienceonline.com | **Explore It!** Animation

I will know the three categories of rocks and how they are formed.

Words to Know

igneous   metamorphic

sedimentary

Classifying Rocks

Earth's crust is made of rocks. Huge boulders are rocks. So are single grains of sand. The bits of rock that make up silt and clay can be too small to see without a microscope.

Rocks are nonliving, but they can change form both above and below Earth's surface. It can take millions of years for some rocks to form. Other rocks can form very quickly. One important way scientists classify rocks is based on how they are formed. The changes that form rocks produce three main kinds: igneous, sedimentary, and metamorphic rocks.

1. ◉ **Draw Conclusions** Use these two facts from the text above to draw a conclusion.

Facts

Huge boulders are rocks.

The bits of rock that make up silt and clay can be too small to see without a microscope.

Conclusion

....

....

....

Igneous Rocks

Some rocks form from other rocks that have melted. Rock below Earth's crust can be so hot that it is partially melted. This melted, or molten, rock is called magma. Rocks that form from molten rock are called **igneous** rocks. Igneous rocks may form above or below Earth's surface.

Magma Cooling Quickly

If you have seen pictures of a volcano erupting, you have seen magma exploding onto Earth's surface. After it reaches the surface, the molten rock is called lava. Sometimes lava oozes from a volcano like a red-hot river. Or, it may fly from a volcano in hot, gooey globs. Either way, the lava on the surface cools quickly. It may harden into solid igneous rock in just a few minutes to days.

As the lava cools, mineral crystals form. But when lava cools quickly, there is not much time for crystals to form. Any crystals that do form are very small. Pumice is an igneous rock that forms when air quickly cools lava.

Water can also cool lava. Basalt is an igneous rock that often forms under the ocean. The ocean water quickly cools the lava.

2. **Analyze** *Igneous* comes from the Latin word *ignis*, meaning "fire." Study the photo of a lava flow on these pages. Why is *igneous* a good name for this type of rock?

....

....

Pumice forms from lava that has lots of trapped gas bubbles. Crystals do not have time to form in pumice.

Granite has large crystals of quartz, feldspar, and mica. Its crystals are easy to see.

Obsidian is volcanic glass. It has no crystals.

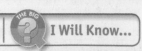

myscienceonline.com | THE BIG ? | I Will Know...

Magma Cooling Slowly

When magma slowly rises toward Earth's surface, it fills in cracks and melts the surrounding rock or forces it aside to make space. The magma cools slowly. As it hardens, crystals of minerals form in the rocks. These crystals are large. The longer it takes magma to cool, the larger mineral crystals can get. The cooling and hardening of magma into igneous rock below Earth's surface is a very slow process. It can take more than a million years!

3. ◉ **Draw Conclusions** If you needed a microscope to see an igneous rock's crystals, what would that tell you about how the rock cooled?

....
....
....
....
....

4. **Classify** Study the photos and captions of igneous rocks on these pages. (Circle) the rocks that cooled quickly. Draw an ✗ on the rocks that cooled slowly.

Basalt is one of the most common igneous rocks. It often has small, fine crystals.

Gabbro is similar in makeup to basalt, but has larger crystals.

Pegmatite contains the same minerals as granite. It often has very large crystals.

211

Sedimentary Rocks

Look at the sandstone cliffs shown on these pages. What do you notice? The cliffs may look like a stack of pancakes or sheets of paper. These layers show that the cliff is made of sedimentary rock. **Sedimentary** rocks form when layers of sediments settle on top of one another and harden. Sediments are made up of soil, shells, bits of rock, and dead plant and animal matter.

Water, wind, ice, and gravity make and move sediments from one place to another. Over time, sediments settle in layers on land or on the bottom of oceans, rivers, and lakes. Newer layers press the older layers together. The weight of the layers, sticky clay minerals in the sediment, and natural chemicals hold the particles together.

Scientists classify sedimentary rocks according to the materials in the sediment. Some sedimentary rock forms from materials that were once living things. Limestone, for example, is often made of hard skeletons and shells of sea animals that lived long ago. Sandstone is another type of sedimentary rock. It is usually made up of bits of quartz that are each about the size of a grain of sand. A third kind of sedimentary rock is made of very tiny particles. These particles usually settle at the bottom of lakes or oceans. Shale and mudstone are two examples of this kind of rock.

Conglomerate can form from rounded rocks that are the size of pebbles or larger.

Limestone often forms from tiny bits of skeletons and shells.

Sandstone can form from quartz sands.

5. ⊙ **Compare and Contrast** Look at the sedimentary rock samples on the previous page. How are conglomerate and sandstone alike? How are they different?

....

....

....

....

....

The layers of sedimentary rock are easy to see in these sandstone cliffs.

6. Identify Label a layer of sedimentary rock in the cliff on these pages.

Metamorphic Rocks

High temperatures deep inside Earth can change rocks. The rock is also under pressure from the weight of the rocks above it. These forces can cause rocks to change form completely. Rocks that have changed as a result of heat and pressure are known as **metamorphic** rocks.

As metamorphic rocks form, they can change in several ways. Heat and pressure may cause the mineral crystals in the rock to change. Sometimes the chemicals in the rock form new types of minerals. For example, the mineral graphite is made entirely of carbon. Enough heat and pressure can turn graphite into diamond.

Metamorphic rocks can form from sedimentary, igneous, and other metamorphic rocks. Limestone, a sedimentary rock, can become the metamorphic rock marble. The igneous rock granite can become the metamorphic rock gneiss. The next page shows how rock that has already been changed sometimes goes through even more changes.

7. **Identify** Based on the text, draw an arrow on the page to show a possible direction of the pressure that formed this metamorphic rock cliff.

Lightning Lab

Rock Model
Make a loose "brick" from different-colored layers of clay. What type of rock have you modeled? Now put the brick between two sheets of plastic wrap and press down hard with the heel of your hand to flatten it. Peel off the wrap. What type of rock have you modeled?

Sedimentary

Shale

Metamorphic

Slate

Metamorphic

Phyllite

Metamorphic

Schist

Shale

Tiny clay sediments settle on the bottom of oceans and lakes, forming shale. Shale is a soft sedimentary rock that often contains fossils. Shale that is exposed to heat and pressure can turn into much harder rock called slate.

Slate

Slate does not usually have fossils because the heat and pressure destroys them. The minerals in slate are arranged so that it splits easily into layers. Heat and pressure can change slate into other metamorphic rocks, such as a rock called phyllite.

Phyllite

Layers of the minerals mica and chlorite give phyllite a silky look. More heat and pressure can change phyllite into yet another kind of metamorphic rock! It can become a rock called schist.

Schist

Schist has larger grains than phyllite or shale. You might expect the cycle to end here, but it does not. Deep within Earth, schist and other rocks get hot enough to melt. If the melted schist cools, it can become new igneous rock!

8. **Summarize** How can shale become schist?

....

....

....

9. ◎ **Compare and Contrast** What feature do these four rocks have in common?

....

....

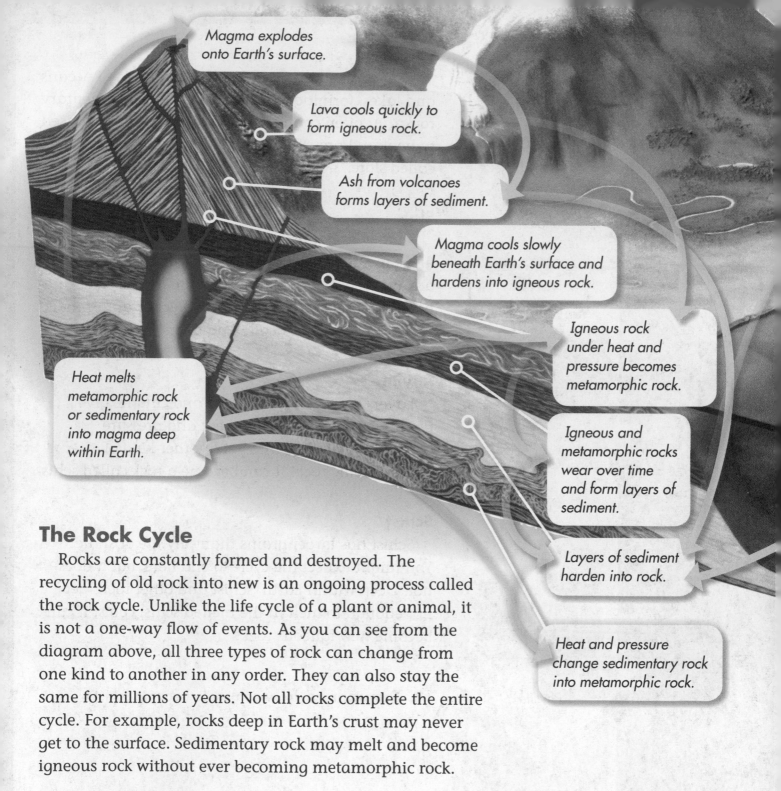

Magma explodes onto Earth's surface.

Lava cools quickly to form igneous rock.

Ash from volcanoes forms layers of sediment.

Magma cools slowly beneath Earth's surface and hardens into igneous rock.

Igneous rock under heat and pressure becomes metamorphic rock.

Heat melts metamorphic rock or sedimentary rock into magma deep within Earth.

Igneous and metamorphic rocks wear over time and form layers of sediment.

Layers of sediment harden into rock.

Heat and pressure change sedimentary rock into metamorphic rock.

The Rock Cycle

Rocks are constantly formed and destroyed. The recycling of old rock into new is an ongoing process called the rock cycle. Unlike the life cycle of a plant or animal, it is not a one-way flow of events. As you can see from the diagram above, all three types of rock can change from one kind to another in any order. They can also stay the same for millions of years. Not all rocks complete the entire cycle. For example, rocks deep in Earth's crust may never get to the surface. Sedimentary rock may melt and become igneous rock without ever becoming metamorphic rock.

10. Describe Study the illustration above. What materials from volcanoes can eventually become rock? What kinds of rock can those materials become?

....

....

....

myscienceonline.com | Got it? 60-Second Video

11. Explain Complete the caption on the diagram.

Some ....
rock wears away to form new layers of sediment.

12. CHALLENGE Can magma ever directly become sedimentary rock? Why or why not?

....

....

....

....

....

....

Got it?

13. Describe What kind of rock is being formed in the *Envision It!* photo at the start of this lesson?

....

14. Recognize What forces can form the particles that make up sedimentary rock?

....

....

⬜ **Stop!** I need help with ....

⏸ **Wait!** I have a question about ....

▶ **Go!** Now I know ....

What are weathering and erosion?

Envision It!

Tell what you think is shaping this beach.

Inquiry **Explore It!**

How does a rock wear away?

☐ **1.** Shake chalk and rocks in a jar for 1 minute. Look for changes in the chalk. Shake for 3 more minutes. **Observe.**

☐ **2.** Empty the jar. Fill it half full with water. Repeat Step 1 using the rocks and 4 new chalk pieces.

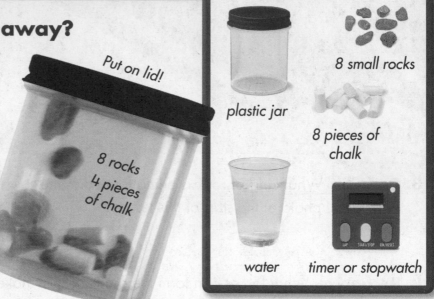

Put on lid!

8 rocks 4 pieces of chalk

Materials

plastic jar

8 small rocks

8 pieces of chalk

water   timer or stopwatch

Explain Your Results

3. How did the chalk change after being shaken with rocks for 1 minute? for 3 more minutes?

....

....

4. Infer Compared with shaking the chalk with only rocks, what effect did shaking with both rocks and water have on the chalk?

....

mYscienceonLine.com | **Explore It!** Animation

UNLOCK THE BIG ?

I will know how weathering, erosion, and deposition can change Earth's surface.

Words to Know

landform   erosion
weathering

Earth's Surface

The outer surface of Earth is a layer of rock called the crust. The crust covers all of Earth. In places such as the ocean, the crust is underwater.

A mountain is one of many different landforms that Earth's crust can have. A **landform** is a natural land feature on Earth's surface. Landforms can be different sizes and shapes. Plains are flat landforms on high or low ground, and plateaus are flat landforms on high ground. Along coasts, landforms such as peninsulas extend into the water. Valleys and canyons are also landforms.

Some landforms take shape quickly, while others form over a long time. A mountain may take millions of years to form. But rocks rolling down the side of that mountain can change it in a hurry. Think of what happens to the large amounts of soil that a flood carries from one place to another.

1. **Describe** What landforms are near where you live?

....

....

....

....

....

....

Earth's crust is miles thick, but if Earth were the size of a peach, the crust would only be as thick as the peach's skin.

myscienceonline.com | **Envision It!**

Weathering

Earth's landforms change constantly. Water, ice, temperature changes, wind, chemicals, and living things can all cause changes. Often, these changes occur over a long time.

Rocks in Earth's crust are slowly broken into smaller pieces in a process called **weathering.** There are two types of weathering, chemical weathering and physical weathering.

Chemical Weathering

During chemical weathering, chemicals cause rocks to change into different materials and break down. For example, rainwater mixes with carbon dioxide in the air to form a weak acid. When it rains, the acid combines with the rock material to form a new chemical. Gradually the new chemical breaks down the rock.

Animals and plants give off chemicals that can cause weathering. Sometimes the activities of people also add chemicals to the environment.

Water and warm temperatures are important for chemical weathering. Warmer areas or areas with a lot of rain have more chemical weathering than drier or colder areas.

2. **Analyze** (Circle) the evidence of weathering in this picture.

myscienceonline.com I Will Know...

Physical Weathering

In physical weathering, rocks are broken into smaller pieces of the same kind of rock. Water is one cause of physical weathering. Flowing water can carry particles of rock, soil, and sand. The particles scrape against larger rocks. The rocks gradually become smaller and smaller. The force of waves pounding against rocks on a shore can also cause rock to break down. Wind can carry small particles that can weather rocks.

Ice can also cause physical weathering. Water can seep into cracks in rocks. If this water freezes, it forms ice. Ice in rock takes up more space than the water does. The ice can make the cracks in the rock deeper. The rock may eventually split.

Temperature changes to a rock's surface may also cause weathering. When a rock's surface gets hotter, it expands, or grows larger. When it gets colder, the surface contracts, or gets smaller. Some scientists think that many temperature changes can weaken the surface of rock.

Living things can cause weathering too. Plants can sprout in a crack in a rock. As these plants and their roots get bigger, they can cause the rock to split.

3. **CHALLENGE** How can water cause both chemical and physical weathering?

....

....

....

Water contributed to the weathering of these rocks.

5. **CHALLENGE** Read the text on these pages and study the photo below. Based on the erosion and deposition patterns, which way do you think the river flows? Draw an arrow to indicate direction.

Erosion

Gravity, wind, water, and ice can all move bits of weathered rock. The process of carrying away weathered bits of rock is called **erosion.**

Moving water erodes, or carries away, materials from the land. As water moves faster, it can carry along heavier pieces of rock. Moving water can slowly carve grooves into the land as it carries away weathered material. Over a very long time, these grooves may become deep canyons.

Waves constantly change the shape of a shoreline. They pound against cracks in the rocks on the shore. Gradually, pieces of rock break off. The waves carry away the pieces. As parts of the shoreline erode, new landforms, such as beaches, develop.

In colder parts of Earth, moving ice erodes landforms. Glaciers are huge sheets of ice. Most glaciers move very slowly as gravity pulls them downhill. As glaciers move, they wear away bits of rock and soil.

4. ◉ **Draw Conclusions** What does a muddy river tell you about erosion?

....

....

Erosion carved this canyon along the Colorado River in Utah.

Deposition

As parts of Earth's surface are broken down, other parts are built up. The forces that carry away bits of weathered rock during erosion must drop them somewhere else. This laying down of pieces of rock is called deposition.

As moving water slows, the larger pebbles in the water settle to the bottom first. Then smaller sand-sized pebbles sink. Finally, the smallest bits of silt and clay sink too. Rivers deposit large amounts of materials where they flow into the ocean. The deposited material forms an area called a delta.

In deserts and near beaches, wind moves grains of sand into mounds called sand dunes. Winds may move a sand dune or change its size and shape. The size and shape of a sand dune also depend on the amount of sand and the number of plants in an area.

6. **Analyze Underline** the sentence that explains what deposition is.

sand dunes

delta

Got it?

7. **Explain** Describe how a canyon forms.

....

....

8. **UNLOCK THE BIG ?** Think about what you read in this lesson. Explain how Earth's surface changes slowly.

....

....

....

⬛ **Stop!** I need help with ....

⏸ **Wait!** I have a question about ....

▶ **Go!** Now I know ....

How can Earth's surface change rapidly?

Tell how the shape of the land is changing.

my PLANET DIARY

Science Stats

Most earthquakes occur at points where two plates, or two large pieces of Earth's surface, meet. But faults, or cracks in rock where Earth's crust can move, can form anywhere in Earth's crust and mantle. The Wabash Valley Fault System is a series of underground faults along the southern border of Illinois and Indiana. Movement along the faults caused medium-sized earthquakes in 1968, 2002, and 2008. The 2008 earthquake was felt in 16 states and in places more than 720 kilometers away.

Scientists cannot predict earthquakes. However, they can study patterns in Earth's crust to try to find out where earthquakes have occurred and how severe they were. By examining Earth's crust, scientists found evidence that the region has had earthquakes for at least 20,000 years.

How might people in the Wabash Valley Fault System prepare for earthquakes?

....

....

....

....

....

....

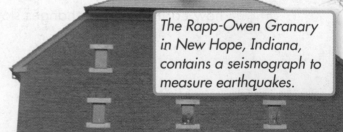

The Rapp-Owen Granary in New Hope, Indiana, contains a seismograph to measure earthquakes.

Word to Know

fault

Earth's Moving Plates

Earth's outer crust rests on top of another layer called the mantle. The crust and the top of the mantle are divided into very large pieces called plates. The plates move all the time. This movement can cause rapid changes in Earth's surface. Volcanoes and earthquakes often occur along or near places where the plates come together.

Look at the picture. It shows an area in Iceland where two plates are moving away from each other. The land on the left is part of the North American plate. This is the same plate that most of the United States is on. The land on the right is part of the plate that much of Europe and Asia are on. Iceland has many volcanoes and earthquakes because it is on top of these two plates.

1. ◎ **Draw Conclusions**
Suppose that an area experiences frequent earthquakes. What might you conclude about that area?

....

....

....

....

3. Predict Ash and other particles from an eruption may fill the sky and block sunlight. How might this change Earth's temperature?

....

....

Volcanoes

A volcano is a landform that forms at an opening in Earth's crust where magma reaches the surface. Magma is very hot, partly melted rock.

When a volcano erupts, the magma reaches the surface and is called lava. Lava is still very hot, perhaps more than 1,100°C (2,000°F). The temperature and the kind of rock that makes up the magma determine the type of eruption. Sometimes the pressure builds up so that the gases in the magma explode. Hot rocks, gases, ash, and other particles burst from the openings, called vents. Sometimes magma oozes upward and flows from the volcano.

Lava and ash can spread over a wide area. Nearby forests or cities may be covered. The volcano and surrounding area may be reshaped. An eruption can also cause floods, landslides, and tsunamis, which are huge ocean waves.

2. ⊙ Draw Conclusions Look at the pictures of the Kilauea Volcano. Tell how the volcano's eruptions have changed the surrounding area.

The Kilauea Volcano in Hawaii erupts frequently.

Earthquakes

Earthquakes occur along a fault. A **fault** is a break or crack in rocks where Earth's crust can move suddenly. Sometimes rocks along a fault get stuck. The plates continue their slow movement. This puts stress on the rocks. If the stress becomes strong enough, the rocks can break. Then the plates move suddenly. The sudden movement that causes Earth's crust to shake is an earthquake. The place underground where the earthquake begins is the focus. The point on Earth's surface that is directly above the focus is the epicenter.

Most earthquakes are small. You might feel a slight shake. A few earthquakes are powerful enough to damage buildings, roads, and bridges. The damage is often greatest near the epicenter. Like volcanoes, earthquakes sometimes cause tsunamis and landslides.

4. Demonstrate (Circle) the area in the picture where the most damage would occur from the earthquake.

5. Infer Where would earthquakes that cause tsunamis probably happen?

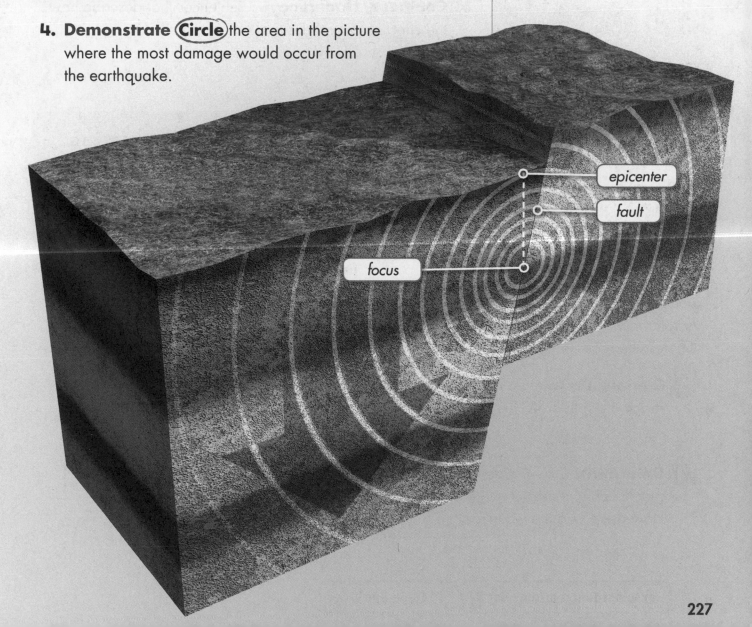

epicenter

fault

focus

Landslides and Floods

Heavy rains or earthquakes may loosen material on a steep slope. Gravity then pulls the loosened material downward. Bits of rock and soil may travel slowly downhill a little at a time. But sometimes they travel rapidly. The rapid downhill movement of a large amount of rock and soil is a landslide. Buildings, cars, trees, and other objects are sometimes carried along with the sliding soil.

Floods also can produce rapid changes. Fast moving water in flash floods can uproot trees, carry away big rocks, and change where rivers flow. Floods also can leave land covered with sand and mud. In 1993, huge amounts of rain caused the Mississippi and Missouri Rivers to overflow. Some areas were flooded for almost 200 days. The floods left thousands of acres covered with sand and mud.

6. Compare Underline two sentences that describe how the effects of landslides and floods are similar.

damage from landslide in Topanga Canyon, California

Do the math!

Read a Graph

The Missouri River flows through the city of Kansas City, Missouri. In early July 1993, the river flooded its banks after months of heavy rain. The river in Kansas City reaches flood stage when the water is 32 feet deep. The graph shows what happened in the weeks that followed, as the river continued to rise.

1 Identify On what day did the river reach a depth of 40 feet?

2 Determine On what day did the river reach its highest point, called the crest? How deep was the water?

3 Calculate How many feet did the river rise overall between the first day of the flood and the crest?

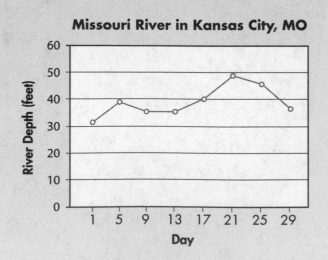

Missouri River in Kansas City, MO

mysci enceonLine.com | Got *it?* | 60-Second Video

Droughts

Sometimes an area experiences a period of weather that is much drier than usual. Periods of unusually low rain or snowfall are called droughts. A severe drought can change the surface of Earth by reducing the amount of water in rivers and lakes. Droughts can destroy farmland and kill trees and other plants. Droughts increase soil erosion too. In the 1930s, the United States experienced a severe drought. As crops died, high winds blew away the dry soil. Winds sometimes carried great, dark clouds of dust thousands of miles away.

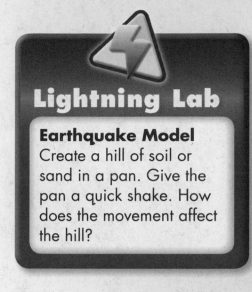

Lightning Lab

Earthquake Model
Create a hill of soil or sand in a pan. Give the pan a quick shake. How does the movement affect the hill?

7. Infer Why does drought increase the possibility of soil erosion?

....

....

....

Got it?

8. Recognize How can the actions around a fault cause an earthquake?

....

....

9. UNLOCK THE BIG ? Think about what you read in this lesson. Explain how Earth's surface changes rapidly.

....

....

⬛ **Stop!** I need help with ....

⏸ **Wait!** I have a question about ....

▶ **Go!** Now I know ....

Where is Earth's water?

Where is this water and steam coming from?

Inquiry Explore It!

Where is Earth's water?

☑ **1.** Label 4 plastic cups as shown.

☑ **2.** Look at the chart. Find the amount of water shown for the atmosphere. Put that much water in the labeled cup.

Earth's Water	Amount
Atmosphere (fresh water)	about $\frac{1}{2}$ drop
Lakes, rivers, streams (fresh water)	about 4 drops
Groundwater (fresh water)	13 mL
Icecaps and glaciers (fresh water)	47 mL
Oceans and seas (salt water)	2139 mL

☑ **3.** Repeat for the next three places on the chart. **Measure** the water.

☑ **4.** Label the 2 L bottle "oceans and seas".

Explain Your Results

5. Use your **model.** Make an **inference** about the amount of fresh water available for human use.

Materials

plastic bottle (2L with cap) filled with water

4 clear plastic cups

masking tape

graduated cylinder

funnel

plastic dropper

ice caps and glaciers

groundwater

lakes, rivers, streams

atmosphere

myscienceonline.com | **Explore It!** Animation

Water on Earth

Think about a globe. When you look at a globe, you see much more blue water than green land. That is because almost $\frac{3}{4}$ of Earth's surface is covered with water.

Water exists as a solid, liquid, and gas. Ice is solid water. Some of Earth's water is frozen in glaciers and polar ice caps. You see liquid water in rivers, lakes, the ocean, and other bodies of water. When water gets hot enough, it turns into an invisible gas called water vapor. Some of the water near Earth's surface is water vapor in the air. The water vapor rises from water on Earth's surface and becomes part of the atmosphere.

An iceberg is a large piece of floating ice. Icebergs form when pieces break off of glaciers.

1. **Clarify** Create a circle chart. Color the circle to show how much of Earth is covered with water and how much is covered with land. Label the parts of the circle.

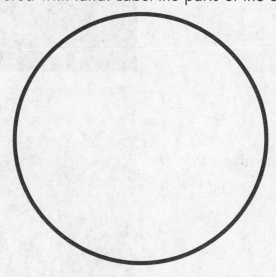

Surface Water

Surface water is any water that is above the ground on Earth. You can see it, splash in it, or swim in it. The pictures to the right show different bodies of surface water. You can classify water bodies by the type of water they contain: salt water or fresh water.

Salt Water

"Water, water, everywhere, Nor any drop to drink." These lines in a famous poem describe a crew on an ocean ship that has run out of drinking water. Water is all around them. How could they run out of drinking water?

If you have ever tasted ocean water, you know the answer. It tastes very salty. However, taste is not the main problem. Ocean water is not healthy for drinking.

More than $\frac{97}{100}$ of Earth's water is salty water in the ocean and seas. Why is the ocean salty? Ocean water is a mixture of water and dissolved salts. These salts come mostly from rocks on land. As rivers flow over land, they dissolve salts from rocks. They carry the salts to the ocean.

Fresh Water

Only $\frac{3}{100}$ of Earth's water is fresh water. People need fresh water for drinking, cooking, growing crops, and many other activities. Most of Earth's fresh water is frozen in glaciers and ice caps. People cannot use that water. People depend on the small amount of fresh water available in rivers and lakes. People also get drinking water from underground.

2. ◉ **Compare and Contrast** Write how the ocean and a pond are alike and different.

....

....

3. **Identify** (Circle) the names of bodies of water that can contain salt water. Draw an ✗ on the body of water that contains most of Earth's fresh water.

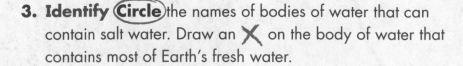

Ocean and Seas

The ocean is a large body of salt water. Seas are smaller areas of the ocean that are partly surrounded by land.

Lakes and Ponds

Land surrounds lakes and ponds, which are smaller than the ocean. Lakes are generally larger than ponds. Almost all lakes and ponds contain fresh water, but a few lakes and ponds contain salt water.

Rivers

A river is flowing fresh water. Water in rivers moves downhill. Rivers flow into the ocean, lakes, and other rivers.

Glaciers and Ice Caps

A glacier is a large body of slowly moving ice. Glaciers form when more snow falls than melts in an area. The polar ice caps are large areas of ice at the North and South Poles.

Groundwater

When it rains, water falls into bodies of water and onto the ground. Some water that falls on the ground runs into bodies of water. This water is called runoff. But some water soaks into the ground. **Groundwater** is any water that is underground. Groundwater fills the spaces and cracks in underground soil and rock.

Think about all of the lakes, rivers, and ponds on Earth's surface. Although it is hard to imagine, there is more fresh liquid water underground than on Earth's surface. Groundwater is not trapped underground. It can flow slowly through most types of soil. In some places, groundwater may flow out of the ground and into a lake, pond, or river. A spring is a place where groundwater comes to the surface of the land. People also dig wells to reach water stored underground.

4. Infer Why do people dig wells to reach groundwater?

....

....

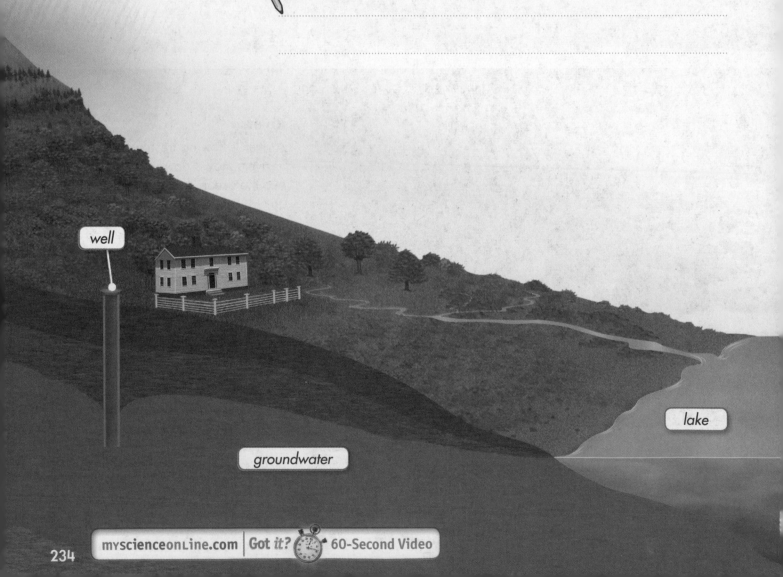

well

groundwater

lake

Clean Drinking Water

People need clean water for drinking, cooking, and other activities. But fresh water from under the ground and from surface water bodies is not always clean. For example, water in lakes and rivers can contain germs that could make people sick. Chemicals used to grow crops can wash into bodies of water. Fresh water must usually be cleaned before people can drink it.

In some places, people get drinking water from their own wells. They must filter the water to remove chemicals and dirt. Many cities have water treatment plants. In these plants, drinking water goes through a cleaning process that removes dirt and other materials and kills germs. The clean water then travels in pipes to people's homes and businesses.

water treatment plant

5. **Name** Write two things that are removed from water at a water treatment plant.

....

Got it?

6. **Identify** Name three places where Earth's fresh water is found. Which of these places has the most fresh water?

....

....

7. **UNLOCK THE BIG ?** Think about what you have learned about the amount of fresh water available for drinking. Why is it important to save water and keep it clean?

....

....

○ **Stop!** I need help with ....

❙❙ **Wait!** I have a question about ....

▷ **Go!** Now I know ....

What is the water cycle?

Envision It!

Draw arrows to show where the water goes when the sun's energy heats it.

Inquiry **Explore It!**

How can water move in the water cycle?

☑ **1.** Seal the cup in a resealable plastic bag without spilling the water. Tape the bag to a sunny window. **Predict** what will happen.

....

☑ **2.** **Observe** the bag after 2 days and after 3 days. **Record** what you observe each time.

....

....

....

....

Explain Your Results

3. **Infer** where water comes from when it rains.

....

....

Materials

plastic cup with water

resealable plastic bag

tape

myscienceonline.com | **Explore It!** Animation

Words to Know

precipitation
water cycle

Recycled Water

There is only a certain amount of water on Earth. Earth's water is constantly being recycled. Water moves from Earth's surface into the atmosphere. Water in the atmosphere falls back to Earth's surface.

Earth's water exists in three different phases: solid, liquid, and gas. Water changes phases as it is recycled. The sun's energy powers this process. The sun heats liquid water on Earth's surface. The water changes into a gas called water vapor. This process is called evaporation. Water vapor rises into the air and cools. As it cools, the water vapor changes into droplets of liquid water. This process is called condensation.

Clouds form when water droplets and ice crystals gather in the atmosphere. These droplets and crystals can combine and grow larger. Eventually they fall back to Earth. Any form of water that falls to Earth is called **precipitation.** Types of precipitation include rain, snow, sleet, and hail.

1. **Analyze** Look at the rain. Could the water falling as rain fall again in the future as snow? Explain.

....

....

....

The Water Cycle

The movement of water from Earth's surface to the atmosphere and back again is called the **water cycle.** This diagram shows the steps in the water cycle.

2. Fill in the Blanks Complete the captions in the diagram. Fill in each blank with the correct word.

Evaporation

Energy from the sun heats liquid water on

Earth's surface. The water changes to a gas

called _____ .

Storage

Precipitation falls into water bodies or onto land. Water that falls on land may soak into the ground and collect as groundwater. Some water runs off the land and collects in rivers, lakes, and the ocean.

3. Underline four places where water collects after it falls as precipitation.

Condensation

Water vapor cools and changes into droplets of liquid water. Water droplets and ice crystals gather in the air, forming ....

Precipitation

The water droplets and ice crystals combine and become larger. Eventually they become so heavy that gravity pulls them to Earth. Precipitation is any form of .... that falls to Earth.

Lightning Lab

Water Droplets
Suppose that you just took a hot shower at home. The mirror in your bathroom would probably be foggy. Work with a partner to explain why you see droplets of water on the mirror.

4. CHALLENGE Suppose hail falls on a warm day. What can you infer about the air temperature high in the atmosphere?

....

....

....

5. ⊙ **Draw Conclusions** Look at the pictures. Draw an ✕ on the type of weather you would expect if there was more evaporation than precipitation over a long period of time.

Water Cycle and Weather

You watch the local weather report. Will the weather be cloudy? Will there be rain? The answer to these questions depends partly on the water cycle. The water cycle is a main factor that causes daily weather conditions such as clouds and precipitation.

Weather is the result of how water, air, and temperature interact. For example, the temperature of air in the atmosphere affects the type of precipitation that falls. Water falls as rain when air in the atmosphere is above freezing. If the air near Earth's surface is colder than air higher up, rain may freeze as it falls. Sleet is rain that has frozen on its way to Earth.

Snow may form when the air in the atmosphere is very cold. Snow forms when water vapor changes directly into ice crystals. The crystals eventually grow large enough to fall out of the clouds. Hail can also develop at freezing temperatures. Hail forms when drops of water in clouds freeze and are coated with multiple layers of ice.

The pictures below show other types of weather that relate to the water cycle.

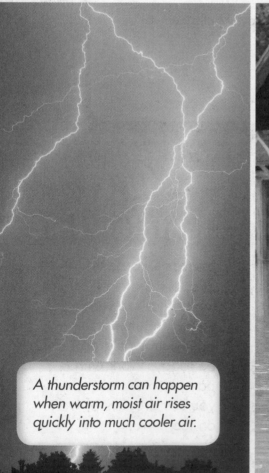

A thunderstorm can happen when warm, moist air rises quickly into much cooler air.

Long periods of rainfall or heavy storms can cause flooding.

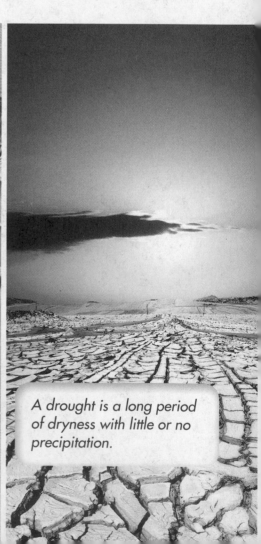

A drought is a long period of dryness with little or no precipitation.

myscienceonline.com | Got it? ⏱ 60-Second Video

Water Cycle and Climate

Climate is the pattern of weather in a place over many years. Some places have a wet climate. Other places have a dry climate. Just as the water cycle affects daily weather conditions, it also affects climate.

For example, places near the ocean often receive a lot of precipitation. This weather pattern is caused by the water cycle. The sun's energy causes a lot of water to evaporate from the ocean. Wind carries the water vapor in the air over land. That land is likely to get more rainfall than a place that is not near a large body of water.

6. **Infer** Temperate rain forests can receive 100 inches of rain in a year. Tell why you think these forests receive so much rain.

Temperate rain forests grow along the northwestern coast of North America.

Got it?

7. **Explain** How does water move through the water cycle?

....

....

....

....

8. **Summarize** Why is the sun important to the water cycle?

....

....

⬛ **Stop!** I need help with ....

⏸ **Wait!** I have a question about ....

▶ **Go!** Now I know ....

How does the steepness of a stream affect how fast it flows?

Follow a Procedure

☐ **1. Make a model** of a stream. Have one student hold a piece of tubing up. Set the stream angle to 10°. Place a cup at the low end of the stream.

☐ **2. Measure** 50 mL of water into a graduated cylinder.

☐ **3.** Attach a funnel to the top of the tubing. Start a timer as you pour the water into the tubing. Stop the timer when all the water has flowed into the cup. **Record** the time.

☐ **4.** Change the stream angle to 25°, 40°, and 55° and repeat Steps 2 and 3.

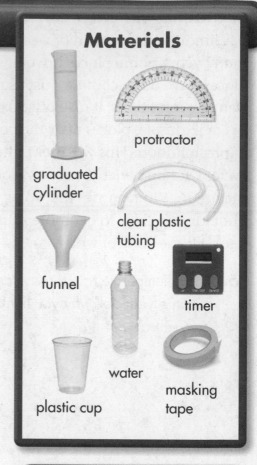

Materials

graduated cylinder

protractor

funnel

clear plastic tubing

timer

plastic cup

water

masking tape

Inquiry Skill

Recording data on a chart can help you make **inferences** based on the data.

Be careful! Wipe up spills with paper towels!

5. Record your **data** below.

Observations of Model Stream	
Stream Angle (°)	Flow Time (seconds)
10	
25	
40	
55	

Analyze and Conclude

6. Communicate by summarizing your results.

....

....

....

....

7. UNLOCK THE BIG ? **Infer**   Where might you find a stream that flows at a 55° angle? Where might you find a stream that flows at a 15° angle?

....

....

....

The Galápagos Islands

The Galápagos Islands are a chain of islands located in the Pacific Ocean. This chain of islands is about 1,000 kilometers (600 miles) west of Ecuador, a country in South America. The chain has more than 100 islands in all. Some of the major islands have their own names.

The Galápagos Islands have not always existed. They were formed by volcanoes and are probably no more than five million years old.

How do volcanoes form islands? Volcanoes can erupt underwater as well as on land. Each time volcanoes erupt, more lava builds up. Eventually, volcanoes can build up above the surface of the ocean and form volcanic islands such as the islands that make up the Galápagos Islands.

Galápagos Islands

Can you think of another group of islands that was formed by volcanoes?

Vocabulary Smart Cards

mineral
luster
hardness
streak
cleavage
igneous
sedimentary
metamorphic
landform
weathering
erosion
fault
groundwater
precipitation
water cycle

Play a Game!

Work with a partner. Choose a Vocabulary Smart Card. Hold up the card with the word side facing your partner. Have your partner use the word in a sentence. Provide the definition if necessary.

Have your partner repeat with another Vocabulary Smart Card.

245

streak

surco

mineral

mineral

cleavage

fractura

luster

brillo

igneous

ígnea

hardness

dureza

natural, nonliving solid crystals that make up rocks

Draw an example. Label your drawing.

cristal natural, sólido y sin vida del que se componen las rocas

---

color of the powder that a mineral leaves when it is scratched across a special plate

Draw an example.

color del polvo que sale de un mineral cuando se le rasga en una placa especial

---

Interactive Vocabulary

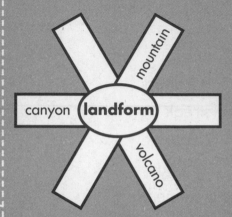

Make a Word Wheel!

Choose a vocabulary word and write it in the center of the Word Wheel graphic organizer. Write synonyms or related words on the wheel spokes.

---

the way the surface of a mineral reflects light

Write a sentence using this word.

reflejo de la luz en la superficie de un mineral

---

property of minerals to break along smooth, flat surfaces

Draw an example.

propiedad que les permite a los minerales romperse por superficies lisas y planas

---

how easily the surface of a mineral can be scratched

What is the suffix of this word?

facilidad con la que se puede rasgar la superficie de un mineral

---

rocks that form from molten rock

Write a sentence using this word.

rocas que se forman a partir de roca derretida

 246

groundwater

agua subterránea

weathering

meteorización

sedimentary

sedimentaria

precipitation

precipitación

erosion

erosión

metamorphic

metamórfica

water cycle

ciclo del agua

fault

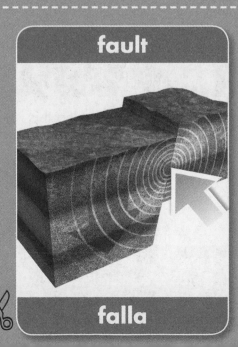

falla

landform

accidente geográfico

rocks that form when layers of sediments settle on top of one another and harden

What is the suffix of this word?

....

rocas que se forman cuando varias capas de sedimento se acumulan, una sobre otra, y se endurecen

---

process of rocks in Earth's crust slowly being broken into smaller pieces

Write a sentence using the verb form of this word.

....

....

proceso de las rocas de la corteza terrestre que se van rompiendo en trozos más pequeños

---

any water that is underground

Write a sentence using this word.

....

....

....

....

agua que está debajo del suelo

---

rocks that have changed as a result of heat and pressure

What is the prefix of this word and what does it mean?

....

....

....

rocas que han cambiado a causa del calor y la presión

---

process of carrying away weathered bits of rock

Draw an example.

proceso por el cual se transportan pedacitos de roca desgastada

---

any form of water that falls to Earth

Write a sentence using the verb form of this word.

....

....

....

cualquier forma de agua que cae a la Tierra

---

a natural land feature on Earth's surface

Draw an example. Label your drawing.

formación natural en la superficie terrestre

---

a break or crack in rocks where Earth's crust can move suddenly

Write a sentence using this word.

....

....

fisura o grieta en las rocas donde la corteza terrestre puede desplazarse en forma repentina

---

the movement of water from Earth's surface to the atmosphere and back again

Write a word related to this term.

....

....

recorrido de ida y vuelta que realiza el agua entre la atmósfera y la superficie de la Tierra

Study Guide

Lesson 1

How are minerals classified?

- Minerals are natural, nonliving crystals that make up rocks.
- Color, luster, hardness, streak, shape, and cleavage are some properties of minerals.

Lesson 2

How are rocks classified?

- Rocks are classified as igneous, sedimentary, or metamorphic, based on how they form.
- A cycle of heat, pressure, and chemical reactions can change rocks.

Lesson 3

What are weathering and erosion?

- Wind, water, ice, changes in temperature, and chemical changes can weather, or break down, rock.
- Erosion carries weathered rock away.

Lesson 4

How can Earth's surface change rapidly?

- Volcanic eruptions, earthquakes, landslides, and floods can cause Earth's surface to change rapidly.
- Earthquakes occur when Earth's plates move suddenly along faults.

Lesson 5

Where is Earth's water?

- Earth's fresh water exists as lakes, ponds, rivers, glaciers, and groundwater.
- Most of Earth's water is salt water in the ocean.

Lesson 6

What is the water cycle?

- The water cycle is the constant movement of water from Earth's surface to the atmosphere and back again.
- Evaporation, condensation, and precipitation are parts of the cycle.

Chapter Review

Lesson 1

How are minerals classified?

1. **Classify** The table shows five minerals and their Mohs ratings. List the minerals in order from softest to hardest.

Mineral	Mohs Rating
Augite	5.5
Cinnabar	2.5
Emerald	7.5
Magnetite	6
Sapphire	9

Lesson 2

How are rocks classified?

2. **Identify** What causes sedimentary rock to turn into metamorphic rock?

3. **Vocabulary** What type of rock is formed from molten rock?
   A. shale
   B. igneous
   C. metamorphic
   D. magma

Lesson 3

What are weathering and erosion?

4. ● **Draw Conclusions** Read the paragraph and fill in the graphic organizer.

Several processes work to shape Earth's surface. The process of weathering wears away rocks and particles. However, during another process, erosion, the weathered material is moved away. Various forces move the weathered material. Yet some of the same forces may work together to drop the rocks and particles in a new location. This process is called deposition.

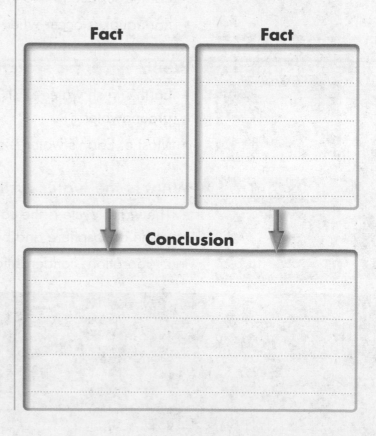

Fact

Fact

Conclusion

Lesson 4

How can Earth's surface change rapidly?

5. Describe How can a flood cause Earth's surface to change?

....

....

....

....

....

Lesson 5

Where is Earth's water?

6. Write About It Explain where fresh water and salt water exist on Earth's surface.

....

....

....

....

....

Lesson 6

What is the water cycle?

7. Illustrate Draw and label a diagram that shows the steps of the water cycle.

8. **APPLY THE BIG ?** **How do Earth's resources change?**

Think of a rocky cliff on a beach. What natural forces have shaped this landform? What forces continue to change it?

....

....

....

....

Benchmark Practice

Fill in the bubble next to the answer choice you think is correct for each multiple-choice question.

1 The chart below shows some mineral properties. Use the chart to identify the mineral sample.

Mineral	Hardness	Luster	Color	Streak
Galena	2.5	metallic	lead-gray	gray
Hematite	5–6	metallic or nonmetallic	silver-gray or red	reddish brown
Hornblende	5–6	silky	dark green to black	pale gray to gray
Magnetite	5.5–6	shiny, metallic	black	black

A mineral sample is black and has a rank of 6 on the Mohs Scale. It has a silky luster. This mineral is

Ⓐ hornblende.

Ⓑ hematite.

Ⓒ galena.

Ⓓ magnetite.

2 A rock with uneven layers of minerals is probably which kind of rock?

Ⓐ an ore

Ⓑ igneous

Ⓒ sedimentary

Ⓓ obsidian

3 Which of these landforms is probably the result of erosion caused by flowing water?

Ⓐ a mountain

Ⓑ a canyon

Ⓒ a glacier

Ⓓ a sand dune

4 The point on Earth above the focus of an earthquake is the

Ⓐ fault.

Ⓑ epicenter.

Ⓒ volcano.

Ⓓ plate.

5 What are two ways that water on Earth and the water cycle are related to weathering and erosion?

....

....

....

....

....

....

STEM

Robotic Fish

A robotic fish can swim like a real fish. It uses its back tail to swim through water like a real fish.

Have you ever seen fish swimming in a lake, river, or ocean? One of the fish may not be real! Scientists and engineers developed a robotic fish! A robotic fish can be used to detect and collect data on pollution. The robotic fish uses sensors to identify the pollutant and its cause. The cause can include chemical spills. This technology allows officials to learn more about the impact of pollution on lakes, rivers, or oceans. The robotic fish was built so it cannot get caught in nets easily. Also, the fish has internal tracking systems. These systems help it avoid collisions with boats. You might wonder if sharks can mistake these robotic fish for prey. The answer is no! The robot has an electromagnetic field. An electromagnetic field is a force that can be felt by other living things around the fish. It seems to make sharks and other predators uneasy.

Determine How could the robotic fish help detect oil spills?

What makes the moon GLOW?

Earth and Space

The moon shines brightly as it appears to move across the night sky. The sun and other stars also appear to move across the sky.

 Predict Do you think these objects in space will move? Why or why not?

....

....

....

THE BIG ? What are some patterns in space?

What is one cause for the seasons?

☑ **1. Make a Model** Set up the light and globes. Tilt the globes. Each is a model of Earth with its axis tilted. On each globe, put a red dot where you live (Northern Hemisphere) and blue dot on the Southern Hemisphere.

Materials

2 inflatable globes

2 plastic cups

2 red dots
2 blue dots

light bulb and holder

stack of books

sun

Winter Globe

Summer Globe

☑ **2.** Have a partner rotate the Winter Globe on its axis. **Observe** the red and blue dots. Which hemisphere has a longer day?

Inquiry Skill You can **make models** to understand how things happen.

☑ **3.** Repeat with the Summer Globe. Which has a longer day? Which does the light strike straight on?

☑ **4.** Work with your group to make a model of Earth without a tilted axis. Compare the day length in summer and winter.

Explain Your Results

5. **UNLOCK THE BIG ?** **Use a Model** Based on your observations, explain one way that Earth's tilt causes seasons.

⊙ Cause and Effect

- A **cause** is why something happened. An **effect** is what happened.
- Writers sometimes signal cause and effect with words such as *because, since, so,* and *as a result.*

Seasons

Earth spins like a top. At the same time, it travels around the sun. However, Earth's axis—the imaginary line it spins around—is tilted compared with Earth's path around the sun.

Each half of Earth tilts toward the sun for about half of the year. Sunlight reaching that hemisphere heats it more. Also, because the sun is higher in the sky, there are more hours of daylight. So, the temperatures are higher in many parts of this hemisphere. During the rest of the year, this half of Earth tilts away from the sun. There are fewer hours of daylight, and temperatures are lower. As Earth revolves around the sun, these differences in temperature and the hours of daylight cause the seasons.

Practice It!

Find causes and effects in the example paragraphs. Write two examples of each in the graphic organizer.

Cause

Effect

How does Earth move?

This series of photos shows the sun over the course of 24 hours from the same spot.

MY PLANET DiARY

Connections

Can you think of some activities that you repeat every seven days or once a month? Maybe there is a class that you only take on Fridays or a sport that you play every Saturday. We schedule our time by watching the calendar. Ancient people created calendars by watching the sky!

The sun, the moon, and the planets appear to move across the sky in patterns that repeat after regular periods of time. The Mayan people kept track of the date by observing and recording the positions of the sun, moon, and stars. One of their calendars followed the sun. In this calendar each year lasted 365 days, just like the sun's cycle. But the Maya also had a calendar that followed the motion of the planet Venus. One year in this calendar lasted only 260 days!

Venus can be seen from Earth.

What are some skills that the Mayans needed in order to create a calendar?

....

....

....

I will know Earth revolves around the sun and rotates on its axis. I will know Earth's rotation is related to the apparent movement of the sun, moon, and stars.

Words to Know

rotation   orbit
revolution   ellipse

Tell why you think it is called the Midnight Sun.

Earth Moves

You cannot feel Earth's movement, but you are moving along with Earth. Even though you cannot sense its motion, you can make observations to know that it moves. You can observe that the sun and the stars seem to move across the sky. This happens because Earth is turning. You can also observe that the seasons change during the year for most places away from the equator. The equator is the imaginary line that divides the north and south halves of Earth. In some regions, the difference in seasons is more noticeable than in other regions. The seasonal changes are partly caused by the way Earth moves around the sun.

1. ⊙ **Cause and Effect** Write one cause and two effects related to Earth's movement.

Cause	Effect

2. **Show** In the picture above, the globe is turning on its axis. Draw an arrow on the equator in the picture to show which way you think Earth rotates.

3. Apply In the illustration to the right, is it day or night where you live? How do you know?

....

....

Sunlight

Earth's Rotation

Earth turns around its axis. An axis is an imaginary line that goes through its center. Earth's axis passes through the North Pole, the center of Earth, and the South Pole.

The spinning of a planet, moon, or star around its axis is called its **rotation.** Each time Earth makes a full turn around its axis, it has made one rotation. Earth takes 23 hours and 56 minutes to make one rotation. When Earth rotates, it turns from west to east. Earth's rotation causes day to change into night and night into day. When a place on Earth is turned toward the sun, it has daytime.

Because of Earth's rotation, objects such as the sun, other stars, and the moon appear to move from east to west in the sky. You cannot see the stars in the daytime because the light from the sun is too bright. If you watch for several clear nights, and if you are in a place that does not have many bright lights, you can see the stars appear to change their positions in the sky.

4. ◉ **Cause and Effect** Explain how Earth's rotation causes day and night.

....

....

....

....

....

....

....

....

Shadows Change

Another result of Earth's rotation is that shadows change their positions and sizes during the day. When light shines on an object and does not pass through it, the object casts a shadow. As Earth rotates, sunlight shines on an object from different angles. The length and position of the object's shadow change.

5. Explain Why is the shadow in the middle of the day shorter than the shadow in the morning and evening?

....

....

....

Lightning Lab

Make a Sundial
Cut a 9-inch circle from posterboard. Draw a line through the center of the circle and write *noon* at one end. Stand a pencil up in the center with a ball of clay. Place your sundial in the sunlight with the word *noon* pointing north. Watch the pencil's shadow move around the circle over time. Mark as many hours as you can.

The flagpole's shadow is longest in the morning and in the evening. It is shortest at noon.

6. Analyze (Circle) the photo that was taken closer to noon. How do you know?

....

....

Earth's Revolution

As Earth rotates, it travels around the sun.
The movement of one object around another is a
revolution. A complete trip around the sun by Earth is
one revolution. The path an object follows as it revolves
around another object is its **orbit.**

Earth takes one year, or about 365 days, to complete
a revolution. During that year, Earth and everything
on it travel about 940,000,000 kilometers at an average
speed of about 107,000 kilometers per hour.

Earth's orbit is an ellipse. An **ellipse** is like a
circle stretched out in opposite directions. As Earth
moves in its orbit, its distance from the sun changes.
Earth is farther from the sun in some parts of its
orbit. It is closer to the sun in other parts. The
moon's orbit around Earth is also an ellipse.

Gravity is a force that pulls two objects toward
each other. The gravity between Earth and the sun
keeps Earth revolving around the sun.

7. **Locate** In the last paragraph, (circle) a cause
   and **underline** an effect.

8. **Draw** Using everyday objects, draw a picture that
   represents Earth rotating and revolving around the sun.

June The Northern
Hemisphere is tilted
toward the sun.

March Neither pole is tilted toward the sun.

The tilt of Earth's axis affects how directly the sun shines on Earth as it travels in its orbit.

December The Northern Hemisphere is tilted away from the sun.

.... Neither pole is tilted toward the sun.

9. CHALLENGE Study the illustration and captions. One of the captions is missing a month. Write the name of the month in the space provided.

10. **Demonstrate** (Circle) the illustration of Earth in which the Southern Hemisphere is receiving the most direct sunlight.

Earth's Seasons

Earth's axis is always tilted. As Earth revolves around the sun, its axis is always tilted in the same direction. The end of the axis at the North Pole points toward Polaris, the North Star. This tilt affects how places on Earth receive sunlight. In different parts of Earth's orbit, different places directly face the sun.

In late June, the Northern Hemisphere tilts toward the sun. It is summer, and day is longer than night. But it is winter in the Southern Hemisphere. Nights are longer than days.

In late December, the Southern Hemisphere tilts toward the sun. Now, it is winter in the Northern Hemisphere and summer in the Southern Hemisphere.

In spring and fall, Earth's axis is not tilted toward the sun. The lengths of day and night in both hemispheres are more nearly equal in spring and fall.

Do the math!

Patterns and Averages

In the Northern and Southern Hemispheres, the number of hours of daylight changes with the seasons. The illustration and captions provide examples.

1 What pattern in the data exists for these three cities?

2 In June, how many more hours of daylight are there in Chicago than in Rio de Janeiro?

3 Find the average number of hours of daylight in Chicago for January and June.

Chicago, USA
January: 9.5 hours
June: 15.2 hours

Quito, Ecuador
January: 12.1 hours
June: 12.1 hours

Rio de Janeiro, Brazil
January: 13.4 hours
June: 10.8 hours

In December, the North Pole tilts away from the sun. The Northern Hemisphere receives the least amount of direct sunlight at this time of year. Temperatures drop, and winter sets in.

The sun's rays strike Earth more directly near the equator. The rays are less spread out. More direct sunlight gives this region warm weather all year long.

The Northern Hemisphere gets more direct sunlight when it tilts toward the sun. Direct sunlight heats this hemisphere more, and daylight lasts longer. As a result, temperatures are higher. It is summer.

At the same time, the Southern Hemisphere tilts away from the sun. The days are shorter, and temperatures are lower. It is winter. In spring and fall, temperatures are more moderate in both hemispheres.

11. Predict What would happen to the seasons if Earth were not tilted on its axis as it orbits the sun?

....

12. Analyze Explain what causes Earth's seasons.

....

....

....

Got it?

13. Understand In what ways does the Earth move? How long do these movements take?

....

....

14. UNLOCK THE BIG ? How does Earth's rotation cause the apparent movement of the sun, the moon, and the stars?

....

....

⬛ **Stop!** I need help with ....

⏸ **Wait!** I have a question about ....

▶ **Go!** Now I know ....

How do star patterns change?

Envision It!

Connect the stars to show a pattern in the sky.

Inquiry Explore It!

What star patterns can you see?

☑ **1.** Use the Star Finder Pattern to make a Star Finder.

☑ **2.** Set the dial for 7 P.M. on November 1. **Record** the star groups you could **observe** at that time. Now set the dial for 11 P.M. Record the star groups.

7 P.M.

11 P.M.

Materials

Star Finder Pattern

Star Wheel

folder

scissors

stapler

glue

A finished Star Finder

Explain Your Results

3. Infer Which star group could you see at 11 P.M. but not at 7 P.M.? Explain why.

myscienceonline.com | **Explore It!** Animation

UNLOCK THE BIG ?

I will learn that patterns in the sky stay the same but appear to change nightly and throughout the year.

Word to Know

constellation

Tell what the differences are between the patterns in the two seasons.

Stars

Scientists estimate that there may be 70 billion trillion stars in the universe! The sun is the star that is nearest Earth and is most important for us. It provides energy and light to living things on Earth.

Like all stars, the sun is a hot ball of gas. Although it seems to be the brightest star in the sky, many stars are much bigger, brighter, or hotter than the sun. Others are smaller, dimmer, and cooler.

During the day, you cannot see stars because the sun is so bright. Even at night, if you are in a city that has many lights, or if the sky is not clear, you may be able to see only a few of the brightest stars. The light from stars that are very far away appears faint when it reaches Earth. Many stars in the sky are so faint or far away that you cannot see them at all with only your eyes. But you could see some of them through a telescope.

Our Milky Way Galaxy has billions of stars!

2. Apply What is one way that we can learn more about the stars in the Milky Way?

....

....

....

....

....

1. 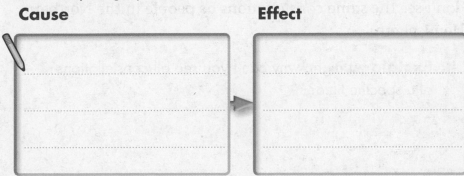**Cause and Effect** List a cause and its effect from the last paragraph.

Cause

Effect

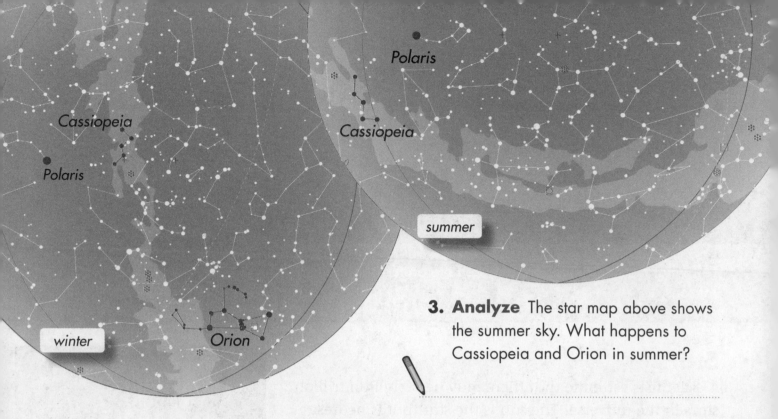

Cassiopeia

Polaris

Polaris

Cassiopeia

summer

winter

Orion

3. Analyze The star map above shows the summer sky. What happens to Cassiopeia and Orion in summer?

....

....

During late fall and winter in the Northern Hemisphere, Cassiopeia is almost directly overhead. Orion is low in the sky.

Star Patterns

For thousands of years, people have noticed that the stars appear in shapes and patterns in the sky. These star patterns are called **constellations.** Astronomers divide the sky into 88 constellations. People often identify the stars by the constellations they are part of. The constellations are so far away from Earth that the stars appear to be near each other. Actually, they may be very far apart in space.

As Earth turns on its axis, stars appear to move across the sky. As Earth orbits the sun during the year, constellations appear to move as well. Some constellations are only visible during certain seasons. For example, Orion is a bright winter constellation in the Northern Hemisphere. In the summer, Orion drops too low in the sky for you to see. People in the Southern Hemisphere don't see the same constellations as people in the Northern Hemisphere.

4. Explain At night, why can't you see all constellations at a specific time?

....

At-Home Lab

Pictures in the Sky
With an adult, locate a star pattern in the night sky. Use a star map or the star finder from the *Explore It!* activity. Write down the date and the direction you are facing. Draw the star pattern.

The North Star

In the Northern Hemisphere, the North Star, or Polaris, appears in the sky above the North Pole. Earth spins on its axis, and the North Pole is at the northern end of the axis. Polaris stays within the same small region of the sky. The stars near it do not rise or set. They seem to revolve around Polaris. They include stars in the constellations Ursa Major (the Great Bear) and Ursa Minor (the Little Bear).

Seven stars in Ursa Major make up the Big Dipper. The two stars that form the end of the dipper's bowl can help you find Polaris. Use the star maps on the previous page to see how the positions of the constellations change during the year.

5. **Investigate** Research a constellation in the summer sky. Connect the stars and label the constellation in the star maps on the previous page.

Got **it?**

6. **Recall** How will the constellations move across the sky if you are standing at the North Pole?

....

....

7. **UNLOCK THE BIG ?** How do the stars and constellations appear to change throughout the year from winter to summer?

....

....

....

■ **Stop!** I need help with ....

Ⅱ **Wait!** I have a question about ....

▶ **Go!** Now I know ....

Lesson 3

What are the phases of the moon?

Quarter Moon

Full Moon

Color in the moon in its different phases.

Inquiry **Explore It!**

Why is the new moon hard to see?

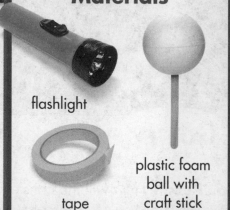

Materials

flashlight

tape

plastic foam ball with craft stick

1. Use a ball as a **model** of the moon, a flashlight for the sun, and you can be Earth.

Sun

One student holds the flashlight.

New Moon Position

One student holds the ball.

Earth

You are here. First, look at the new moon.

Full Moon Position

After you **observe** the new moon, turn 180 degrees and look at the full moon. First the student holding the ball will need to move the ball to the Full Moon Position.

2. In what position does all of the Earth-facing part of the moon look bright?

....

Explain Your Results

3. **Draw a Conclusion** Why is the new moon hard to see?

....

....

....

myscienceonline.com | **Explore It!** Animation

Crescent Moon

New Moon

I will describe the phases of the moon.

Words to Know

eclipse
lunar eclipse
solar eclipse

Sun, Moon, and Earth

Sometimes you can see the moon at night. Sometimes you can even see it during the day. The moon looks as if it is shining with its own light, just as the sun does. But the moon does not really produce its own light. You can see the moon because sunlight reflects off the moon's surface.

The gravity between the moon and Earth keeps the moon in its orbit. Because it moves, the moon stays in its orbit and doesn't crash into Earth. The moon makes a complete trip around Earth in about 27.3 days.

The moon spins around an axis. Each time the moon completes a spin, it also travels once around Earth. As a result, the same side of the moon is always facing Earth. That is the only side you can see from Earth.

1. **Calculate** About how many times does the moon revolve around Earth in one year?
Hint: $\frac{365 \text{ days}}{27.3 \text{ days}}$

2. **Conclude** Study the illustration below. Notice that part of the moon is in a shadow. Tell what you think the yellow arrow represents.

Phases of the Moon

If you look at the moon at different times of the month, its shape appears to change. Half of the moon faces the sun, and sunlight is reflected from the surface of that half. When the lighted half of the moon directly faces Earth, the moon appears as a full circle of light. It is called a full moon.

We see a full moon only briefly each time the moon revolves around Earth. The rest of the time, only part of the lighted half of the moon faces Earth. Then, you can see only part of the full circle of light. For a short time, you cannot see any of the lighted part of the moon. So, you do not see the moon at all. Between the times you see the full moon and the time you cannot see any moon at all, the moon appears to have different shapes. All the moon's shapes are called the phases of the moon.

Last-quarter moon: Gradually, you see less and less of the moon. About a week after the full moon, the moon appears as half of a circle. You see half of the lighted half, or one quarter of the entire moon.

3. **Explain** What causes the changing appearance of the moon over the course of a month?

....

....

4. **Infer** During a full moon, what can you infer about the opposite side of the moon?

....

5. **Diagram** Draw a picture that shows the moon revolving around Earth and the parts of the moon that are visible from Earth as it rotates.

Crescent moon: A sliver of lighted moon appears.

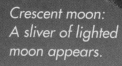

myscienceonLine.com | THE BIG ? | I Will Know...

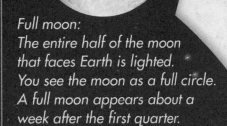

At-Home Lab

Moon Phases
Draw the moon this
evening. Label its phase.
Do this with an adult.

Full moon:
The entire half of the moon
that faces Earth is lighted.
You see the moon as a full circle.
A full moon appears about a
week after the first quarter.

First-quarter moon:
One half of the lighted
half of the moon, or one
quarter of the entire
moon, is visible.

New moon:
Since the moon's dark, unlighted
side faces Earth, you cannot see
a new moon. The new moon
begins a new set of phases.

6. **Explain** Study the other
moon phases on these
pages. The moon in this
box is in which phase?

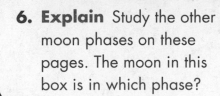

....

This time-lapse photo shows the path of the moon during a lunar eclipse.

Eclipses

When one object in space gets between the sun and another object and casts its shadow on the other object, an **eclipse** occurs. Eclipses happen when the moon passes through Earth's shadow and when the moon's shadow falls on part of Earth.

Lunar Eclipses

Most of the time, reflected sunlight lights up the moon. However, during some full moons, the moon and the sun are on opposite sides of Earth. Often, the moon passes above or below Earth's shadow. A **lunar eclipse** occurs when the moon passes through Earth's shadow.

If only part of the moon is in Earth's shadow during the eclipse, the moon might look as if something took a bite out of it. This is a partial eclipse. If the whole moon is in Earth's shadow, the eclipse is a total lunar eclipse. A lunar eclipse can last as long as 100 minutes. It can happen several times in the same year. Each eclipse is visible only in certain places. Where on Earth the eclipse can be viewed depends on the moon's position in Earth's shadow.

Although the moon is in Earth's shadow during a total lunar eclipse, it stays visible.

7. **Contrast** How is a total lunar eclipse different from other lunar eclipses?

....

....

....

8. **Describe** What factors contribute to producing a total lunar eclipse?

....

....

....

myscienceonline.com | Got it? 60-Second Video

Solar Eclipses

When the moon passes between the sun and Earth and casts its shadow on Earth, a **solar eclipse** occurs. From Earth, this looks like something slowly covering up the sun. A solar eclipse can be seen only at the places on Earth where the moon casts its shadow.

During a total solar eclipse, the day can become as dark as night. Total solar eclipses last up to 7.5 minutes. Solar eclipses occur two to five times each year.

During a total solar eclipse, the sun may not be visible at all. Sometimes in a solar eclipse a thin, bright ring of sunlight appears to circle the moon.

9. **Order** In what order are the sun, Earth, and moon positioned during a solar eclipse?

Got it?

10. **Compare** How are lunar and solar eclipses similar?

11. **Explain** How does the observable shape of the moon change over the course of about a month?

⬛ **Stop!** I need help with ....

⏸ **Wait!** I have a question about ....

▶ **Go!** Now I know ....

What is the solar system?

Envision It!

This picture shows the surface of Mercury. **Tell** one reason why there is most likely no life on Mercury.

MY PLANET DIARY

FunFact

The images on this page show Pluto and its moon Charon. Photographs of Pluto are blurry because it is so far from Earth.

Charon

For a long time, people used simple sentences to remember the order of the planets in the solar system. "My very energetic mother just served us nine pizzas" is one example. Each word starts with the same letter as the name of a planet: Mercury, Venus, Earth, Mars, Jupiter, Saturn, Uranus, Neptune, and Pluto.

In 2006, however, the number of planets in the solar system changed from nine to eight. Scientists had observed that Pluto is much smaller than the other planets. Scientists decided that Pluto is actually a dwarf planet. A dwarf planet is a small, round body that orbits a star. Pluto is no longer considered a planet like Earth or Saturn.

Pluto

Write a sentence that will help you remember the order of the remaining eight planets.

....

....

....

UNLOCK THE BIG ?

I will know that the sun, the planets and their moons, and other objects are part of the solar system.

Words to Know

solar system	asteroid
planet	comet

Our Solar System

The **solar system** includes the sun, the eight planets and their moons, and other objects. The sun, a medium-sized star, is at the center of the solar system. The planets and other objects revolve around, or move around, the sun. The path that each object follows is its orbit.

The sun's gravity keeps planets in their orbits. Gravity is the force that pulls objects toward each other. Because the sun is so massive, its gravity is the strongest in the solar system. The sun's gravity pulls planets toward it. As a result, the planets do not move in straight lines. They move in curved paths around the sun. A planet's orbit is shaped like an ellipse, a slightly stretched-out circle.

1. **Cause and Effect** What causes the planets to revolve around the sun?

....

....

....

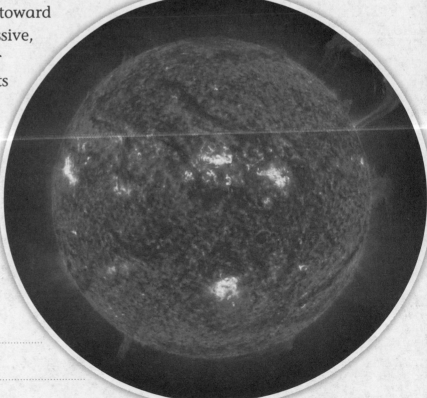

The sun is the largest object in the solar system.

comet

asteroid

Objects in the Solar System

A **planet** is a very large, round object that moves around a star. Each planet orbits on a clear path. This means that there are no other objects in a planet's path as it moves around a star. Dwarf planets are small, round objects that move around the sun. Unlike planets, dwarf planets do not orbit on a clear path. One dwarf planet, Pluto, was once considered the ninth planet in the solar system.

An **asteroid** is a rocky object that orbits the sun but is too small to be called a planet or a dwarf planet. The asteroid belt is a region between Mars and Jupiter that contains many asteroids.

Comets are another type of object in the solar system. A **comet** is a frozen object that orbits the sun. Comets are made of ice, gases, dust, and bits of rock. They are much smaller than planets.

2. ◉ **Compare and Contrast** Tell how asteroids and comets are similar to planets. Tell how they are different.

asteroid belt

Jupiter

Earth

Mars

Venus

Mercury

Sun

278

Planets and Moons

The diagram shows the eight planets in our solar system. Planets are cooler and smaller than stars. They do not produce their own light. At night, planets may appear to shine because they reflect light from the star they orbit.

Moons are satellites of planets. A satellite is an object that orbits another object in space. All of the planets in the solar system except Mercury and Venus have moons.

3. **⊙ Cause and Effect <u>Underline</u>** the sentence that tells you why planets shine at night.

4. **Identify** Look at the diagram. Four of the planets have a particular feature in common. Draw an ✗ on those four planets. Describe the feature they share.

....

....

....

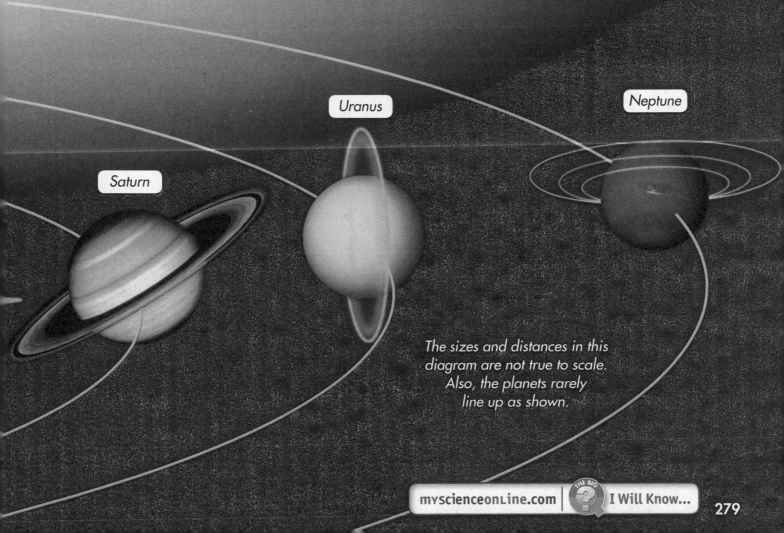

Saturn

Uranus

Neptune

The sizes and distances in this diagram are not true to scale. Also, the planets rarely line up as shown.

Mercury

Diameter: 4,879 km (3,032 mi)
Average surface temperature: 179°C
Moons: 0

Mercury is the planet closest to the sun. It is about two-fifths the size of Earth. Mercury's surface is dry and covered with craters, or dents. The craters formed when rocks from space crashed into Mercury long ago. During the day, temperatures on Mercury can reach 427°C (800°F)! But at night temperatures can drop below −170°C (−275°F).

Venus

Diameter: 12,100 km (7,520 mi)
Average surface temperature: 465°C
Moons: 0

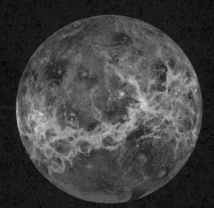

Venus, the second planet from the sun, is about the same size as Earth. Like Mercury, Venus is extremely hot and dry. Its surface has craters, mountains, and valleys. Venus has an atmosphere made of thick, swirling clouds. Unlike Earth's clouds, the clouds on Venus are burning hot and poisonous. They also reflect light from the sun. This makes Venus one of the brightest objects in Earth's night sky.

The sizes of the planets pictured here are not true to scale.

Inner Planets

The four planets closest to the sun are known as the inner planets. Mercury, Venus, Earth, and Mars are all small, rocky planets. But there are many differences among them. Read the descriptions of the planets on these pages. Then complete the activities.

5. [CHALLENGE] Give two reasons why Earth's living things could not survive on Venus.

....

....

6. ◎ **Sequence** List the inner planets from smallest to largest.

....

Earth

Diameter: 13,000 km (8,000 mi)
Average surface temperature: 15°C
Moons: 1

Our home, Earth, is the third planet from the sun and the largest of the inner planets. Earth is the only planet that has liquid water on its surface. Earth's atmosphere and its closeness to the sun help keep the planet warm enough for life. Earth is the only planet in the solar system known to support life.

Mars

Diameter: 6,800 km (4,200 mi)
Average surface temperature: −60°C
Moons: 2

Mars, the fourth planet from the sun, is about half the size of Earth. Mars is known as the "Red Planet" because certain minerals make its rocks and soil appear red. Mars has an atmosphere, but there is not enough oxygen in it to support life. Winds cause dust storms that can cover the whole planet. Mars has mountains, volcanoes, and canyons. Scientists have found evidence that water once flowed on Mars.

---

7. **Apply** A planet's average surface temperature is somewhere between its hottest and coldest temperatures. Could Earth's hottest temperature be less than 15°C? Why or why not?

....

....

8. ◎ **Cause and Effect** A planet's atmosphere can hold in warmth from the sun. Mercury has almost no atmosphere. How does this affect the planet's temperature?

....

....

Go Green

Solar Power
The sun provides energy that helps plants grow and heats Earth. Energy from the sun, called solar energy, can also power devices such as calculators and cars! Work with a partner to brainstorm a list of ways people can use solar energy instead of electricity.

Jupiter

Diameter: 142,984 km (88,846 mi)
Moons: At least 63

Jupiter is the fifth planet from the sun. It is so large that all of the other planets in the solar system could fit inside it! Jupiter's cloudy atmosphere is mainly hydrogen and helium. A huge storm has been raging for hundreds of years in its atmosphere. The storm is called the Great Red Spot.

Saturn

Diameter: 120,540 km (74,900 mi)
Moons: At least 62

Saturn is the sixth planet from the sun. It is the second-biggest planet in the solar system, about ten times the size of Earth. Like Jupiter, Saturn has a thick, cloudy atmosphere instead of a solid surface. Saturn's rings can be seen only through a telescope. Saturn has the clearest rings of the outer planets.

Outer Planets

Jupiter, Saturn, Uranus, and Neptune are known as the outer planets. They are all very large planets made mostly of gases and liquids. Instead of solid rock, dense clouds cover their surfaces. They all have many moons and rings made of dust, ice, and rocks.

9. Infer Could a spacecraft land on any of the outer planets? Explain your answer.

....

....

10. Conclude Why are Uranus and Neptune so cold?

....

11. Identify Draw an ✕ on the smallest of the outer planets.

Uranus

Diameter: 51,118 km (31,763 mi)

Moons: At least 27

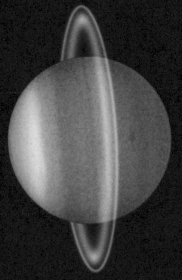

Uranus, the seventh planet from the sun, is a very cold planet. It looks blue-green because of a gas in its cloudy atmosphere. Uranus rotates on its side, like a ball rolling through space.

Neptune

Diameter: 49,528 km (30,775 mi)

Moons: At least 13

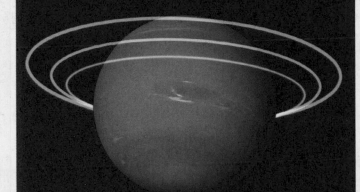

Neptune is the farthest planet from the sun. It takes about 165 Earth years to orbit the sun. A gas in its cloudy atmosphere gives Neptune a blue color. Neptune is a windy, stormy, cold planet.

Got it?

12. UNLOCK THE BIG ? Why do you think scientists are able to predict where in the night sky a planet will be visible?

....

....

13. Compare and Contrast Explain one way the inner and outer planets are similar and one way they are different.

....

....

⬛ **Stop!** I need help with ....

⏸ **Wait!** I have a question about ....

▶ **Go!** Now I know ....

What is the shape of a planet's path?

The path each planet follows around the sun is called its orbit. Every planet's orbit is an ellipse, a slightly stretched-out circle.

Follow a Procedure

☑ **1.** Tape the paper onto the cardboard. Stick a pin in the center. Tie a knot to make a loop of string.

☑ **2.** Put the loop over the pin. Use a pencil and the string to draw a circle. Hold the pencil upright against the stretched string as you draw your circle.

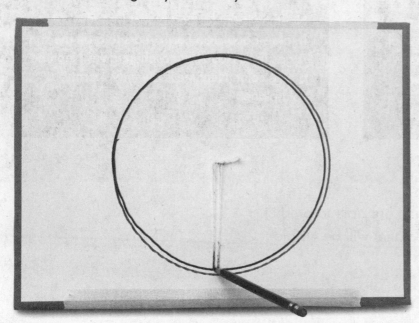

☑ **3.** **Measure** the largest and smallest diameters. Describe the shape. **Record** in the chart.

Materials

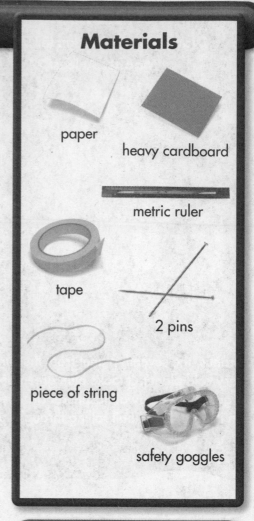

paper

heavy cardboard

metric ruler

tape

2 pins

piece of string

safety goggles

Inquiry Skill

You observe carefully and **interpret data** from models to learn about the real thing.

4. Put a second pin about 5 mm away from the first pin.
Put the loop of string over both pins.
Repeat Steps 2 and 3 with the loop over both pins.

5. Set the second pin about 10 mm away from the first pin.
Put the loop of string over both pins.
Repeat Steps 2 and 3 with the loop over both pins.

Orbit Measurement Chart

Distance Between Pins (millimeters)	Largest Diameter	Smallest Diameter	Shape (circle or ellipse)
0			
5			
10			

Analyze and Conclude

6. Interpret Data How did the shape of the orbits change in your **model**?

....

....

....

7. UNLOCK THE BIG ? Relate the pattern you **observed** in this activity to the observed orbits of the planets.

....

....

....

....

Kitt Peak National Observatory

Observatories are places where scientists can observe the universe. One of the best observatories in the world sits on a remote mountaintop in the Sonoran Desert of Arizona. The Kitt Peak National Observatory has twenty-six telescopes. Most of the telescopes detect light. Two of the telescopes detect radio waves.

Scientists from many places come to Kitt Peak National Observatory to study the universe. You may think that the universe changes very little, but as seen from these powerful telescopes the universe is always changing. Stars die in explosions bigger than you can imagine. New stars are born. Some bright stars in the night sky are not what they seem. With a telescope you may find that these bright stars are actually many stars clustered together.

You can visit Kitt Peak National Observatory during the day to learn about its many telescopes. There are also times when you can visit the observatory at night to observe the universe yourself.

APPLY THE BIG ?

How do you think telescopes can help scientists learn about patterns in the sky?

....

....

....

Vocabulary Smart Cards

rotation
revolution
orbit
ellipse
constellation
eclipse
lunar eclipse
solar eclipse
solar system
planet
asteroid
comet

Play a Game!

Cut out the Vocabulary Smart Cards.

Work with a partner. Choose a Vocabulary Smart Card. Say as many words as you can think of that describe that vocabulary word.

Have your partner guess the word.

ellipse

elipse

rotation

rotación

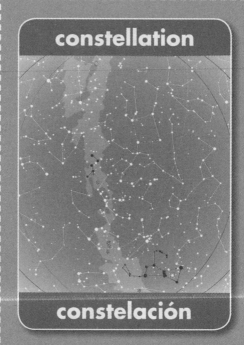

constellation

constelación

revolution

traslación

eclipse

eclipse

orbit

órbita

spinning of a planet, moon, or star around its axis

Write two synonyms of this word.

....

....

....

giro de un planeta, una luna o una estrella sobre su propio eje

---

a shape that is like a circle stretched out in opposite directions

Draw an example.

forma que parece un círculo alargado

Interactive Vocabulary

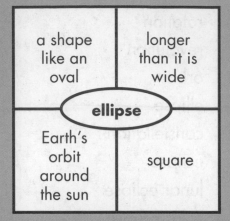

a shape like an oval	longer than it is wide
ellipse	
Earth's orbit around the sun	square

Make a Word Square!

Choose a vocabulary word and write it in the center of the square. Fill the squares with a definition, a characteristic, an example, and something that is not an example.

---

movement of one object around another

Write a sentence using the verb form of this word.

....

....

....

....

movimiento de un objeto alrededor de otro objeto

---

star pattern

Draw an example.

patrón estelar

---

path an object follows as it revolves around another object

Write a sentence using the verb form of this word.

....

....

....

camino que sigue un objeto mientras gira alrededor de otro objeto

---

event in which one object in space gets between the sun and another object

Write another definition for this word, as a verb.

....

....

....

fenómeno en el que un objeto del espacio se interpone entre el Sol y otro objeto

planet

planeta

lunar eclipse

eclipse lunar

asteroid

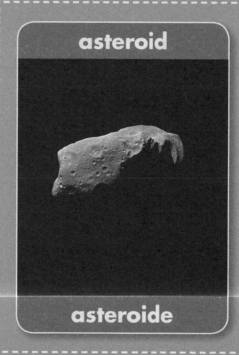

asteroide

solar eclipse

eclipse solar

comet

cometa

solar system

sistema solar

event in which the moon passes through Earth's shadow

Write a sentence using this term.

....

....

....

fenómeno en el que la Luna pasa por la sombra de la Tierra

---

a very large, round object that moves around a star

Write a sentence using this word.

....

....

....

....

cuerpo grande y redondo que orbita una estrella

....

....

....

---

event in which the moon passes between the sun and Earth

Write a sentence using this term.

....

....

....

fenómeno en el que la Luna pasa entre el Sol y la Tierra

---

a rocky object that orbits the sun but is too small to be called a planet or a dwarf planet

Write a sentence using this word.

....

masa rocosa que orbita alrededor del Sol pero que es demasiado pequeña para ser llamada planeta o planeta enano

---

....

....

....

---

the sun, the eight planets and their moons, and other objects

Write two words related to this term.

....

....

....

el Sol, los ocho planetas y sus lunas, y otros objetos

---

a frozen object that orbits the sun

Draw an example.

objeto helado que orbita alrededor del Sol

....

....

....

Study Guide

Lesson 1
How does Earth move?

- Earth's movements cause changes in patterns that are seen in the sky.
- Earth makes a rotation on an imaginary axis in about 24 hours.
- Earth revolves around the sun in about 365 days.

Lesson 2
How do star patterns change?

- Apparent patterns of stars are called constellations.
- Polaris, the North Star, does not seem to move in the sky, and stars appear to revolve around it.

Lesson 3
What are the phases of the moon?

- The moon's phases depend on where the sun, moon, and Earth are.
- Each time the moon rotates on its axis, it revolves once around Earth.
- In an eclipse, an object in space casts its shadow on another.

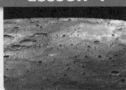

Lesson 4
What is the solar system?

- The solar system includes the sun, planets, moons, and other objects.
- Inner planets are small and rocky.
- Outer planets are large and made of gas and liquids.

Chapter Review

Lesson 1

How does Earth move?

1. **Vocabulary** The spinning of Earth around its axis is called its _____
   A. rotation.
   B. revolution.
   C. orbit.
   D. ellipse.

2. **Infer** How is Earth tilted when it is winter in the Northern Hemisphere?

....

....

....

3. **Explain** How are the noticeable movements of the sun, moon, and stars related?

....

....

....

....

....

Lesson 2

How do star patterns change?

4. **Explain** What is a constellation?

....

....

....

....

....

5. **Summarize** Why do stars appear to move across the sky?

....

....

....

....

....

6. **Analyze** Why can some different stars be seen in different seasons?

....

....

....

....

....

....

Lesson 3

What are the phases of the moon?

7. ⦿ **Cause and Effect** Write a cause and its effect in the correct box below.

> Like Earth's orbit around the sun, the moon's orbit around Earth is shaped like an ellipse. The gravity between the moon and Earth keeps the moon in its orbit. Because it moves, the moon stays in its orbit and doesn't crash into Earth. The moon makes a complete revolution around Earth in about 27.3 days.

Cause

Effect

Lesson 4

What is the solar system?

8. **Write About It** Explain how the sun's gravity affects the orbits of the planets.

9. **APPLY THE BIG ?** **What are some patterns in space?**

What kinds of motion cause solar eclipses? Explain.

Fill in the bubble next to the answer choice you think is correct for each multiple-choice question.

1 When Earth spins, it turns around an imaginary line called a(n)

Ⓐ rotation.

Ⓑ axis.

Ⓒ orbit.

Ⓓ ellipse.

2 Constellations are

Ⓐ star patterns.

Ⓑ recognized stars.

Ⓒ star circles.

Ⓓ recognized planets.

3 What do moons orbit?

Ⓐ comets

Ⓑ planets

Ⓒ stars

Ⓓ asteroids

4 A _____ is the phase of the moon when the entire half of the moon that faces Earth is lighted.

Ⓐ quarter moon

Ⓑ first quarter

Ⓒ new moon

Ⓓ full moon

5 The diagram below shows how Earth tilts. Describe how this tilting affects seasons on Earth.

....

....

....

....

....

....

Stargazing

You can go stargazing where you live. Choose a clear night. Then, go outside with a parent or guardian and look up at the stars. Do you see any groups of stars? Draw them in the box below. Then, use your school's library or media center to research constellations. Can you find a constellation that looks like your drawing? What is the name of the constellation?

Let's see... one, two, three, four... I count ten stars in this part of the sky!

Name of Constellation:

295

Materials

gloves and masking tape

2 containers and soil

small paper cup and two books

small paper clip and foam cup

water

graduated cylinder (or measuring cup)

metric ruler

Inquiry Skill

A **hypothesis** is a statement that explains an observation. It can be tested by an experiment.

What affects how soil erodes?

Moving water can change the land. It can carry soil from one place to another.

Ask a question.

How does the amount of water that falls on soil affect the amount of soil erosion?

State a hypothesis.

1. Write a **hypothesis** by circling one choice and finishing the sentence.
   If more water falls on soil, then (a) *more,* (b) *less,* (c) *about the same amount of* soil will be eroded because

....

....

Identify and control variables.

2. In an **experiment,** the **variable** you observe is called the **dependent variable** because it changes depending on the variable you change. In this experiment what is the dependent variable?

....

3. The variable you change is called the **independent variable** because you choose how to change it. It does NOT depend on anything except your choice. What is the independent variable?

....

4. In an experiment, there are factors that could be changed but must not be changed. These are called **controlled variables** because you control the experiment to make sure they do not change. List two controlled variables.

....

Design your test.

☑ **5.** Draw how you will set up your test.

☑ **6.** List your steps in the order you will do them.

Do your test.

☑ **7.** Follow the steps you wrote.

☑ **8.** Make sure to **measure** accurately. **Record** your results in a table.

☑ **9.** Scientists repeat their tests to improve their accuracy. Repeat your test if time allows.

Be careful! Wear safety goggles.

Work Like a Scientist

Scientists work with other scientists. They compare their methods and results. Talk with your classmates. Compare your methods and results.

Collect and record your data.

☑ **10.** Fill in the chart.

Interpret your data.

☐ **11.** Use your data to make circle graphs.

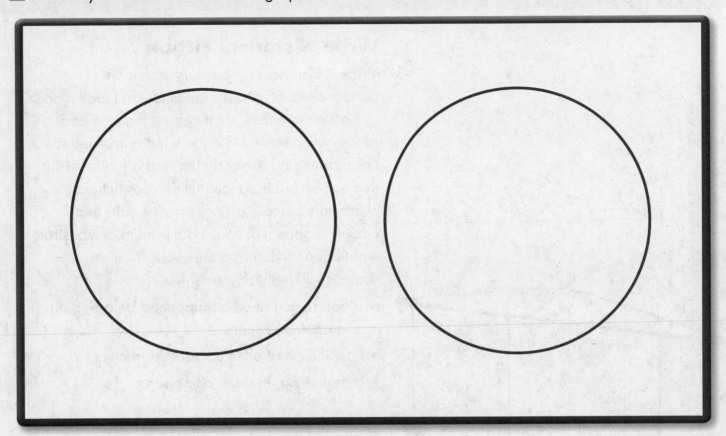

☐ **12.** Look at your graphs closely. Analyze how the amount of water that fell affected the amount of soil the water moved. Identify the evidence you used.

....

....

....

State your conclusion.

13. Communicate your conclusion. Compare your **hypothesis** with your results. Compare your results with others.

....

....

....

....

Write Historical Fiction

Write a historical fiction story about an earthquake, volcano, or landslide that took place in the United States. Write about the time and place of the event. Describe what happened to the surrounding areas during and after the event. Remember that historical fiction uses fictional characters but tells a story about events that actually happened. Make a model to demonstrate what happened during the event. Your story should include these elements:

- a description of what happened before, during, and after the event
- how the event affected your characters
- a beginning, middle, and end

Super Model

Using materials such as wire, string, or foam, create a model of the sun, Earth, and the moon. Use the model to demonstrate these things:

- Earth's rotation and its revolution around the sun
- changes in the moon's appearance and in star patterns as Earth moves

Using Scientific Methods

1. Ask a question.
2. State your hypothesis.
3. Identify and control variables.
4. Test your hypothesis.
5. Collect and record your data.
6. Interpret your data.
7. State your conclusion.
8. Try it again.

Plan an Investigation

Design an experiment to identify a sampling of rocks and minerals. Identify which properties you will test and the tools you will use. Use the numbered Scientific Methods steps as your guide. Then conduct your experiment.

Physical Science

Can you UNPOP popcorn?

Matter

Chapter 7

Can you unpop popcorn?

Predict Can the popcorn be kernels of corn again?
Why or why not?

....

....

....

THE BIG ? How can matter be described and measured?

What properties can be used to classify matter?

Use tools and your senses to observe properties of matter.

Materials

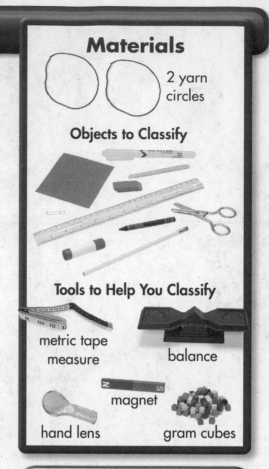

2 yarn circles

Objects to Classify

Tools to Help You Classify

metric tape measure

balance

magnet

hand lens

gram cubes

Follow a Procedure

☑ **1. Observe** ways the objects are alike and different.
List 3 of these properties.

....

☑ **2. Classify** Observe how the objects are alike.
Sort the objects into 2 groups.
Put a yarn circle around each group.
What property is alike for the objects in each loop?

....

....

Inquiry Skill

You **classify** objects when you sort them according to properties you observe.

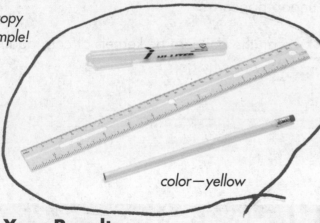

Do not copy this example!

color—yellow

color—not yellow

Explain Your Results

3. Look at what other groups did.
Infer three properties they used to **classify** their objects.

....

4. **UNLOCK THE BIG ?** How can you use properties to describe matter?

....

◉ Compare and Contrast

- When you **compare** you say how things are alike.
- When you **contrast** you say how things are different.

Lab Report

Day	Action	Observations
1	We put water in the freezer.	Water was liquid.
2	We put the frozen ice into a glass of water.	The ice floated on the water.
3	We waited one day.	There was no more ice in the water.

Practice It!

Write ways that water and ice are alike and different.

water   ice

What are properties of matter?

Envision It!

Tell how you can use your senses to find something at the grocery store.

MY PLANET DiARY

FunFact

You can bounce a rubber ball. But can you stretch it? Can you copy pictures with it? Can you model it like clay? Can you snap it apart? You can do all of these things with bouncing putty.

Bouncing putty is a silicone-based substance. It was invented by scientist James Wright in 1943. He was trying to make artificial rubber.

The putty is clearly fun, but it has some serious uses too. The putty is used for physical therapy by people with hand and arm injuries. People squeeze the putty to help strengthen muscles.

What changes would you make to the putty that would make it better for therapy?

....

....

....

I will know how to compare objects based on their physical properties. I will know that magnets attract and repel objects.

Words to Know
....

property
density

Properties of Matter

Matter is anything that has mass and takes up space. Scientists use different properties to identify matter. A **property** is a characteristic of an object. You can identify many properties of matter by using your senses. For example, you can look at the color, size, and shape of some matter. You can touch matter to decide if its texture is rough or smooth, soft or hard. You can also recognize some matter by its odor or taste.

Look at the fruits and vegetables in the picture. The banana is yellow and green. It has a smooth texture. The pineapple is green and brown, but it has a rough texture.

1. **Circle** six properties used to identify matter.

2. **◉ Compare and Contrast** How are the banana and pineapple alike and different?

Pineapple   **Banana**

3. **Describe** Name one of the fruits or vegetables shown in the picture below. What properties can you use to describe it?

....

....

....

....

....

....

....

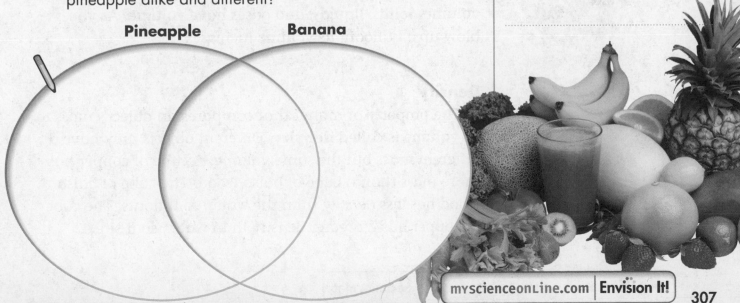

More Properties of Matter

Some properties of matter, such as mass, weight, volume, and density, are measurable. Scientists use tools to measure these properties. For example, a balance can be used to measure mass, and a scale can be used to measure weight.

Mass and Weight

Sometimes people confuse mass and weight. These two properties of matter are different. An object's mass is the amount of matter that makes it up. The mass of an object does not depend on the object's shape. A piece of paper has the same mass whether it is flat on a desk, folded in half, or shaped into a paper airplane.

Weight is a measure of the force or pull of gravity between an object and Earth. Weight can change if an object is moved to a place where the pull of gravity is different than on Earth. The mass of an object stays the same even if it is put on the moon.

Gravity on the moon is less than the gravity on Earth. The pull of gravity on the moon is $\frac{1}{6}$ of that on Earth. Suppose the astronaut shown below has a weight on Earth of 180 pounds. On the moon, the astronaut's weight would be about 30 pounds. The astronaut's mass on Earth and on the moon is the same.

4. Explain Why is your mass the same wherever you go?

....

....

Volume

The amount of space that matter takes up is called volume. Solids, liquids, and gases have volume. As you blow up a balloon, its volume increases.

Density

The property of matter that compares an object's mass to its volume is called **density.** Different objects may have a different mass but the same volume. A cube of copper has more mass than a cube of balsa wood. The cube of balsa wood has less density than the water, so it floats. The cube of copper has a greater density than water, so it sinks.

Attraction to Magnets

Another property of matter is attraction to magnets. Several metals, such as iron and nickel, are attracted to magnets and can be made into magnets. Iron and nickel are described as magnetic. Copper, another metal, is not attracted to magnets, so it is not described as magnetic.

All magnets have the property of magnetism. Magnetism is a force that acts on moving electric charges and magnetic materials. You can observe magnetism when a magnet is placed near a magnetic material. A magnet can attract a magnetic material such as iron filings. A magnet can also attract or repel another magnet depending on the positions of the magnets.

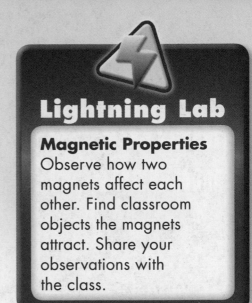

Lightning Lab

Magnetic Properties
Observe how two magnets affect each other. Find classroom objects the magnets attract. Share your observations with the class.

5. ◉ **Compare and Contrast** How are iron and copper alike and different?

....

....

Got it?

6. **Examine** What are some properties of a paper clip?

....

7. **UNLOCK THE BIG ?** Why is it useful to learn about the many different properties of matter?

....

....

⬛ **Stop!** I need help with ....

⏸ **Wait!** I have a question about ....

▶ **Go!** Now I know ....

How is matter measured?

Envision It!

Observe the group of toy blocks on each page. **Tell** how the two groups are alike and different.

Inquiry Explore It!

How does dividing clay affect its mass?

☑ **1. Measure** and **record** the mass of the clay. ____ g

☑ **2.** Break the clay into 2 pieces.
   Estimate the mass of each. ____ g and ____ g

☑ **3.** Measure the mass of each piece. ____ g and ____ g

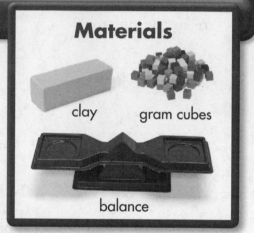

Materials

clay   gram cubes

balance

Explain Your Results

4. Interpret Data Compare the total mass of the clay before and after breaking it apart.

....

5. Predict how breaking the clay into 6 pieces would affect its total mass.

....

mys𝗰ienceonLine.com | **Explore It!** Animation

Mass

Matter is anything that has mass and takes up space. **Mass** is the measure of the amount of matter that makes up an object. Mass is a property that can be measured. Scientists use mass because they want a measurement that will not change if the object is moved to a different location. The mass of an object does not change unless matter is added to or removed from it. An empty plastic bottle has a specific mass. If that same plastic bottle were crushed, it would still have the same mass.

Anything that is made of matter has mass. Solid objects have mass. Water and other liquids also have mass. Even the air we breathe has mass.

You can use a pan balance to compare a mass that you know with one that you do not know. When the pans are level, the two masses are equal.

You can lay a sheet of aluminum foil flat or crumple it into balls of different sizes, but it still has the same mass.

1. **Recognize** (Circle) an instrument used to measure mass. **Underline** what that tool does.

2. **Analyze** A magazine is put through a paper shredder. Does it have more mass before or after it is shredded? Why?

....

....

....

Law of Conservation of Mass

The law of conservation of mass states that the parts of an object will have the same total mass as the whole object.

Suppose you measured the mass of the toy in the picture and discovered it was 23 grams. Next you took the toy apart and measured the mass of each part separately. If you added together the masses of all the parts, the total would be 23 grams, or the same as the mass of the assembled toy.

Suppose someone who did not see the toy takes all of the parts and makes a toy that looks very different from the one you see. What do you think is the mass of this new toy? That is right, 23 grams. The only way to change the toy's mass is to add parts or not use all of them. This is because the only way to change the total mass of an object is to either add matter or take it away.

3. **CHALLENGE** Suppose you measured the mass of a wet sponge. Then you wrung out the sponge and measured it again. Would the mass be different? Why or why not?

....

....

....

....

Measure and Compare Mass

Scientists use metric units when they measure and compare matter. The gram is the base unit of mass in the metric system. Some of the metric units that are used to measure mass are milligram (mg), gram (g), and kilogram (kg). Like our place-value system, the metric system is based on tens. Prefixes change the base unit to larger or smaller units. For example, 1,000 milligrams is equal to 1 gram, and 1,000 grams is equal to 1 kilogram.

6. **Calculate** The mass of a nickel is about 5 g. About how many nickels are needed for a mass of 1 kg? Remember that 1 kg = 1,000 g.

Each cube on this balance has a mass of 1 g. The mass of the eraser equals 22 g.

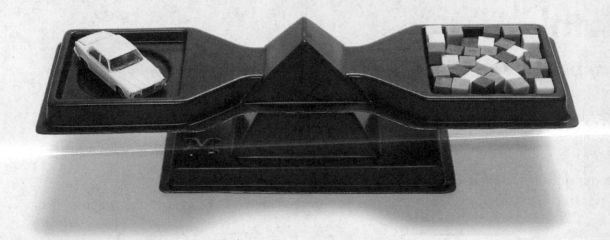

4. **Determine** What is the mass of the toy car?

....

5. **Compare** How does the mass of the eraser compare to the mass of the toy car?

....

....

length = 2 cm

width = 2 cm

height = 2 cm

Volume

Like mass, volume is also a property of matter that can be measured. **Volume** is the amount of space that matter takes up. If a solid has the shape of a rectangular box, one way to measure its volume is to use a ruler to measure the solid's length, width, and height. Then multiply the measurements. Look at the photos to the left. To find the volume of the cube, use this equation:

volume = length × width × height

volume = 2 cm × 2 cm × 2 cm

volume = 8 cm³

So the volume of the cube is 8 cubic centimeters (cm³).

7. Support Will the volume of a wooden cube change if you cut the cube in half? Why or why not?

....

....

Do the math!

Measuring Volume

To measure the volume of a box, you multiply its length, height, and width. For example, the volume of Box A would be 2 cm × 3 cm × 4 cm, or 24 cm³.

Use a metric ruler to measure Box B. Then answer the following questions.

1 What is the volume of Box B? Show your work.

2 Which box has a greater volume, A or B? _____

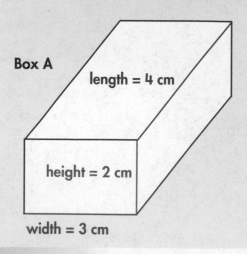

Box A

length = 4 cm

height = 2 cm

width = 3 cm

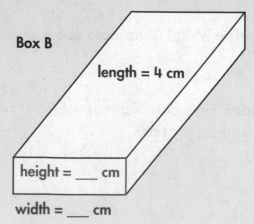

Box B

length = 4 cm

height = ___ cm

width = ___ cm

314

Volume of Liquids and Solids

Liquids do not have a definite shape. To measure a liquid, you use a measuring container, such as a graduated cylinder. A graduated cylinder is marked with metric units. Some metric units used to measure volume are milliliter (mL) and liter (L). One liter is equal to 1,000 milliliters. The units marked on this graduated cylinder are milliliters (mL).

A graduated cylinder can be used to find the volume of solids that sink in water. To measure the volume of a ball, for example, put some water into a graduated cylinder. Record its volume. Then place the ball into the cylinder, and record the volume of the water again. The ball has pushed away some of the water. The water level has risen the same number of milliliters as the volume of the ball. A volume of 1 mL is the same as 1 cm³.

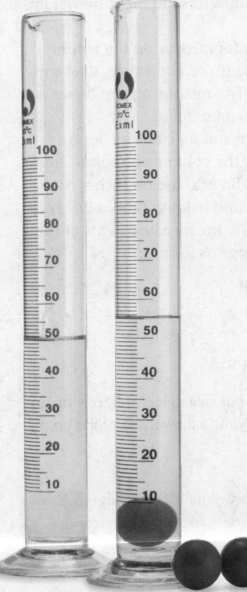

Volume A   Volume B

The volume of the water is 50 mL.

The volume of the ball and water is 55 mL.

volume = volume B − volume A
volume = 55 mL − 50 mL
volume = 5 mL
The ball's volume is 5 mL, or 5 cm³.

8. **Calculate** The volume of the water is _____ mL.
The volume of the water and the cube is _____ mL.
The volume of the cube is _____.
How does the volume of the cube compare to the volume of the ball?

....

....

length = 1 in.

width = 1 in.

height = 1 in.

U.S. System of Measurement

You have probably used the U.S. system of measurement to measure the properties of matter. This system uses units known as ounces (oz) and pounds (lbs.) to measure weight. One pound is 16 ounces.

The units of the U.S. system for measuring the volume of a liquid include fluid ounces (fl. oz.) and cups. One cup is the same as 8 fluid ounces. The measuring cup below is used for measuring the volume of a liquid.

The U.S. system uses units including cubic inches (in.³) and cubic feet (ft³) to measure the volume of a solid. One way to find the volume of a solid is to use an inches ruler to measure the length, width, and height of the solid. Then multiply the measurements. Use the measurements of the cube at the left to find its volume as follows:

volume = length × width × height
volume = 1 in. × 1 in. × 1 in.
volume = 1 in.³

So, the volume of the cube is 1 in.³

9. **Calculate** Suppose a box has a length of 4 ft, a width of 2 ft, and a height of 3 ft. What is the volume of the box?

....

10. **Understand** If a toy has a weight of 2 pounds, what is its weight in ounces?

....

11. **Interpret** Look at the height of the liquid in the measuring cup. What is the volume of the liquid in cups and in fluid ounces?

....

....

Compare Measurements

You can use either the metric or U.S. system to measure properties of objects. Suppose you measure your height in inches and then in centimeters. How do the two heights compare? The numbers and units used to tell the height will be different. However, the height is the same. That is because the choice of units does not affect the actual height.

height
1 in., or
about 2.5 cm

width
8.5 in., or about 22 cm

length
11 in., or
about 28 cm

12. Determine How would the volume of the book change if you calculated it in cm³ and then in in.³?

....

....

....

....

....

Got it?

13. Apply If the length of an object decreases while its width and height remain unchanged, will its volume increase or decrease? Explain.

....

....

14. **UNLOCK THE BIG ?** How can volume and mass be measured?

....

....

⬛ **Stop!** I need help with ....

⏸ **Wait!** I have a question about ....

▶ **Go!** Now I know ....

Lesson 3

What are phases of matter?

Tell why you think this person can climb up this waterfall.

Inquiry **Explore It!**

How does freezing affect the volume of water?

☑ **1.** Use a graduated cylinder to **measure** 40 mL of water.
Record two properties of liquid water.

....

....

☑ **2.** Freeze the water overnight.

☑ **3.** After freezing the water, **observe** and record its
volume. .... mL.
Record 2 properties of frozen water.

....

Materials

plastic graduated   plastic bottle
cylinder   with water

balance and
gram cubes (optional)

Explain Your Results

4. Draw a Conclusion How did freezing affect the volume?

....

5. How do you think freezing affects the water's mass?

With your teacher's permission, you may wish to make and carry out a plan.

   mYscienceonLine.com | **Explore It!** Animation

UNLOCK
THE BIG
?

I will know that heating
and cooling affect the
motion of particles.

Words to Know
....
phase of matter
melting point
boiling point

Phases of Matter

Scientists have learned that all matter is made up of tiny
particles. These particles are arranged in different ways and
also move. The form in which particles are arranged and
move is called a **phase of matter.** Three phases of matter
are solids, liquids, and gases.

Most substances on Earth exist naturally in only one
phase. For example, gold and lead exist naturally as solids
on Earth. Oxygen and helium exist naturally as gases on
Earth. However, rock exists as a liquid inside Earth and as a
liquid or solid on Earth's surface. Water exists naturally in
three phases. Liquid water is the same substance as the solid
called ice and the gas called water vapor.

1. ⊙ **Compare and Contrast** Write in the graphic
organizer how the phases of gold and oxygen on Earth
are alike and different.

2. **Compose** Write a
caption for the picture
and include two phases
of matter.

....
....
....
....

Gold   Oxygen

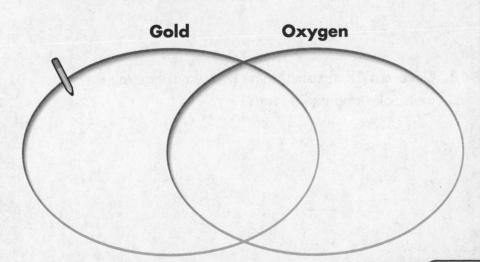

You cannot see the individual particles in a solid. This drawing shows that they are tightly packed and held in place.

Solids

At a temperature of 0°C or below, the shape of an ice cube is the same whether it is on a plate or in a container. A solid is matter that has a definite shape and usually takes up a definite amount of space. Its particles are closely packed together. The particles have some energy. They move back and forth, but they do not change places with each other.

You cannot see the particles in a liquid either. The particles are close to each other, but they are not held tightly in place.

Liquids

Water takes the shape of the container it is in. If you pour water from a pitcher into a glass, the shape of the water changes. The volume of water stays the same. Matter that does not have a definite shape but takes up a definite amount of space is a liquid. In a liquid, the particles are not held in place as in a solid. The particles of a liquid are able to slide past one another. In many substances the particles are packed more tightly in the solid state than in the liquid state. Water is an exception. The particles in liquid water are a little closer together than in solid water.

The particles in a gas are far apart. Even if you could see them, you would not see the particles arranged in any special way.

Gases

In the gas state, water is called water vapor. It is invisible. Water vapor and several other gases make up the air that is all around us. Like a liquid, a gas takes the shape of its container. Unlike a liquid, a gas expands to fill whatever space is available. A gas always fills the container it is in. The particles in a gas are very far apart from one another and move in all directions. Particles in a gas move more easily and quickly than those in a liquid.

3. **Give an Example** Name two ways that you use water in its solid and liquid forms.

....

....

4. Arrange Label the three phases of matter in this photo. Explain how the particles in each phase are arranged. Draw how the particles might look in the circles below.

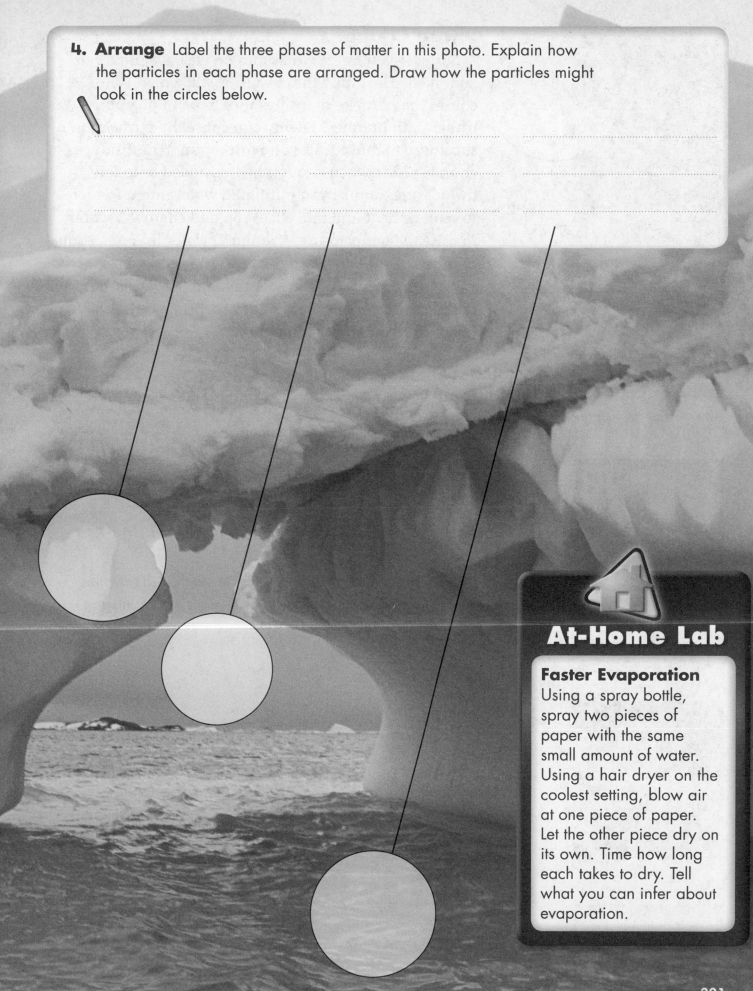

At-Home Lab

Faster Evaporation
Using a spray bottle, spray two pieces of paper with the same small amount of water. Using a hair dryer on the coolest setting, blow air at one piece of paper. Let the other piece dry on its own. Time how long each takes to dry. Tell what you can infer about evaporation.

100°C
Water boils.
Water vapor condenses.

Between 0°C and 100°C, water is a liquid.

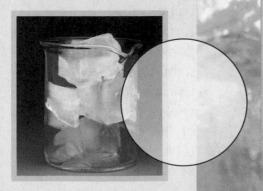

0°C
Water freezes into ice.
Ice melts into water.

Phase Changes

Suppose you freeze water into an ice cube and then let it melt. The liquid that results is still water. What causes the particles of a substance to be in one phase rather than another? Energy can cause the particles in a substance to move faster and farther apart. Substances change phase when enough heat is added or taken away. For example, you put liquid water into a freezer to remove heat and make ice. You add energy to water to raise the temperature. If you boil water in a pot, some of the water becomes water vapor. Phase changes are examples of physical changes that can be reversed by adding or removing energy. Every substance changes phases at a different temperature.

5. **Compare** What do ice, liquid water, and water vapor all have in common?

....

....

....

6. **Illustrate** Draw in the circles to the left how the particles might look. Which particles are moving the most? The least?

....

....

....

myscienceonline.com | Got it? 60-Second Video

Melting and Boiling Points

The melting point and boiling point of a substance are physical properties that help identify the substance. The **melting point** is the temperature at which a substance changes from a solid to a liquid. The temperature at which a substance melts is the same temperature at which it freezes, or changes from a liquid to a solid.

The **boiling point** is the temperature at which a substance changes from a liquid to a gas. This temperature is also the temperature at which the substance changes from a gas back into a liquid.

Substances have different melting and boiling points. For example, tin melts at approximately 232°C. It boils at approximately 2270°C. These are different from the melting and boiling points of water.

7. Compute Read about different temperatures. Find the difference between the melting point of iron and the temperature of the human body. Show your work.

surface of the sun: 6000°C

melting point of iron: 1538°C

boiling water: 100°C

human body: 37°C

melting ice: 0°C

food in a freezer: −18°C

Got it?

8. Cause and Effect How does the energy of particles relate to their motion?

....

....

9. Differentiate How does taking away heat cause changes in matter?

....

....

⬛ **Stop!** I need help with ....

⏸ **Wait!** I have a question about ....

▶ **Go!** Now I know ....

What are mixtures?

Tell what parts you see mixed together in this photo.

my planet diary

FunFact

You probably do not have to think about where your water comes from or how much of it you drink. This is not the case for astronauts. Water is heavy, so only a small amount can be carried into space. The rest of the water that astronauts drink comes from the astronauts themselves.

Astronauts use a system that gets drinkable water from their urine. The system removes water from urine in several steps. To separate pure water from the waste products in urine, the solution is heated to make the water evaporate. As water evaporates, waste products are left behind. Then the water vapor is cooled and purified. Iodine is added to the water to kill any bacteria. Eventually, pure water that used to be part of the urine is left for astronauts to drink!

> For what other purpose might the astronauts use the filtered water?
> ....
> ....

Words to Know

mixture   evaporation
filtration   condensation

Mixtures

You may have eaten a salad made from a mixture of lettuce, cucumbers, and tomatoes. Each ingredient in this mixture keeps its own taste and shape.

A **mixture** is a combination of two or more substances. Substances in a mixture can be separated. This means that they are not chemically combined. Peas, carrots, and corn can be combined in a mixture. In fact, you can buy a bag of frozen mixed vegetables at the store. Each vegetable can be sorted into separate piles. The peas, carrots, and corn taste the same whether they are separated or mixed together. Since parts of a mixture are not joined together chemically, each substance keeps its own properties. All substances that are separated out of a mixture have the same properties as when they were mixed.

1. **Underline** why substances in a mixture can be separated.

2. **Generalize** Why does a tomato taste the same whether it is separated or in a mixture?

....

....

....

A garden salad is a mixture of many fruits and vegetables.

Lightning Lab

Step by Step
Write a numbered set of instructions for separating a mixture of paper clips, wood chips, gravel, and sugar.

Separating Mixtures

A mixture is often easy to separate into its parts. You can use the properties of the substances in a mixture to separate them from each other.

Magnetism

A magnet can be used to separate substances that are attracted to a magnet. You can use a magnet to separate safety pins that are mixed with other objects in a drawer.

Filtration

The process of separating substances with a filter is **filtration.** Filtration can be used to separate some solids from liquids and big objects from small objects. You can separate sand from water if you pour the mixture into a filter.

Evaporation

Some mixtures of solids and liquids can be separated by evaporation. **Evaporation** is the change from a liquid into a gas. To make salt, salty ocean water can be put in a tray. After evaporation occurs, the salt is left in the tray.

3. **Interpret** Look at the photos on these pages. Complete each caption.

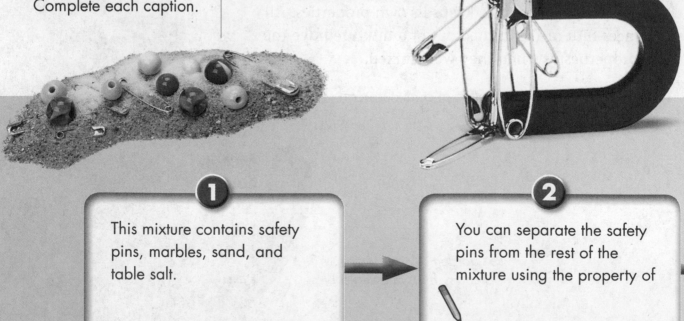

1 This mixture contains safety pins, marbles, sand, and table salt.

2 You can separate the safety pins from the rest of the mixture using the property of

....

myscienceonline.com | I Will Know...

Condensation

What if you want the evaporated water back? You can use condensation. **Condensation** is the process of a gas changing into a liquid. You can lower the temperature to cause condensation. When you have a cold glass of lemonade outside on a warm day, the water vapor in the air separates from the other gases in air. The water vapor condenses into beads of water on the glass.

condensation

4. Compare What do evaporation and condensation have in common?

....

....

....

5. Recall Describe how to use condensation to separate a mixture.

....

....

....

....

....

6. [CHALLENGE] In step 3, why does the salt in the water not get trapped in the filter?

....

....

....

....

salt in the bottom of glass

3

You can stir the rest of the mixture into water. Then you use the process of

....

4

The salt will be left after

.... occurs.

7. ⊙ **Compare and Contrast** How are a solute and a solvent alike? How are they different?

....

....

....

....

Solutions

If you stir salt and water together, you make a mixture. You cannot see the salt in this mixture because it has broken into very small particles. The salt has dissolved in the water. The salt and the water form a special kind of mixture called a solution.

In a solution, one or more substances are dissolved in another substance. The most common kind of solution is a solid dissolved in a liquid, such as salt in water. In a solution, the substance that is dissolved is the solute. A solvent is the substance that takes in, or dissolves, the other substance. Usually there is more solvent than solute.

In the ocean, salt and other minerals are dissolved in water. Ocean water is a solution. But a solution does not have to be a liquid. The air you breathe, for example, is a solution made up of gases. The steel used for buildings and cars is a solution of two solids, carbon and iron.

8. Classify Below each picture, write the name of the solute and the solvent.

When making steel, carbon and iron are melted into liquid form. Then, the carbon is dissolved in the iron.

Solute ....

Solvent ....

Solute ....

Solvent ....

Solubility

The ability of one substance to dissolve in another is called its solubility. Solubility is a measure of the amount of a substance that will dissolve in another substance. The solubility of materials can be high or low. The solubility of sand in water is very low.

Sometimes raising the temperature of the solvent can speed up the process of dissolving the solute. This is true for most solids. For example, you can dissolve sugar more quickly in warm water than you can in cold water.

Another way to make a solute dissolve more quickly is to crush it. If you drop a sugar cube into a cup of water, it may take a while to dissolve. If you crush the sugar cube into tiny crystals, the crystals will dissolve very quickly. More of the sugar particles are touching the water when the sugar is in tiny crystals than when it is in a sugar cube.

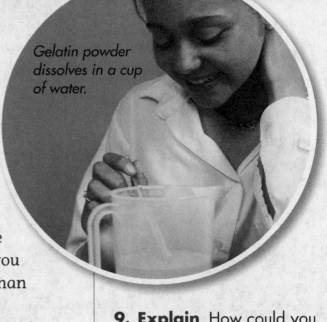

Gelatin powder dissolves in a cup of water.

9. **Explain** How could you make gelatin powder dissolve more quickly?

....

....

Got it?

10. **Describe** How can a safety pin be separated from a mixture?

....

....

11. **Apply** Mud is a mixture of dirt and water. Describe which methods you would use to separate this mixture so you are left with the dirt.

....

....

 Stop! I need help with ....

 Wait! I have a question about ....

 Go! Now I know ....

How does matter change?

Discuss how matter is changing in this photo.

Inquiry Explore It!

How can you tell if a change has occurred?

Materials

plastic cup with vinegar

plastic cup with baking soda

safety goggles

☑ **1. Observe** and **record** two properties of baking soda.

....

☑ **2.** Observe and record two properties of vinegar.

....

☑ **3.** Pour the vinegar into the baking soda. Observe. Record what happens.

....

....

Be careful with chemicals. Wear safety goggles.

Be careful!

Explain Your Results

4. Infer Did a change happen? Explain.

....

....

myscienceonline.com | **Explore It!** Animation

SC.4.L.17.2

UNLOCK
THE BIG
?

I will know that some materials change and become materials with different characteristics.

Words to Know

chemical change

Matter Changes

Matter can undergo many different changes. Sometimes the size, shape, or state of the substance can change. For example, carving a block of wood into a figure changes the block's size and shape. Other times, a change can form a new substance with new properties. For example, burning that block of wood would turn the wood into coals, and then into ashes.

1. **Circle** the main idea. **Underline** the details.

2. ◉ **Compare and Contrast** How are the three photos below alike and different?

....

....

....

A lump of soft clay is used to shape into a pot.

The clay has been shaped to make this pot. The pot is soft.

The pot has been heated at high temperatures. By baking the clay, a new substance called ceramic is formed. The pot is now hard.

A knitter uses a ball of yarn.

The yarn is knitted into a long strip.

The knitted strip can unravel into the same amount of yarn as the original ball.

Physical Changes

If you cut and fold a piece of paper to make an origami sculpture, you change only the size and shape of the paper. You have not changed the particles that make up the paper.

A change in the size, shape, or state of matter is a physical change. A physical change does not change the particles that make up matter. The arrangement of the particles, however, may be changed.

Examples of Physical Changes

Are you causing a physical change when you mix nuts and raisins? A mixture of nuts and raisins does not form a new substance. You can separate the nuts and raisins by hand. In a mixture of salt and water, the particles are too small to be separated by hand. However, if the water evaporates, the salt will be left behind. Because the parts of a mixture do not change and can be separated, making a mixture is an example of a physical change.

Breaking a pencil is a physical change. The pieces of the pencil are still made of wood and graphite. If you sharpen the broken ends, you can keep using the pencil. Another physical change is tearing. If you tear a sheet of paper into tiny pieces, it still is made of the same kind of matter.

3. **Identify** (Circle) two examples of physical changes.

4. **Classify** Is a phase change, such as ice melting into a puddle, an example of a physical change? Why or why not?

....

....

....

....

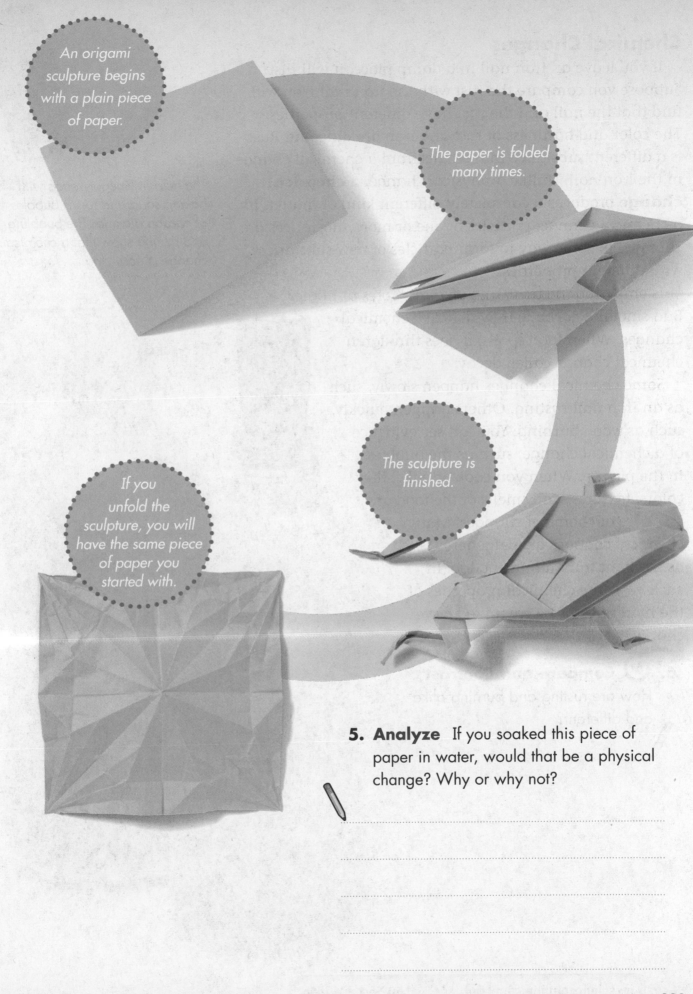

An origami sculpture begins with a plain piece of paper.

The paper is folded many times.

The sculpture is finished.

If you unfold the sculpture, you will have the same piece of paper you started with.

5. **Analyze** If you soaked this piece of paper in water, would that be a physical change? Why or why not?

....

....

....

....

Chemical Changes

If you leave an iron nail in a damp place, it will rust. Suppose you compare the rust with the iron nail. You will find that the nail and the rust have different properties. The color and hardness of rust and iron are different. Rust is a different substance that results from a chemical change in the iron nail. Unlike a physical change, a **chemical change** produces a completely different kind of matter. In a chemical change, particles of one or more substances are changed in some way to form particles of new substances with different properties.

Is emptying the trash one of your chores at home? Bad-smelling garbage is evidence of chemical changes. When food spoils, it goes through a chemical change called decay.

Some chemical changes happen slowly, such as an iron nail rusting. Others happen quickly, such as wood burning. You can see evidence of a chemical change, such as the bubbles in the picture. When you cook or bake, the colors, textures, and smells of the food are evidence of chemical changes. Many chemical changes give off energy, such as the light from a burning log. In each case, the chemical properties of the materials that were mixed have changed.

The acid in vinegar reacts with baking soda and forms bubbles of carbon dioxide. The bubbling and fizzing show that a chemical change is occurring.

6. ◉ **Compare and Contrast**
   How are rusting and burning alike and different?

   ....

   ....

   ....

   ....

7. **Evaluate** Write whether the following changes are physical or chemical.

Bacteria cause the decay of dead plant and animal matter.

....

A cook slices a yellow pepper to put in a salad.

....

Burning wood reacts quickly with oxygen in the air. The new substances formed by this change include ashes, carbon dioxide, and water vapor.

....

At-Home Lab

Shiny Pennies
Wear safety goggles. Measure 100 mL of vinegar and 25 mL of water. Pour them into a bowl. Add a pinch of salt. Stir. Find a penny. Describe it. Drop it into the solution. Wait a few minutes. Observe any changes.

Got it?

8. **Justify** Identify a change in a substance that results in a new material. Tell how the properties of the new substance are different.

....

....

9. **Explain** How does a chemical change occur?

....

....

■ **Stop!** I need help with ....

❚❚ **Wait!** I have a question about ....

▶ **Go!** Now I know ....

Does steel wool rust faster in water or vinegar?

Materials

safety goggles

2 pieces steel wool

2 plastic cups

masking tape

water

vinegar (whole class use)

clock with a second hand

2 paper towels

Follow a Procedure

☑ **1. Observe** the properties of steel wool. **Record.**

☑ **2.** Fill one cup $\frac{1}{3}$ full with water.
Fill the other cup $\frac{1}{3}$ full with vinegar.

☑ **3.** Put a piece of steel wool in each cup. Wait 1 minute.

Be careful! **Wear safety goggles. Do not breathe in vinegar fumes.**

Label the cups.

Inquiry Skill
You can use what you observe to make **inferences.**

☑ **4.** Take the steel wool out of each cup. Squeeze out any extra liquid. Place each piece of steel wool on a paper towel in front of its cup.

Wait 5 minutes.

5. Observe the properties of the steel wool. Look at it. Feel it. Record.

	Observations
Steel wool	
Steel wool 5 minutes after soaking in water	
Steel wool 5 minutes after soaking in vinegar	

Be careful! Wash your hands when finished.

Analyze and Conclude

6. Interpret Data Which piece of steel wool rusted faster?

....

7. Infer Based on your **observations,** is rusting a physical change or chemical change? Explain using what you observed.

....

....

....

8. UNLOCK THE BIG ? Why might it be important for scientists to describe how the properties of matter change during an investigation?

....

....

Materials Scientist

As a materials scientist, your job would be to study the atomic or molecular structure of different materials. Many materials scientists work mainly with metals. Others concentrate on plastics. Some work with semiconductors—materials important in computers. Still others combine a variety of materials for different uses.

Materials scientists design new materials. They test how well the materials work in different products. Sometimes they figure out the best ways to manufacture the materials. Materials scientists often work in a lab. They need good math and science skills. They usually work with a team. Therefore, they need to be able to communicate well face-to-face. They also need to report about their work, so they must know how to write well.

For this career, you will need a degree in physics, chemistry, or engineering. Even after you have a job, you will need to continue your education. This will help you keep learning about the new materials that are always being produced.

 APPLY THE BIG ? How does understanding how matter is described and measured help materials scientists design new materials?

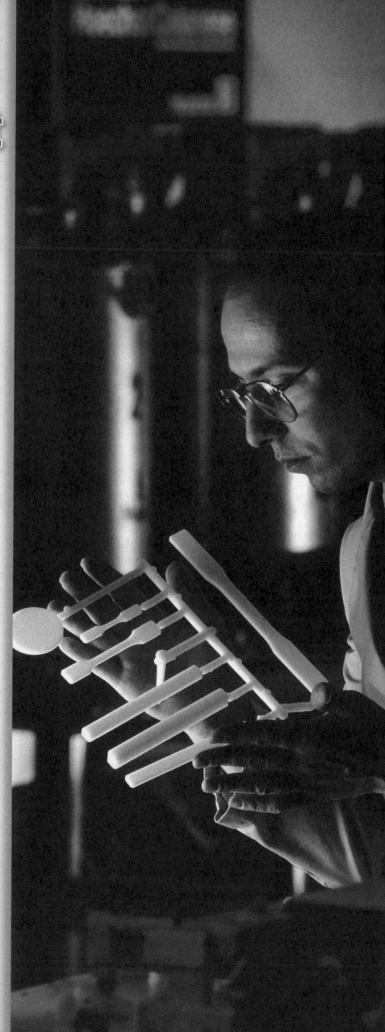

Vocabulary Smart Cards

property
density
mass
volume
phase of matter
melting point
boiling point
mixture
filtration
evaporation
condensation
chemical change

Play a Game!

Cut out the Vocabulary Smart Cards.

Work with a partner. Write a sentence using the vocabulary word. Draw a blank where the vocabulary word should be.

Have your partner fill in the blank with the correct vocabulary word. Have your partner repeat with another Vocabulary Smart Card. Take turns.

volume

volumen

property

propiedad

phase of matter

fase de la materia

density

densidad

melting point
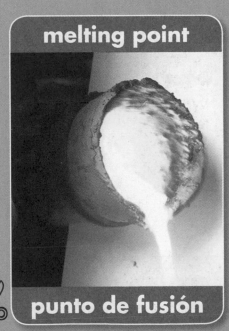
punto de fusión

mass

masa

Interactive Vocabulary

a characteristic of an object

Use a dictionary. Find as many synonyms for this word as you can.

....

....

....

característica de un objeto

---

the amount of space that matter takes up

Write another definition for this word.

....

....

....

cantidad de espacio que la materia ocupa

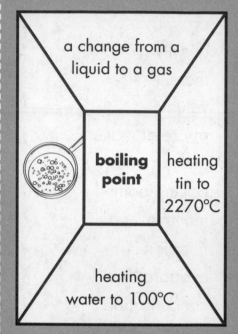

boiling point

a change from a liquid to a gas

heating tin to 2270°C

heating water to 100°C

---

the property of matter that compares an object's mass to its volume

Write three other forms of this word.

....

....

....

propiedad de la materia que compara la masa de un objeto con su volumen

---

the form in which particles are arranged and move

Write three examples.

....

....

....

manera en que están dispuestas y se mueven las partículas

Make a Word Frame!

Choose a vocabulary word and write it in the center of the frame. Write or draw details about the vocabulary word in the spaces around it.

---

the measure of the amount of matter that makes up an object

Write a sentence using this word.

....

....

....

medida de la cantidad de materia de la que está compuesto un objeto

---

the temperature at which a substance changes from a solid to a liquid

Write a sentence using this term.

....

....

....

temperatura a la cual una sustancia cambia de sólido a líquido

evaporation

evaporación

boiling point

punto de ebullición

condensation

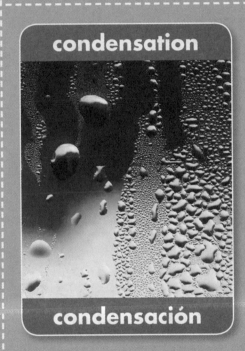

condensación

mixture

mezcla

chemical change

cambio químico

filtration

filtración

the temperature at which a substance changes from a liquid to a gas

Write a sentence using this term.

....

....

....

temperatura a la cual una sustancia cambia de líquido a gas

---

the change from a liquid into a gas

Draw a picture.

cambio de líquido a gas

....

....

....

---

a combination of two or more substances

Write an example of this word.

....

....

....

combinación de dos o más sustancias

---

the process of a gas changing into a liquid

Write a sentence using this word.

....

....

....

proceso por el cual un gas se convierte en líquido

....

....

....

---

the process of separating substances with a filter

Write the verb form of this word.

....

....

....

proceso de separar sustancias con un filtro

---

a change that produces a completely different kind of matter

Draw an example.

cambio por el cual se produce un tipo de materia completamente diferente

---

....

....

....

Chapter 7
Study Guide

REVIEW THE BIG **?** How can matter be described and measured?

Physical Science

Lesson 1

What are properties of matter?

- Matter is anything that has mass and takes up space.
- There are many properties of matter including color, shape, texture, odor, taste, mass, weight, volume, density, and magnetism.

Lesson 2

How is matter measured?

- Mass is the amount of matter in an object.
- Volume is the amount of space taken up by an object.
- The metric and U.S. systems can be used to determine measurements.

Lesson 3

What are phases of matter?

- Three phases of matter are solids, liquids, and gases.
- Heating and cooling affect the motion of particles in different phases of matter.

Lesson 4

What are mixtures?

- A mixture is two or more substances that are not chemically joined.
- Methods to separate a mixture into its parts include filtration, magnetism, evaporation, and condensation.

Lesson 5

How does matter change?

- Matter can undergo physical and chemical changes.
- A physical change does not change the particles that make up matter.
- Chemical changes produce new substances with different properties.

Lesson 1

What are properties of matter?

1. **Vocabulary** What do you call the characteristics of an object?
   A. volume
   B. properties
   C. mass
   D. states

2. **Apply** What could you do to identify an object in a closed box?

Lesson 2

How is matter measured?

Do the math!

3. Suppose you have 50 mL of water in a graduated cylinder. After you place a marble in the cylinder, the water level rises to 78 mL. What is the volume of the marble?

4. **Calculate** What is the volume of a cardboard box that is 11 in. long, 3 in. wide, and 7 in. high? Show your work.

5. **Recall** What are two systems for measuring matter?

Lesson 3

What are phases of matter?

6. **Write About It** When warm water is cooled, the tiny particles of matter that make up the liquid slow down. Why does this happen?

Lesson 4

What are mixtures?

7. **Vocabulary** The change in phase from a gas into a liquid is called
   A. filtration.
   B. evaporation.
   C. solution.
   D. condensation.

8. **Describe** Why is filtration useful to separate a mixture of water and sand?

Lesson 5

How does matter change?

9. ◉ **Compare and Contrast** Explain how physical and chemical changes are alike. How are they different?

10. **APPLY THE BIG ?** **How can matter be described and measured?**

Think about a book in your classroom. How would you describe and measure it? Use the term *property*.

Fill in the bubble next to the answer choice you think is correct for each multiple-choice question.

1. What is the volume of the box?

   Ⓐ 9 cm³

   Ⓑ 11 cm³

   Ⓒ 6 cm³

   Ⓓ 15 cm³

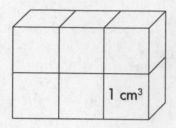

1 cm³

2. The phase of matter with no definite volume or shape is a

   Ⓐ liquid.

   Ⓑ solid.

   Ⓒ gas.

   Ⓓ phase.

3. Which method would you use to separate salt that is dissolved in water?

   Ⓐ magnetism

   Ⓑ evaporation

   Ⓒ solubility

   Ⓓ filtration

4. The parts of an object will have the same total mass as

   Ⓐ the volume of the object.

   Ⓑ the object's densities.

   Ⓒ the phases of matter.

   Ⓓ the whole of the object.

5. A chemical change results in a

   Ⓐ loss of matter.

   Ⓑ solution.

   Ⓒ phase change.

   Ⓓ different kind of matter.

6. What happens to the motion of particles when a liquid becomes hotter?

Making Orange Juice

BigWorld My World

Big World

Many people drink orange juice for breakfast. Have you ever wondered how orange juice is made?

Many oranges grown in Florida are used to make orange juice. Making large amounts of orange juice is a complex process. The oranges go through a lot of changes before becoming orange juice. Large machines at processing plants remove the peels from the oranges, squeeze the oranges to remove the juice, and also strain out the seeds.

Then the orange juice can either be frozen or pasteurized. Pasteurization is a process used to kill bacteria in some foods. Next, the pasteurized orange juice is bottled and shipped. You can buy a bottle of orange juice at your local grocery store. Then you can pour yourself a tall glass of refreshing orange juice any time.

What are some of the changes made to oranges before they become orange juice?

....

....

....

....

He is drinking orange juice.

My World

347

What puts the

BOOM

in fireworks?

Energy and Heat

Chapter 8

Try It! What are some forms of energy?

Lesson 1 What are forms of energy?

Lesson 2 What is sound energy?

Lesson 3 What is light energy?

Lesson 4 What is heat?

Investigate It! Which material is the better heat conductor?

When fireworks go off they can be louder than a jet engine. Even if you watch from a safe distance, a fireworks display can be loud enough to make you shake!

Predict What forms of energy are at work in a fireworks display?

....

....

....

THE BIG ? How does energy cause change?

What are some forms of energy?

Energy is the ability to cause motion or create change.

☑ **1.** Use each of the Forms of Energy Cards.
Record your **observations**.

Materials

Forms of Energy
Cards A, B, C

wind-up toy

white paper

flashlight

safety goggles

color
change ring

sound can

Forms of Energy Cards

Card	Energy Observations
A	
B	
C	

Inquiry Skill

You can use observations and previous experience to help make an **inference.**

Explain Your Results

2. **UNLOCK THE BIG ?** **Infer** Use your **observations** to tell how energy caused the changes you observed.

Station A ....

Station B ....

Station C ....

⊙ Main Idea and Details

- The **main idea** is the most important idea in a reading selection.
- **Details** help to explain or support the main idea.

A Hot Job!

Steelworkers work in one of the world's hottest jobs. At the mill where they work, iron ore is heated with other substances in giant furnaces to become liquid steel. Workers must wear suits that protect them from heat, but they can still sense the warm air around them.

Practice It!

Complete the graphic organizer below to show the main idea and two details in the example paragraph.

Main Idea

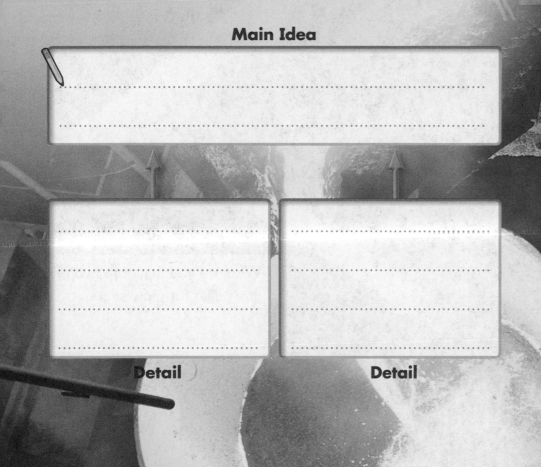

Detail   Detail

Lesson 1

What are forms of energy?

Tell what sounds and movements you think this plane might make.

MY PLANET DIARY

FunFact

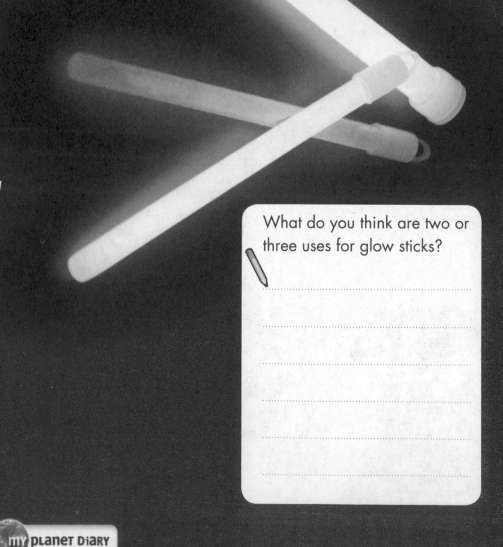

Fireflies know the secret, but eventually people discovered it. The secret is how to make light with a chemical reaction that does not produce much heat.

Glow sticks are made in two sections. One chemical, along with a dye, fills the outer section. Another chemical fills the inner section. When the glow stick is bent, the inner section breaks open. This lets the chemicals mix. The reaction that follows gives off energy in the form of light. The light can last for hours.

What do you think are two or three uses for glow sticks?

....

....

....

....

....

....

I will know what energy is and some forms it can take. I will know what energy can do.

Words to Know
....
energy
kinetic energy
potential energy

Energy

Turn on a light switch. Rub your hands together to warm them. Roll a pencil across your desk. You are using energy! **Energy** is the ability to cause motion or create change. Whenever the position, chemical structure, or look of something changes, energy is required.

There are many forms of energy. Some energy takes the form of light or sound. Electrical energy is another type of energy you use every day.

1. ◎ **Main Idea and Details** Complete the graphic organizer below. Write details about energy.

2. **Analyze** What is changing about the dog and the toy?

....

....

....

....

....

....

....

Main Idea

Energy is the ability to cause motion or create change.

Detail

Detail

Forms of Energy

Energy cannot be made or destroyed. It is transferred from form to form. Energy also moves from one object to another. Energy can exist in many forms. Here are some common forms of energy.

Electrical energy is energy caused by the movement of electrically charged particles. When you flip on a light switch or use the toaster, you are using electrical energy. Electricity flows through the devices to power them.

3. **Describe** Write an example of electrical energy in your home.

....

Thermal energy is energy due to randomly moving particles that make up matter. You can feel the flow of thermal energy as heat. The faster particles move, the more thermal energy is produced. People use thermal energy to heat or cook food. The thermal energy causes changes in the food as the food cooks.

Sound energy is the energy of vibrations carried by air, water, or other matter. You use sound energy when your alarm clock wakes you up, or when you listen to your favorite music.

Kinetic energy is the energy of motion. Anything moving has this kind of energy. A moving swing at the playground or a hurricane both have kinetic energy.

4. **Describe** Write an example of kinetic energy in school.

....

Light energy travels as waves and can move through empty space. Some light energy comes from the sun and travels to Earth. These sunflowers use this light energy to help make their own food.

Potential energy is energy that is stored in an object. When an object is in motion, its potential energy is released as other forms of energy. For example, when a truck burns fuel, the potential energy in gasoline is released as sound, heat, and motion.

5. **Conclude** (Circle) the names of the forms of energy in use when you turn on a fan in your home.

Where is the energy?

6. Look for examples of these forms of energy.
Write a total number.

thermal energy ....

sound energy ....

light energy ....

electrical energy ....

kinetic energy ....

Go Green

Energy Savers
Look around your classroom. Describe some forms of energy. How could you save energy? Write a list. Share your list with the school.

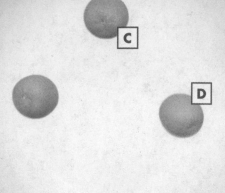

Energy and Motion

All moving things have kinetic energy. The amount of kinetic energy depends on the speed and mass of the object. Look at the time-lapse photo of the boy tossing an orange. The harder he throws the orange, the more kinetic energy it has. An object with greater mass would also have more kinetic energy.

When the boy throws the orange, he gives it kinetic energy. As the ball rises, it slows down. Its kinetic energy is gradually converted to potential energy. As the orange falls, the potential energy is converted back to kinetic energy.

7. Explain Use the photo at left to complete the captions.

Forms of Potential Energy

There are different forms of potential energy. Some forms have to do with an object's position. Other forms have to do with an object's makeup.

Gravitational

A raised object has what is called gravitational potential energy. The orange the boy is throwing has this kind of potential energy. The higher or heavier an object is, the more gravitational potential energy it has.

8. Hypothesize Does the orange have more gravitational potential energy in the boy's hand or high in the air? Explain.

....

....

Chemical

Chemical potential energy is stored in the connections that hold particles together. A car uses chemical energy when it burns gasoline. The food you eat has chemical energy. When your body digests food, chemical energy turns into other forms of energy that you use to move, talk, and live.

A The orange is at rest in the boy's hand. He gives the orange kinetic energy when he throws it.

B As the orange rises, its kinetic energy changes to

....

C At the top of the throw, the orange has its maximum potential energy.

D As the orange falls, its potential energy changes back into

....

myscienceonline.com | Got it? | 60-Second Video

Elastic

A stretched rubber band or a compressed spring have potential energy. This is called elastic potential energy. The more a rubber band is stretched, the more potential energy it has. If you bounce, kick, or hit a ball, the ball also has this kind of potential energy. The ball's material and the air inside it compress like a spring. Elastic potential energy can change into sound energy and kinetic energy.

The golf club's kinetic energy is transferred to the ball as elastic potential energy. The club compresses the ball.

9. **Hypothesize** Look at the picture of the golf club striking the golf ball. Will the ball's elastic potential energy change into kinetic energy? Explain.

....

....

....

....

Got it?

10. **Categorize** What forms of energy taught in this lesson are produced by a television set?

....

....

11. **Analyze** Suppose you throw a basketball in the air. Instead of catching it, you let it bounce on the court. What kinds of energy are in use as the ball travels?

....

....

⬜ **Stop!** I need help with ....

⏸ **Wait!** I have a question about ....

▶ **Go!** Now I know ....

Lesson 2
What is sound energy?

Circle the instruments that you think make a high sound.
Draw boxes around those that make low sounds.

MY PLANET DIARY

How does an acoustic guitar make sound? It starts with plucking the guitar's strings. Plucking causes the strings to vibrate. The vibrations first move through the saddle. Then they move through the bridge to the soundboard. The soundboard is the wooden piece that makes up the front of the guitar's body. The entire soundboard then vibrates. The body of the guitar is shaped in a way that makes the sound louder. These sounds come out through the sound hole, producing the sound you hear when someone plays a guitar.

Fun Fact

strings

sound hole

soundboard

saddle

bridge

Look closely at the different parts of the guitar.
Suppose the sound hole were covered up.
How do you think the sound would change?

....

....

....

UNLOCK THE BIG ?

I will know what sound energy is and how it is produced.

Words to Know

sound   pitch
frequency   volume
wavelength   amplitude

Sound Energy

The blare of an alarm clock, the beep of a car horn, the quack of a duck, and the rumble of thunder during a storm are all sounds. **Sound** is energy in the form of vibrations passing through matter. A vibration is a quick back-and-forth movement. Sounds occur when objects vibrate. Sound travels through solids, liquids, and gases. Sound cannot travel through empty space, where there is no matter.

Pluck a guitar string, and the string starts to vibrate. The vibrating string passes energy to the air around it. The sound energy travels outward as sound waves. A sound wave is a disturbance that moves sound energy through matter. When the waves reach your ears, the waves make your eardrum vibrate, and you hear the sound made by the guitar string.

1. **Underline** words that tell what sound is.

2. **Explain** A plucked guitar string will make a sound until the string stops vibrating. How might you play a short note?

....

....

....

How Sound Travels

As sound waves move through matter, they set particles into motion. The moving particles form a pattern. Areas with groups of particles that are bunched together alternate with areas of particles that are farther apart. The areas where particles bunch together are called compressions.

Sound waves travel at different speeds through matter. Sound waves travel quickly through most solids and liquids. Sound waves tend to travel more slowly in gases.

3. **Identify** (Circle) the compression images in this picture.

4. ⊙ **Main Idea and Details** (Circle) the main idea in the first paragraph above. **Underline** three details.

Do the math!

Read a Graph

This graph shows the speed of sound through some common materials. Use the graph to answer the following questions.

Approximate Speed of Sound

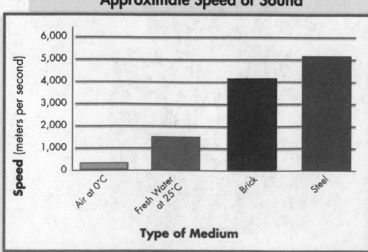

1 **Compare** Does sound travel faster in air or in fresh water?

....

2 **Compute** About how many meters per second faster is the speed of sound in steel than in brick?

....

....

Frequency and Wavelength

Waves can travel in different ways. They can carry different types and amounts of energy. But all waves have certain properties. Frequency and wavelength are two of these properties. The **frequency** of a wave is the number of waves that pass a point in a certain amount of time. Frequency is often described as the number of complete cycles a wave makes in one second. A cycle is one vibration. **Wavelength** is the distance between a point on one wave and a similar point on the next wave.

Studying Sound

One way scientists study sound is by using oscilloscopes. An oscilloscope is a device that takes sound waves and displays the shape of the waves on a screen. Look at the oscilloscope screen below. The signals are displayed onscreen in the form of a wave. Compressions in a sound wave show up on screen as crests, or high points on the wave. The spaces between compressions show up as troughs, or low points on the wave.

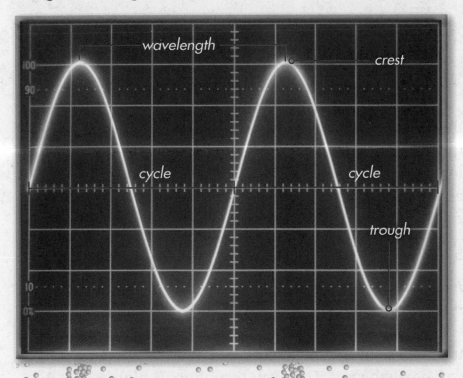

5. Analyze Which has a higher frequency, a wave that makes 6 cycles per second or one that makes 10 cycles per second? Explain your answer.

....

....

....

....

Wavelength can be measured between two crests or between two troughs. The slower an object vibrates, the longer its wavelength and the lower its frequency will be.

If this screen represented one second, this wave's frequency would be 2 cycles per second.

6. Label Where are the compressions in both images to the left?

Pitch

People experience the frequency of sound as its pitch. **Pitch** is how high or low a sound is. Pitch depends on the frequency of the sound wave. Objects that vibrate more quickly have higher frequencies. Those objects have a higher pitch. Objects that vibrate more slowly have a lower frequency and a lower pitch.

The material of the object making the sound and its size and shape affect the pitch you hear. A tuba, for example, is a musical instrument made of many feet of brass tubing. Tubas make low-pitched sounds. Some sounds are too low-pitched or too high-pitched for humans to hear.

7. **Apply** Put your hand on your throat and make a low-pitched sound. Then make a high-pitched sound. Explain how your throat adjusts while making these sounds.

....

....

....

A dolphin communicates by making high-pitched sounds.

8. **Explain** Are dolphin sounds high or low frequencies?

Lightning Lab

Water Music
Fill four bottles with different amounts of water. Blow across the top of each to make a sound. Put the bottles in order from low sounds to high. What do you notice about the sound and the amount of water in each bottle?

Volume

When you describe a sound, probably one of the first things you think about is loudness, or volume. You know that some sounds are louder than others. A jet engine, for example, makes much more noise than a car. What, exactly, is volume? **Volume** is a measure of how strong a sound seems to us. The more energy there is in the sound wave, the louder the sound and the higher the volume.

The volume of a sound is related to its amplitude. **Amplitude** is the height of a wave measured from its midline. The higher the amplitude of a wave, the more energy it has, and the louder it sounds. Suppose you turn down the volume on the TV as soft as it will go. You can barely hear it. Then you turn it up as high as it will go. Now you have to hold your ears so they don't hurt! You have not changed the pitch of the sound. You have changed its amplitude and its volume.

mysCienceonline.com | Got it? 60-Second Video

9. Recall Label the parts of this wave.

midline

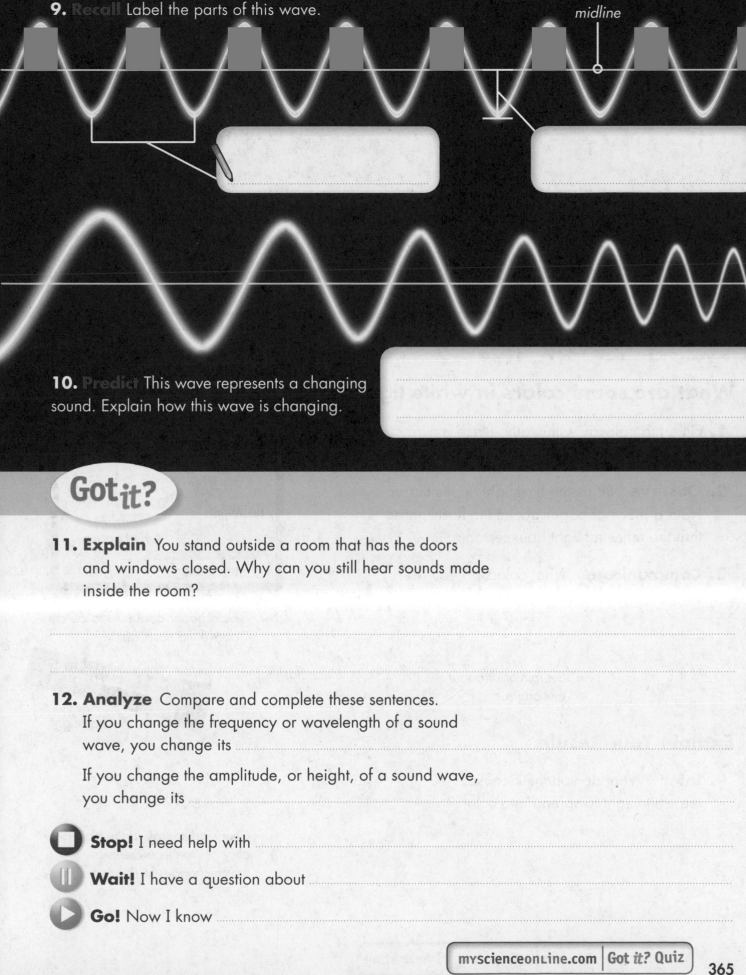

10. Predict This wave represents a changing sound. Explain how this wave is changing.

Got it?

11. Explain You stand outside a room that has the doors and windows closed. Why can you still hear sounds made inside the room?

....

....

12. Analyze Compare and complete these sentences.

If you change the frequency or wavelength of a sound wave, you change its ....

If you change the amplitude, or height, of a sound wave, you change its ....

Stop! I need help with ....

Wait! I have a question about ....

Go! Now I know ....

What is light energy?

Envision It!

Describe how the frog looks. Tell why you think it looks this way.

Inquiry **Explore It!**

What are some colors in white light?

☑ **1.** Fill a tub halfway with water. Place a mirror in the water at an angle.

☑ **2.** **Observe** Shine the flashlight on the mirror. Hold a piece of paper above the flashlight so that the reflected light bounces onto it.

☑ **3.** **Communicate** What colors do you see?

....

....

Explain Your Results

4. **Infer** What do you think causes the white light to spread into colors?

....

....

Materials

mirror

plastic tub
$\frac{1}{2}$ full of water

flashlight

white paper

metric ruler

Hold paper about 30 to 60 cm above the flashlight.

Set mirror at about this angle.

Shine flashlight here.

Put flashlight here.

Chemical energy in the battery changes to electric energy, which changes to light energy.

I will know how light bends when it passes through different materials.

Words to Know

refraction   reflection
absorption

Sources of Light

The sun is an important source of light energy on Earth. Without constant light energy from the sun, Earth would be a dead planet. It would be too cold and dark for any kind of life. For example, plants convert sunlight into chemical energy, which they use to make food. Without plants, animals could not survive.

Besides the sun, there are sources of light on Earth. For example, some animals give off light called bioluminescence. This light is a result of chemical reactions inside the animal's body. In addition, humans discovered long ago that they could make their own light. The discovery of fire changed how people lived. They could light a campfire and work even after dark.

1. ◉ **Draw Conclusions** Write in the graphic organizer facts that support the conclusion about the sun.

firefly

2. **Explain** Describe how this firefly can be a source of light energy.

....

....

....

....

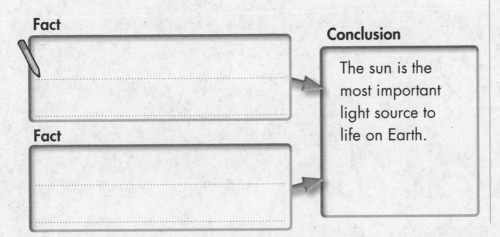

Fact

Fact

Conclusion

The sun is the most important light source to life on Earth.

At-Home Lab

Rainbows in Light
Look at the back of a compact disc in a well-lit room. Describe what you see. How does a compact disc act like a prism?

Light Waves We See

The form of light energy that we can see is called visible light. Light energy travels from its source as waves. Like all waves, light waves have wavelengths and frequencies. White light, such as the light from a lamp or the sun, is actually a blend of colors. The colors are red, orange, yellow, green, blue, and violet. These colors make up the visible light spectrum. The colors of the visible light spectrum always appear in the same order in which they appear in a rainbow and are arranged by their wavelengths and frequencies.

3. **Explain** Why does the visible light spectrum have different colors?

....

....

....

....

 red   orange   yellow   green   blue   violet

Prisms

A piece of glass called a prism separates white light into its different wavelengths. A prism lets you see the colors. As you move from red to blue on the visible light spectrum, wavelength decreases and frequency increases.

4. Describe Explain how raindrops and prisms are similar.

....

....

....

5. Apply Raindrops can cause light waves to bend. What other substances can cause a rainbow to form?

....

....

Light waves bend when they enter the prism at an angle.

Different wavelengths bend at different angles. The different colors separate from each other when light leaves the prism.

6. Describe Light rays refract as they travel from the pencil to the water to the glass to the air. Explain how the pencil looks.

Light and Matter

Light rays travel in straight lines—as long as nothing is in their way! But when light rays strike an object, they may pass through it, reflect off it, or be absorbed by it.

Refraction

Light changes speed when it passes into a new medium. When this happens, the light bends. This bending is called **refraction.** The change in speed causes the light to refract, or bend. Refraction causes the white light striking a prism to bend. The white light separates into individual colors you can see because each color bends differently.

Reflection

Light waves reflect at least a little off most objects. **Reflection** occurs when light rays bounce off, or reflect from, a surface. Objects with smooth, shiny surfaces, such as still water, reflect more light rays than other objects. When you brush your teeth in front of a mirror, the smooth, shiny surface of the mirror reflects almost all the light rays that hit it. All light rays reaching the mirror from the same direction are reflected in the same new direction, so you see a clear image, or reflection, of your toothpaste-filled mouth.

halo

Halos around the sun are formed where ice crystals in Earth's atmosphere refract light.

mYscienceonline.com | Got it? 60-Second Video

Absorption

Objects may absorb some light waves. **Absorption** occurs when an object takes in a light wave. After a light wave is absorbed, it becomes a form of heat. Look at the photo of the pencil in the glass on the previous page. The pencil is an object that absorbs most light waves.

7. ⊙ **Draw Conclusions** What happens to an object that absorbs a lot of light?

....

8. **Explain** Tell what you see in the photo at right. Explain what you see.

....

....

....

Got it?

9. **Describe** What happens during refraction of light as light passes through a prism?

....

10. **Summarize** Describe how light bends, or refracts, when traveling through different objects.

....

....

....

⏹ **Stop!** I need help with ....

⏸ **Wait!** I have a question about ....

▶ **Go!** Now I know ....

What is heat?

In this kind of photograph, different temperatures show up as different colors.

Inquiry Explore It!

How does heat move?

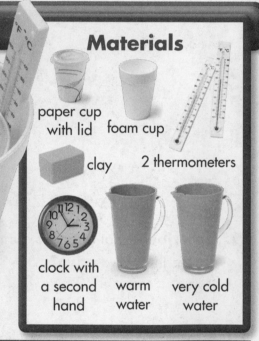

Materials

paper cup with lid   foam cup

clay   2 thermometers

clock with a second hand   warm water   very cold water

1. Fill a paper cup with warm water. Cover it. Push a thermometer through the lid and hold it in place with clay. **Record** the temperature. .... °C.

2. Fill a foam cup $\frac{1}{4}$ full with very cold water. Record the temperature. .... °C.

3. Place the paper cup inside the foam cup. Record the temperature in each cup every minute for 10 minutes.

Heat Movement Observations											
	Water Temperature (°C)										
	Start	1 min	2 min	3 min	4 min	5 min	6 min	7 min	8 min	9 min	10 min
Paper cup											
Foam cup											

Explain Your Results

4. **Observe** What happened to the temperatures? ....

5. **Infer** Tell which way heat moves between objects with different temperatures.

myscienceonline.com | **Explore It!** Animation

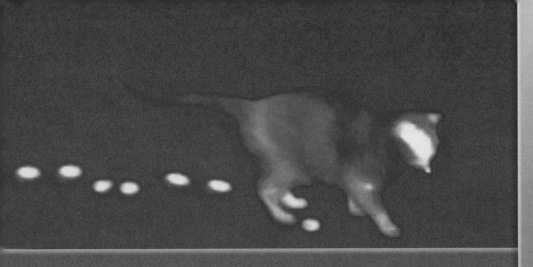

Tell which colors you think represent warmer areas.

I will know that heat flows from hot objects to cold ones. I will know that some materials are good conductors of heat and others are not.

Words to Know

conduction   radiation
convection

Conduction

Thermal energy flows from something warm to something cool. The transfer of thermal energy between matter of different temperatures is heat. A heat source is anything that gives off energy that particles of matter can take in.

When you go to bed at night, does your pillow feel cool on your face? Is the pillow warm when you wake up? That is thermal energy moving! Your body is the heat source. Thermal energy transfers from your body to your pillow. When solids touch, thermal energy moves by conduction. **Conduction** is the transfer of heat that occurs when one thing touches another.

A bird warming its eggs in a nest is another example of conduction. The bird's body is the heat source. Conduction transfers thermal energy from the bird to the eggs, which are cooler.

1. **Visualize** Draw an ice cube sitting on a counter top on a hot day. Draw an arrow showing which direction thermal energy flows. Describe how the heat is transferred.

A Conduction Example

Have you ever eaten hot oatmeal for breakfast? Suppose that you eat a bowl of hot oatmeal with a metal spoon. Why does the metal spoon begin to feel warmer? The particles of the spoon that touch the oatmeal start to move. As they move more quickly, they crash into other particles in the spoon. Soon, thermal energy from the oatmeal moves throughout the spoon. Heat transfer continues until the oatmeal and the spoon are at the same temperature.

2. **Exemplify** How do you know that heat from the oatmeal has moved?

....

....

....

....

3. **Describe** Suppose cold milk is poured into a warm glass. What will happen to the milk's temperature? Why?

Convection

Have you felt how warm a kitchen gets when the oven is on? You feel the heat indirectly as the heat moves through the room from convection. **Convection** is the transfer of thermal energy as matter moves. In convection, a gas or a liquid moves from place to place. The oven heats air inside it. Particles in the warm air move faster and travel upward into the rest of the kitchen. Then cooler air enters the oven to be warmed up.

Radiation

When the sun warms your skin or you sit near a fire, you feel another kind of energy. This energy is radiant energy, or radiation. **Radiation** is energy that is sent out in waves. When radiant energy hits you, the particles in your skin move more quickly. The radiation is converted to thermal energy and you feel warm. Radiation can travel through matter and through empty space.

4. **Summarize** Complete the captions on the greenhouse below.

.... from the sun warms the ground in _____ the greenhouse below.

.... moves warmer air upward.

.... moves cooler air downward.

Glass walls and ceilings let radiation in, but keep warm air from escaping.

The ground warms the air directly above it.

Changes of Other Energy to Heat

Where does heat come from? Sometimes, other forms of energy change and give off heat. This heat can be used in many different ways.

Fossil Fuel to Heat

Fossil fuels are a source of heat. Coal, natural gas, and oil are all fossil fuels. When these fuels are burned, they produce useful heat. People often use this heat in their homes, schools, and other buildings.

Light to Heat

Have you ever noticed that a black T-shirt gets warm on a hot, sunny day? Objects that are black absorb all the colors of visible light. When the light is absorbed, it becomes a form of heat. So, the black T-shirt warms up.

Laser light produces a great deal of heat. A laser is a powerful beam of light. Lasers are often used to cut, drill, and bond materials. Doctors use lasers to treat certain problems with the eye, the skin, and other organs.

The sun's energy also can change to heat. A solar panel absorbs energy from the sun. In a solar heat system, the sun's energy heats a liquid that flows through the solar panels. The heated liquid is pumped through pipes. It can then be used to heat homes and wash clothes.

5. **Predict** What do you think could be one important use of solar panels, such as the ones on this home?

myscienceonline.com | Got it? | 60-Second Video

Friction to Heat

Try rubbing your hands together quickly. The heat you feel is an effect of friction. Friction occurs when two surfaces rub together. As a result of friction, heat is produced. For example, when a person skates on ice, the ice and skate rub together. This friction gives off heat.

6. **Infer** The skates of this ice skater cause friction. What might you see that would show that the friction of an ice skate sliding on ice causes heat?

....

....

Got it?

7. **Classify** How is thermal energy transferred in these examples?

A cold drink left in the sun gets warm. ....

You eat a warm bite of food. ....

After you get out of a long shower, the bathroom is warm. ....

8. **UNLOCK THE BIG ?** How does heat travel during conduction?

....

....

⬛ **Stop!** I need help with ....

⏸ **Wait!** I have a question about ....

▶ **Go!** Now I know ....

Which material is the better heat conductor?

Follow a Procedure

☐ **1.** Place $\frac{1}{4}$ of a spoonful of margarine on the handles of each spoon. Stick a bead into the margarine on each spoon. Place both spoons in an empty cup.

☐ **2.** Pick up the cup filled halfway with very warm water. Gently pour it into the cup with the spoons.

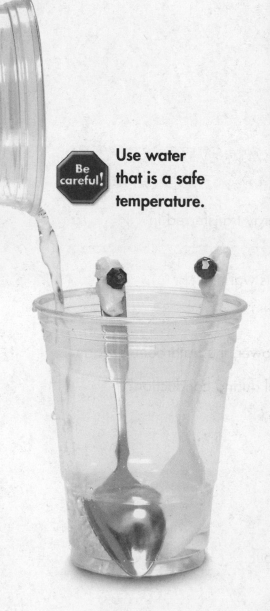

Be careful! **Use water that is a safe temperature.**

Materials

2 small beads

margarine

metal spoon

plastic spoon

plastic cup $\frac{1}{2}$ full of very warm water

timer, stopwatch, or clock with second hand

empty plastic cup

Inquiry Skill
Carrying out an investigation carefully and observing closely help you make accurate **inferences.**

☑ **3. Observe** Watch the beads closely.
Time how long it takes for each bead to fall.

☑ **4. Record** your **data** below.

Heat Conductor Observations	
Material	**Observations and Melting Time**
Plastic spoon	
Metal spoon	

Analyze and Conclude

5. Write an explanation for your **observations.**

....

....

....

6. Infer Which of the materials would be better for a cooking pot? Explain how you made your inference.

....

....

....

7. UNLOCK THE BIG ? What do your observations teach you about how energy moves?

....

....

....

Sound and Temperature

Did you know that you can usually hear sounds better at night than during the day? You can investigate the properties of sound at home. During the day, have a friend stand 50 meters away and make a sound using a whistle. Describe the volume of the sound. During the evening after the temperature has decreased, repeat this activity and describe what you hear. The speed and direction of the sound waves are affected by the temperature of the air. In many places, the temperature of the air is warmer during the day than it is in the evening.

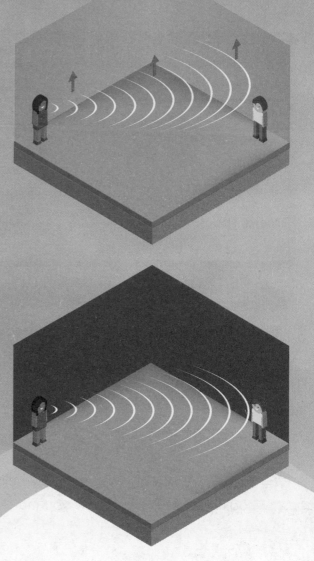

Describe the different volumes you heard during the day and during the evening. If you did not notice a difference, why might this be the case?

....

....

....

....

Vocabulary Smart Cards

energy
kinetic energy
potential energy
sound
frequency
wavelength
pitch
volume
amplitude
refraction
absorption
reflection
conduction
convection
radiation

Play a Game!

Cut out the cards.

Work with a partner. Spread out both sets of Vocabulary Smart Cards on a table. One set should show the definition and the other should show the word.

Have your partner pick a card and find the definition that matches the word.

Have your partner repeat with another word.

sound

sonido

energy

energía

frequency
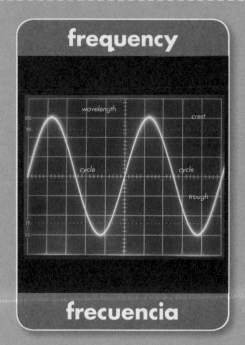
frecuencia

kinetic energy

energía cinética

wavelength
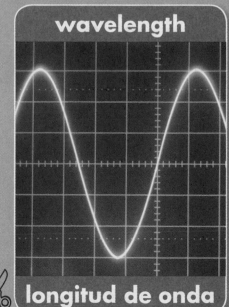
longitud de onda

potential energy

energía potencial

the ability to cause motion
or create change

Write an example.

....

....

....

....

capacidad de producir
movimiento o causar
cambio

---

energy in the form of
vibrations passing through
matter

Draw an example.

energía en forma de
vibraciones que pasa a
través de la materia

Interactive Vocabulary

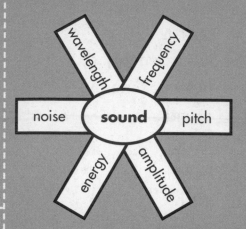

Make a Word Wheel!

Choose a vocabulary word
and write it in the center of
the Word Wheel graphic
organizer. Write synonyms
or related words on the
wheel spokes.

---

energy of motion

Draw an example.

energía de movimiento

---

number of waves that pass
a point in a certain amount
of time

Write three words that
have the same root as the
word.

....

....

número de ondas que
pasan por un punto en un
tiempo determinado

---

energy that is stored in an
object

Write a sentence using
this term.

....

....

....

energía que está
almacenada en un objeto

---

distance between a point
on one wave and a similar
point on the next wave

Draw an example.

distancia entre un punto
de una onda y un punto
similar de la onda que
sigue

conduction	refraction	pitch

conducción	refracción	tono

low pitch

high pitch

convection	absorption	volume
	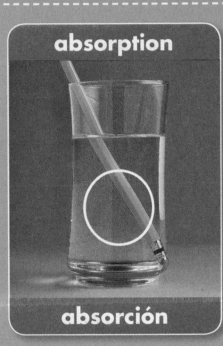	
convección	absorción	volumen

radiation	reflection	amplitude
		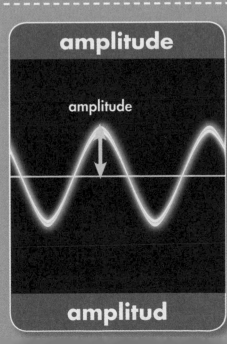
radiación	reflexión	amplitud

amplitude

how high or low a sound is

Write an example.

....

....

....

....

....

cuán agudo o grave es un
sonido

---

the bending of light when it
passes into a new medium

Write a sentence using the
verb form of this word.

....

....

....

desviación que sufre la luz
cuando pasa de un medio
a otro

---

the transfer of heat that
occurs when one thing
touches another

Write a sentence using the
verb form of this word.

....

....

....

transmisión de calor que
ocurre cuando un objeto
toca otro objeto

---

a measure of how strong a
sound seems to us

Write a sentence using this
word.

....

....

....

....

medida de cuán fuerte nos
parece un sonido

---

occurs when an object takes
in light waves

Write a sentence using the
verb form of this word.

....

....

....

....

ocurre cuando un objeto
captura las ondas de luz

---

the transfer of thermal
energy as matter moves

Write an example.

....

....

....

....

transferencia de energía
térmica mientras se mueve
la materia

---

the height of a wave
measured from its midline

Write three words that
have the same root as the
word.

....

....

....

altura de una onda medida
desde su punto medio

---

occurs when light rays
bounce off a surface

Write an example.

....

....

....

....

ocurre cuando los rayos
de luz rebotan en una
superficie

---

energy that is sent out in
waves

Write a sentence using the
verb form of this word.

....

....

....

....

energía transmitida a través
de ondas

Study Guide

REVIEW THE BIG ? How does energy cause change?

Lesson 1

What are forms of energy?

- There are basic forms of energy, including light, sound, electrical, and the energy of motion.
- Energy has the ability to cause motion or create change.

Lesson 2

What is sound energy?

- Sound is produced by vibrating objects. The way an object is made and the way it vibrates affect the type of sound we hear.
- A sound wave's frequency and energy also affect the sound we hear.

Lesson 3

What is light energy?

- Visible light is made up of waves with different wavelengths and frequencies.
- Light can be refracted, reflected, or absorbed.

Lesson 4

What is heat?

- Heat is the transfer of thermal energy.
- Heat can move by conduction, convection, or radiation.
- Other forms of energy can change to heat.

Chapter Review

How does energy cause change?

Lesson 1

What are forms of energy?

1. **Vocabulary** The energy of motion is called
   A. potential energy.
   B. kinetic energy.
   C. chemical energy.
   D. thermal energy.

2. **Analyze** What two kinds of energy are you using when you play on a slide?

....

....

....

....

....

....

....

....

....

....

....

....

Lesson 2

What is sound energy?

Do the math!

3. Sound travels through cold air at about 1,190 kilometers per hour. That means that a sound can travel the length of three football fields in about a second. Some machines, such as jet planes, can travel faster than sound. The world's fastest train can travel 574.8 kilometers per hour. How much faster would it have to go to match the speed of sound in air?

....

4. **Summarize** Sound cannot travel through
   A. water.
   B. metal.
   C. air.
   D. empty space.

Lesson 3

What is light energy?

5. **Write About It** Suppose light waves refract as they pass through a raindrop. Describe what happens to the light.

....

....

....

....

....

6. ⊙ **Main Idea and Details**
Underline the main idea and circle the details in the following paragraph.

Light waves reflect at least a little off most surfaces. Some surfaces reflect more light than others. A smooth, shiny surface reflects more light rays than other surfaces. A mirror has a smooth shiny surface.

Lesson 4

What is heat?

7. **Analyze** Which of these items is the best conductor of heat?
   A. a metal fork
   B. a wooden drawer handle
   C. a solid plastic ladle
   D. a foam plastic drink container

8. ⊙ **Cause and Effect** How are friction and heat related?

....

....

....

9. **APPLY THE BIG ?** **How does energy cause change?**

....

Think back to this morning as you were getting ready for school. Name some of the different forms of energy you used or saw. How did you use them?

....

....

....

....

....

Fill in the bubble next to the answer choice you think is correct for each multiple-choice question.

1 Which of the following is not a basic form of energy?

Ⓐ muscle
Ⓑ electrical
Ⓒ thermal
Ⓓ sound

2 Which statement about energy is true?

Ⓐ Energy is a wave.
Ⓑ Energy cannot travel through a vacuum.
Ⓒ Energy has the ability to cause motion.
Ⓓ Energy cannot change form.

3 A sound wave with a high frequency will also have a high

Ⓐ wavelength.
Ⓑ volume.
Ⓒ amplitude.
Ⓓ pitch.

4 Refraction occurs when a light wave

Ⓐ bends as it moves from one medium to another.
Ⓑ bounces back off an object or a surface.
Ⓒ is taken in by an object.
Ⓓ changes into heat.

5 Explain how the stove burner heats up the metal pot.

Solar Cooking

In some parts of Africa, people use wood to cook food. But wood is sometimes hard to find, and other fuels can be very expensive. Solar Cookers International (SCI) is a group that helps people learn to cook with the sun's energy. SCI needs to know where solar cooking can best be used.

One of NASA's energy management programs uses satellites to study Earth from space. NASA's Surface Solar Energy (SSE) information lets people use their latitude and longitude to learn the amount of solar energy available for cooking and many other purposes.

NASA's SSE information helps people use the sun, a natural resource and great source of energy, to cook. Then the people do not need to hunt for wood or spend what little money they have on fuel.

With the sun's energy, people use solar cookers to prepare meals. The sun is a safe and clean heat source. Solar cooking does not cost much. It does not cause a lot of smoke or air pollution in the environment. Solar cooking helps people harness some of the sun's power!

What properties should solar cookers have to make them work well and be useful?

What LIGHTS the night?

Electricity and Magnetism

 Try It!   What can electricity flow through?

Lesson 1   What is static electricity?

Lesson 2   How do electric charges flow in a circuit?

Lesson 3   How does electricity transfer energy?

Lesson 4   What is magnetism?

Lesson 5   How are electricity and magnetism transformed?

Investigate It!   What is an electromagnet?

This is what the United States looks like at night. Can you find a city near where you live?

 Predict   How does electrical energy help to light the cities of the United States?

....

....

....

THE BIG ?   How are electricity and magnetism used?

Inquiry ▶ Try It!

What can electricity flow through?

☑ **1.** Make the circuit as shown.

☑ **2.** **Predict** Choose one of the objects to complete the circuit. Will it allow the bulb to light up or not? **Record** your predictions for each object.

....

....

....

☑ **3.** Test each object. **Observe.**

Touch the free ends of the wires to the material being tested.

Be careful! **Wear safety goggles.**

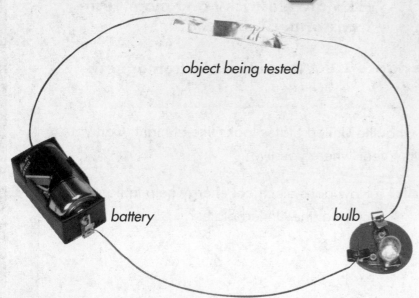

object being tested

battery

bulb

Materials

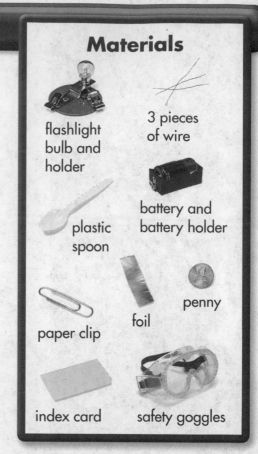

flashlight bulb and holder

3 pieces of wire

plastic spoon

battery and battery holder

paper clip

foil

penny

index card

safety goggles

Inquiry Skill You **classify** objects when you sort them according to properties you observe.

Explain Your Results

4. Classify Electricity flows through ....

....

Electricity does not flow through ....

....

◉ Cause and Effect

- A **cause** is why something happens. An **effect** is what happens.
- When you read, sometimes clue words such as *because* and *since* signal a cause-and-effect relationship.

Heat Lamps and Chicks

A farmer flips the switch on a heat lamp. Electricity begins to flow, the lamp lights up, and the lamp heats up. The farmer puts newly hatched chicks under its warm glow. Because the lamp gives off heat, the chicks will stay warm and be able to grow.

Practice It!

Use the graphic organizer below to list one cause and one effect found in the example paragraph.

Cause

Effect

myscienceonLine.com | Vocabulary Smart Cards

Lesson 1
What is static electricity?

Tell what is causing the light between these two wires.

Inquiry **Explore It!**

What is one effect of static electricity?

☑ **1.** Cut two strips of tissue paper, each about 2 cm × 30 cm.

☑ **2.** Hold the strips together at the top with one hand.

☑ **3.** Put one strip between the middle and pointer fingers of your other hand. Put the second strip between your middle and ring finger. Starting at the top, gently squeeze the strips as you quickly pull your hand down. **Observe.**

Explain Your Results

4. Communicate Describe how the strips hung before and after sliding your fingers through them.

....

....

5. Draw a Conclusion When you finish this lesson, draw a conclusion about the charges on the strips after you slid them between your fingers.

....

Materials

scissors

tissue paper

ruler

left strip ___ ___ right strip

---

myscienceonLine.com | **Explore It!** Animation

I will know what static electricity is and how charged objects behave.

Words to Know

static electricity

Static Electricity

Atoms are the tiny building blocks that make up all matter. Atoms themselves are made of even smaller particles. Some of these particles have an electric charge. Electric charge is a property of matter that can be described as positive or negative. Some particles in atoms have a positive charge (+). Some particles have a negative charge (–). Some particles have no charge. Most matter has the same number of positive particles as negative particles. Because the charges balance, the matter has no overall electric charge. It is neutral.

However, charged particles can move from one object to another. Negative particles often move between objects that are close together or touching. When the numbers of positive and negative particles in an object are not the same, the object is charged. A neutral object can gain negative particles and end up with a negative charge. A neutral object can also lose negative particles and end up with a positive charge. An excess of positive or negative charge in an object is called **static electricity.**

The (+) symbols on these balloons represent positive particles. The (–) symbols represent negative particles.

1. **Analyze** (Circle) the balloon that has a negative charge. How do you know that it has a negative charge?

....

....

....

How Charged Objects Behave

Charged objects behave in predictable ways. If two objects have opposite charges, they attract, or pull toward, each other. Objects with the same charge repel, or push away from, each other. Have you ever noticed that your hair stands on end after you take off a wool cap? That happens because the cap rubs against your hair. When it does, negative charges move from your hair to the cap. The strands of your hair are left with a positive charge. The hairs stand up as they try to push as far away from each other as possible.

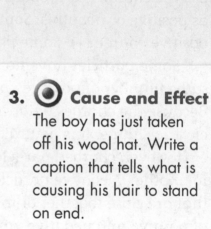

2. Infer How can you tell that these balloons have the same charge?

....

....

....

3. ◎ **Cause and Effect** The boy has just taken off his wool hat. Write a caption that tells what is causing his hair to stand on end.

....

....

....

....

....

396

Electric Force

The pull or push between two charged objects is called an electric force. Electric force gets stronger when the charged objects are close together. Electric force can also exist between charged objects and neutral objects. For this reason, electric force can move lightweight neutral objects or lift them into the air.

If you rub a balloon against your hair and then place the balloon against a wall, the balloon will stick to the wall. Why does this happen? First, the balloon picks up negative particles from your hair. Then, the extra negative particles on the balloon push away some of the negative particles on the wall. The part of the wall close to the balloon is left with an excess of positive particles. These positive particles attract the negative particles on the balloon. An electric force holds the balloon against the wall until the balloon loses its charge.

This balloon is negatively charged.

4. **Illustrate** Draw positive (+) and negative (–) symbols on the balloon to show its overall charge.

5. **Infer** A negatively charged balloon lifts paper scraps but gets pulled toward clothing. Why do you think the balloon responds differently to different objects?

....

....

....

At-Home Lab

Strength of Force
Gather lightweight objects of different sizes, such as scraps of paper and cloth. Set them on a table. Rub an inflated balloon against your hair. Hold the balloon close to the objects. Does the balloon attract any objects? Which ones? What can you conclude about the strength of the balloon's electric force?

6. Summarize Look at the picture. Explain what might happen if the boy picked up negative particles while walking across the carpet.

....

....

....

....

....

....

....

Effects of Static Electricity

You dash across a carpet and touch a metal doorknob. Ouch! A small zap of electricity startles you. During a thunderstorm, you see a big bolt of lightning flash across the sky. How are the small zap and the flash of lightning similar? Both result from the movement of charged particles.

The word *static* means "not moving," and electric charge can stay on an object for some time. But eventually the charge does move. The negative particles on an object with negative charge may move to another object. This movement of charged particles releases electrical energy. You feel this electrical energy when you get a shock, and you see its effects in a lightning bolt.

Small Shocks

Static electricity can build up on all types of objects. It also can build up on you! You can pick up negative particles when you drag your feet on a carpet. You become negatively charged. When you reach for a metal doorknob, the negative particles travel from you to the doorknob. You might even see the spark caused by the release of static electricity!

7. Compare <u>Underline</u> the sentence that tells how a bolt of lightning and a small zap of electricity are similar.

myscienceonline.com | Got it? ⏱ 60-Second Video

Lightning

Lightning is the result of a fast, powerful release of static electricity. In a cloud, water droplets rub against each other. The droplets become electrically charged. Negative charges build up near the bottom of the cloud. The static electricity is released when positive particles on the ground attract the negative particles on the cloud. When the particles move, the electrical energy heats up the air and makes it glow as lightning! Lightning often strikes the tallest object in an area. For this reason it is safer to avoid the high ground during a lightning storm.

8. ⊙ **Cause and Effect** What causes the glow of a lightning bolt?

....

....

....

Got it?

9. **Paraphrase** In your own words, explain what static electricity is.

....

....

10. **Explain** Suppose that you and a friend each rub a balloon against your hair. What would happen if you tried to push the two balloons close together? Why?

....

....

▢ **Stop!** I need help with ....

⚏ **Wait!** I have a question about ....

▷ **Go!** Now I know ....

How do electric charges flow in a circuit?

Envision It!

When you plug a string of light bulbs into an electric outlet, why do you think all the bulbs light up?

Inquiry **Explore It!**

How can a switch make a complete circuit?

☐ **1.** Make a circuit as shown.

☐ **2.** Make a switch as shown.

top side

Punch two fasteners into an index card. Attach a paper clip to one of the fasteners.

bottom side

Wrap a wire around the arms of two metal fasteners.

☐ **3. Predict** what will happen when the paper clip touches the other fastener.

☐ **4.** Use the pencil eraser to touch the paper clip to the other fastener. **Observe.**

 Be careful! Wear safety goggles.

Materials

safety goggles

3 pieces of wire

battery and holder

bulb and holder

paper clip

pencil with eraser

2 fasteners

index card

Explain Your Results

5. Draw a Conclusion How did the paper clip act as a switch?

....

....

myscienceonline.com | **Explore It!** Animation

I will know how electricity is transferred in a circuit.

Words to Know

electric   series circuit
  current   parallel
conductor   circuit
insulator

Electric Currents

When a sweater comes out of the dryer, it often clings to other objects. This is due to electric charges that stay on the sweater for some time. Electric charges can also move from place to place. An electric charge in motion is called an **electric current.** An electric current flows quickly and invisibly from one place to another.

In one type of electric current, electric charges must flow in a loop, or circuit. A power source, such as a battery, causes the electric charges to flow. Wires provide a path for the flow. A current cannot flow if the circuit has any gaps, or breaks. A cut wire and an off switch are examples of breaks. A circuit is open if it has at least one break. It is closed if it has no breaks. For example, if a switch in a flashlight is turned off, the circuit is open.

1. ◎ **Cause and Effect** Complete the graphic organizer below. Write what will happen if a circuit has breaks.

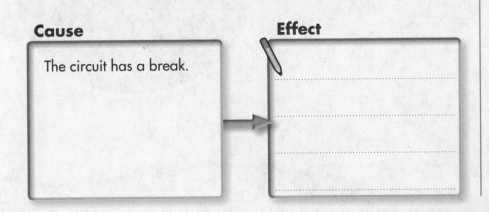

Cause

The circuit has a break.

Effect

2. **Infer** Is the circuit in this flashlight open or closed? Write how you can you tell.

How Electric Charges Flow

The flow of electric charges is not the same in all materials. Some kinds of atoms become charged more easily than others.

Conductors

Materials made of easily charged atoms are conductors. A **conductor** is a material through which an electric charge can move easily. Most metals, such as copper, gold, and silver, are good conductors. Other conductors include metal scissors and the pencil lead, or graphite, in pencils.

3. ◉ **Cause and Effect** In the text, **underline** what causes some materials to be good conductors of electricity.

4. **Explain** The computer part below is made of gold conductors. Will gold allow electric charges to flow easily in this computer part? Why or why not?

....

....

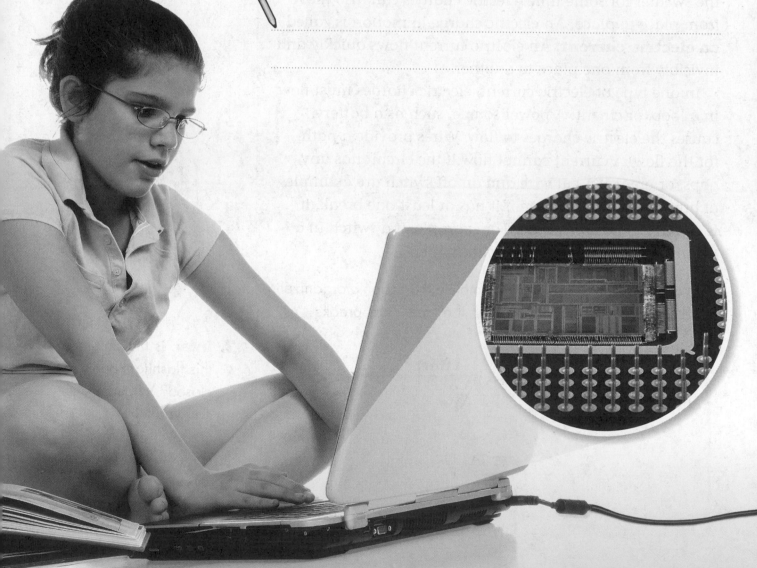

Insulators

Other materials are made of atoms that do not become charged easily. An **insulator** is a material through which an electric charge moves with difficulty. Plastic, rubber, glass, and dry wood are good insulators. Other insulators are the eraser on a pencil and the chalk you may use to draw.

5. **Analyze** Why are glass insulators used on power lines?

....

....

6. **Infer** Electricians often wear special shoes with thick, rubber soles. Why?

....

....

....

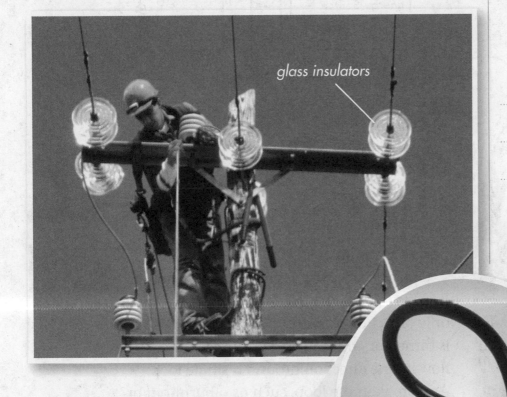

glass insulators

plastic insulator

conductor

The plug and the wires inside this electrical cord are conductors. The plastic insulator makes the cord safe to handle.

Types of Circuits

A circuit has many parts. Its energy source provides the energy to move electric charges through its wires. Batteries and electrical outlets are energy sources. A circuit also has resistors such as light bulbs or machines. Resistors transform energy into other forms of energy. They use the energy that flows through the circuit. A circuit may also have a switch. The symbols below are used to represent the parts of a circuit.

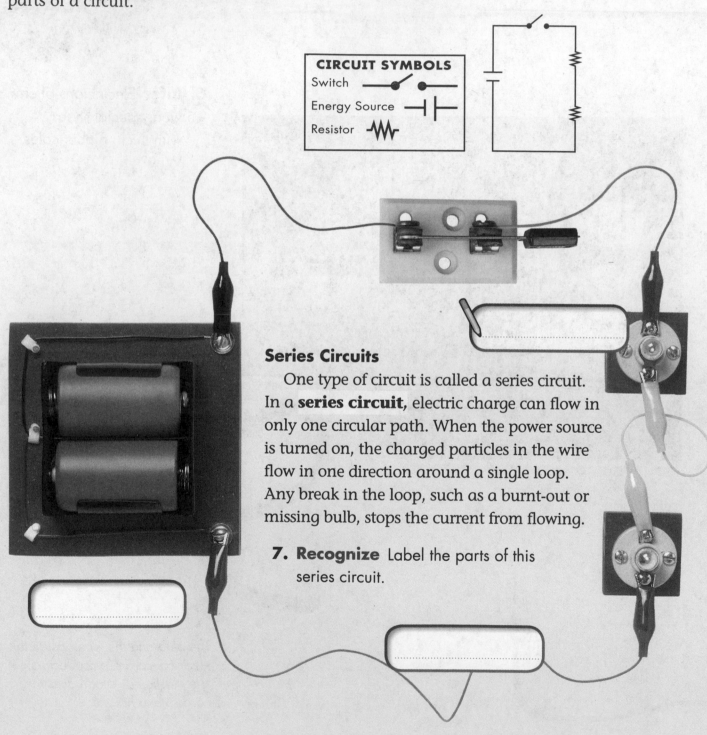

CIRCUIT SYMBOLS

Switch

Energy Source

Resistor

Series Circuits

One type of circuit is called a series circuit. In a **series circuit**, electric charge can flow in only one circular path. When the power source is turned on, the charged particles in the wire flow in one direction around a single loop. Any break in the loop, such as a burnt-out or missing bulb, stops the current from flowing.

7. Recognize Label the parts of this series circuit.

myscienceonline.com | Got it? 60-Second Video

Parallel Circuits

Another type of circuit is a parallel circuit. A **parallel circuit** has two or more paths through which electric charges may flow. Each path leaves from the power source and returns to it. The current that flows through one path does not have to flow through the other paths. Therefore, if one loop in the circuit is broken, the current will still flow through the other loops.

8. **Locate** (Circle) the loop that is broken.

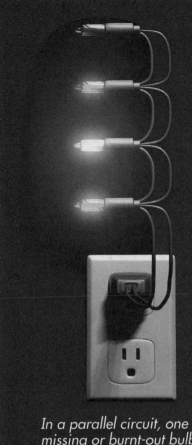

In a parallel circuit, one missing or burnt-out bulb does not open the circuit.

Got it?

9. **Classify** How can you classify materials as conductors or insulators?

....

....

10. **Cause and Effect** Explain how a switch can affect the flow of an electric current in a circuit.

....

....

■ **Stop!** I need help with ....

⏸ **Wait!** I have a question about ....

▶ **Go!** Now I know ....

How does electricity transfer energy?

Envision It!

Tell how electricity is important to the plants in this tank.

my planet diary

VOICES FROM History

Thomas Edison was an American inventor who lived from 1847 to 1931. He developed more than one thousand inventions in his lifetime. One of his most famous inventions was the electric light bulb. Most light bulbs work by sending electricity through a piece of material called a filament. The filament does not conduct electricity well. It heats up and glows. Other scientists besides Edison had tried to develop electric light bulbs. However, the filaments they used burned up too quickly. Edison was able to create a bulb with a long-lasting filament.

Edison once said, "Genius is one percent inspiration and ninety-nine percent perspiration." He meant that hard work is more important to success than having a great idea. Edison worked hard to improve his light bulb, and he finally succeeded!

Do you agree with Edison that hard work is more important to success than having a great idea? Why or Why not?

....

....

....

UNLOCK
THE BIG
?

I will know how energy changes form. I will know how electricity changes to light and gives off heat.

Word to Know

filament

Energy Changing Form

There are many different forms of energy. Electricity, light, sound, and energy of motion are some forms of energy. Energy is never lost. It cannot be made or destroyed. However, energy can transform, or change form. Electricity can change to light. Motion can change to sound. Wind can change to electricity. These examples are only some ways that energy can change.

Many objects transform energy as they work. A lamp transforms electrical energy to light energy. If you pluck a guitar string, the energy of motion transforms to sound energy. A wind turbine transforms wind energy to electrical energy. All of these examples also produce heat.

You experience energy changing form when you rub your hands together quickly. The energy of motion causes friction. Friction is a force that acts when two surfaces rub together. As a result of friction, heat is given off. So, your hands warm up.

A wind turbine transforms energy.

1. **Exemplify** Name an object that transforms electrical energy to sound energy.

....

2. **Recognize** Write what happens when energy is transformed by a wind turbine.

....

energy changes to

....

Light from Electricity

Televisions, computers, and light bulbs all use electricity. These objects are resistors that use the energy in a circuit. Most resistors transform electrical energy to heat and light. The filament in an incandescent light bulb is its resistor. A **filament** is a thin, coiled wire that can get very hot without melting. Most of the electricity passing through the filament is changed into heat. But the filament is a strong resistor. The filament becomes so hot that it glows, also giving off light.

3. ○ Cause and Effect
   Underline the cause of electricity being changed into light in a filament.

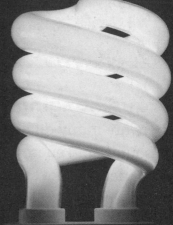

Fluorescent light bulbs do not use a filament. They produce less heat than incandescent light bulbs and use less electricity.

incandescent light bulb

Do the math!

Using Percents

Electrical energy is measured in units called kilowatt-hours. About 10 percent of the energy in an incandescent light bulb is used for light. The rest is heat. About 75 percent of the energy of a fluorescent light bulb is given off as light.

1 If an incandescent light bulb consumes 1,000 kilowatt-hours, how much energy is used for light?

2 If a fluorescent light bulb consumes 1,000 kilowatt-hours, how much energy is used for light?

3 **Conclude** Which bulb is more energy-efficient at producing light?

myscienceonline.com | Got it? 60-Second Video

Heat from Electricity

When electrical current passes through a resistor, it gives off heat. This change is why electrical wires sometimes become hot. Some types of wires are good resistors. Many appliances have coils of these wires. More coils allow an appliance to become hotter. The resistors of some appliances get so hot that they produce a red glow. This glow happens in toasters.

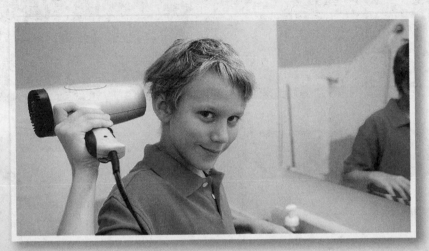

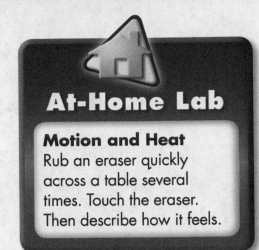

At-Home Lab

Motion and Heat
Rub an eraser quickly across a table several times. Touch the eraser. Then describe how it feels.

4. **Infer** Many hair dryers use heating coils as resistors. Explain why.

....

....

....

Got it?

5. **Summarize** Describe how a filament in an incandescent light bulb transforms electrical energy.

....

....

6. **UNLOCK THE BIG ?** How can objects transform electrical energy?

....

....

⬛ **Stop!** I need help with ....

⏸ **Wait!** I have a question about ....

▶ **Go!** Now I know ....

Lesson 4
What is magnetism?

Envision It!

Tell how you think this train moves.

Inquiry **Explore It!**

How can you make a magnet?

☐ **1.** Pick up one paper clip. Touch it to a second paper clip. **Record** your **observations.**

☐ **2.** Stroke the magnet against the paper clip about 20 times. Stroke in only one direction.

☐ **3.** Hold the paper clip near the second paper clip. Record your observations.

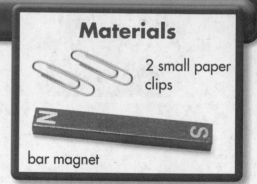

Materials

2 small paper clips

bar magnet

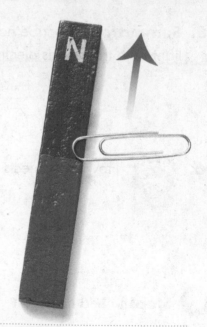

Explain Your Results

4. Infer How can rubbing a paper clip with a magnet change the paper clip?

myscienceonline.com | **Explore It!** Animation

UNLOCK THE BIG ?

I will know that magnets can attract magnetic materials and attract and repel other magnets.

Word to Know

magnetism

Magnetism

Does the door of your refrigerator look like a scrapbook and message center? Papers, photos, notes, and reminders may be held in place by many colorful refrigerator magnets. Magnets attract the magnetic materials, such as steel, found in many refrigerators and paper clips. This attraction is what makes the magnets cling to the refrigerator and to the paper clips.

As you may know, all magnets have the property of magnetism. **Magnetism** is a force that acts on moving electric charges and magnetic materials. So how do magnets support a heavy Maglev train? Electric current produces enough magnetic force to lift the entire train! The pushing and pulling force between the magnets also moves the train along the track.

Magnetic forces lift and move this Maglev train as it speeds along about 1 centimeter above the track.

1. **Recall** Name two objects that are attracted to magnets.

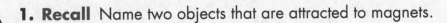

2. **Apply** How do you use magnets in your daily life?

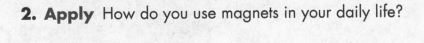

Magnetic Fields

Each magnet has a magnetic field around it. A magnetic field is the space around a magnet in which magnetic forces operate. The magnetic field extends out in all directions from a magnet. The exact shape of the field depends on the shape of the magnet.

Magnetic Poles

The two ends of a magnet are called its magnetic poles. The end of a magnet labeled *north* is pulled to the geographic north by Earth's magnetic field. The end labeled *south* is pulled to the geographic south by Earth's magnetic field. The magnetic field is strongest at the magnet's poles and gets weaker away from the poles.

The north pole of a magnet attracts the south pole of another magnet. The north pole repels the north pole of another magnet. Similarly, the south pole of a magnet attracts the north pole of another magnet. And, the south pole repels another south pole.

3. **Compare** How are the magnetic fields of the bar and horseshoe magnets alike?

....

4. **Draw** Draw two bar magnets in a position so that the magnets are repelling each other. Label each end of each magnet with an "N" for north or an "S" for south.

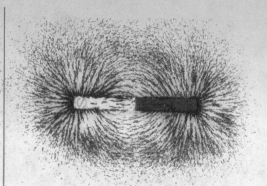

Iron filings near a bar magnet show the magnetic field is strongest near the poles.

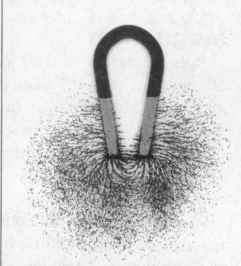

A horseshoe magnet has a magnetic field that looks like a large U-shape.

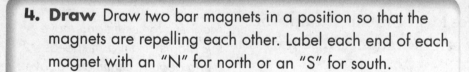

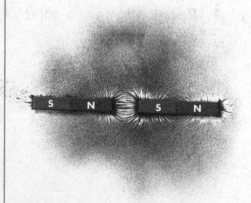

Opposite poles attract. Like poles repel.

myscienceonline.com | Got it? 60-Second Video

Magnetic Compasses

A compass is a helpful, easy-to-carry tool. Wherever you are on Earth, one end of a compass needle will point approximately to Earth's geographic north pole. It follows an imaginary line that connects the magnetic poles of Earth. Once you know which direction is north, you can easily determine south, west, and east.

For a compass to work properly, its needle must be lightweight and must turn easily. The compass cannot be close to a magnet. Otherwise, the needle will respond to the pull of the magnet rather than to Earth's magnetic field.

5. Evaluate Why does one end of a compass needle point north?

....

....

....

Lightning Lab

Make a Compass
Half-fill a small bowl with water. Cut off the bottom of a paper cup. Set it in the water. Touch a magnet to a metal paper clip. Stroke the magnet away from the paper clip 20 times. Put the paper clip in the cup bottom. What happens?

Got it?

6. Infer If you find a metal bar, how can you determine if it is a magnet?

....

....

....

7. Explain How is Earth like a magnet?

....

....

● **Stop!** I need help with ....

❚❚ **Wait!** I have a question about ....

▶ **Go!** Now I know ....

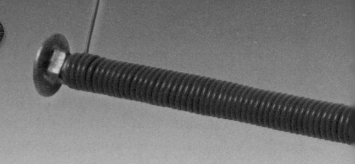

Lesson 5

How are electricity and magnetism transformed?

Envision It!

Tell what force attracts the paper clips to the bolt.

Explore It!

How can energy be transformed and transferred?

☑ **1.** Use the Make a Motor instruction sheet to build a motor.

☑ **2.** Move the magnet near the coil. Move the coil slightly. **Observe. Record.**

Materials

Make a Motor

safety goggles

wire   rubber band

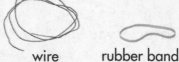
battery and battery holder   bar magnet

sandpaper   2 metal paper clips

Explain Your Results

 Be careful! Wear safety goggles.

3. Communicate How was energy transformed and transferred?

....

....

....

mysciencenonline.com | **Explore It!** Animation

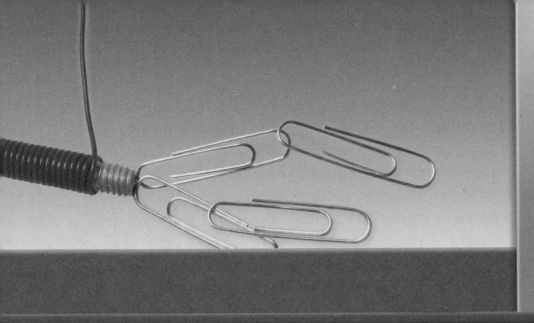

Words to Know

electromagnet
generator

Electric Current and Magnetism

Ordinary magnets work without an electric current, and electric circuits can work without magnets. Scientists used to think that magnetism and electricity did not affect each other. In 1820, Danish scientist Hans Christian Oersted was running electric current through a wire. He noticed that the magnetic needle on a nearby compass moved each time he turned on the current. He wondered why that happened. Oersted realized that the flowing electric current was producing a magnetic field. This magnetic field caused the compass needle to move. Oersted saw that the forces of electricity and magnetism have a lot in common.

1. **Identify** <u>Underline</u> the text that tells what Oersted discovered.

2. **Identify** One of the circuits below has a break in it. (Circle) the break.

When no current flows, all compasses point north.

The compass needles line up with the magnetic field caused by the flowing current.

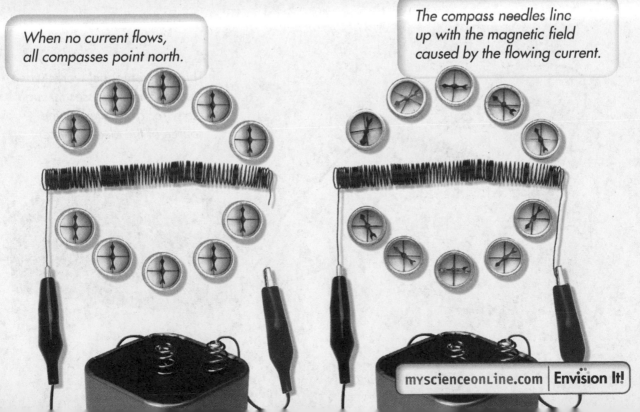

Go Green

Electromagnets in Recycling

Electromagnets are used at recycling centers to separate certain metals from other recycled materials. Make a list of objects that an electromagnet might be able to pick up. Remember that most metals, such as copper and aluminum, are nonmagnetic.

Electromagnets

Hans Christian Oersted's discovery of the relationship between electricity and magnetism led to an important invention—the electromagnet. An **electromagnet** is a magnet that only works when electricity is provided. To make an electromagnet, you pass an electric current through a coiled wire. The moving current creates a magnetic field. The wire loses its magnetism when the current is stopped.

You can change the strength of an electromagnet in several ways. You can make the magnet stronger by coiling the wire around an iron core, such as an iron nail. You can also add more coils of wire. The more coils you add, the stronger the magnetic field. Another way to make an electromagnet stronger is by increasing the amount of electric current running through the wire.

3. Contrast How is an electromagnet different from a refrigerator magnet?

....

....

....

4. Predict Look at the photo of the electromagnet. What would happen if you attached the wire to a stronger battery?

....

....

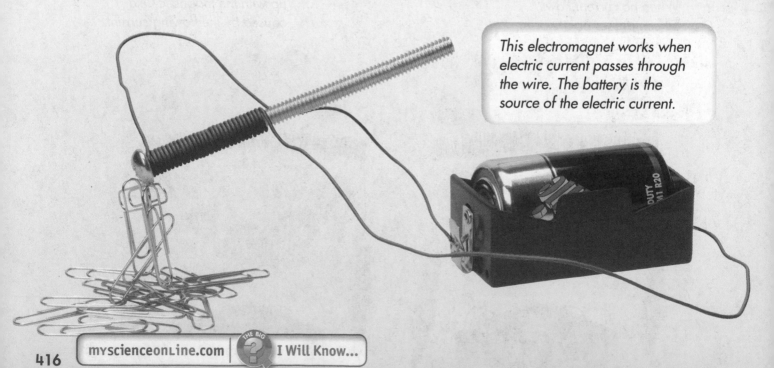

This electromagnet works when electric current passes through the wire. The battery is the source of the electric current.

Uses of Electromagnets

Electromagnets are useful because you can turn them off when you do not want them to attract objects. You can also change the strength of an electromagnet.

You may not know it, but you use electromagnets every day. There are electromagnets in doorbells, computers, and DVD players. Electromagnets are used in these devices to convert electrical energy to other forms of energy. Think of things that spin when you close a circuit by flipping a switch. You might think of a fan or a blender. These electric objects have motors. Motors use electromagnets to create motion. A motor changes electrical energy into mechanical energy, the energy involved in motion.

5. Explain Why do you have to press the button to make a doorbell ring?

....

....

....

....

....

....

....

....

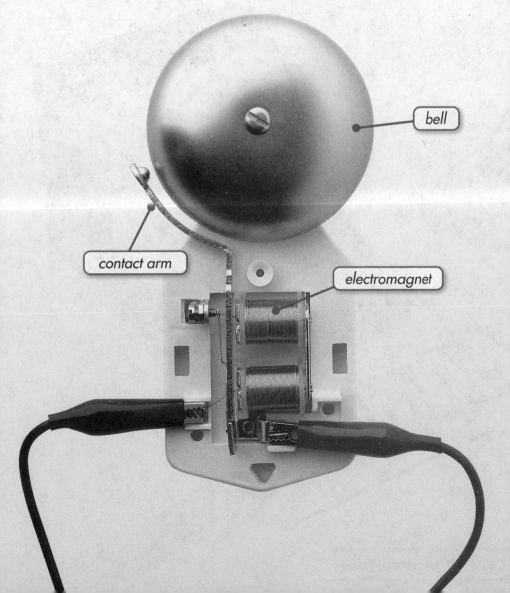

bell

contact arm

electromagnet

How a Doorbell Works

When you press the button to ring a doorbell, you are closing a circuit. Current flows to the electromagnet.

Electromagnet Electricity flowing in the coil of wire magnetizes the electromagnet. This pulls up the contact arm.

Contact Arm The arm is attached to a metal clapper that hits the bell.

Bell This makes the sound.

417

Transforming Magnetism into Electricity

An electric current traveling through a wire can make a magnetic field. Similarly, a magnet moving near a wire can make electricity. Sliding a magnet back and forth within a coiled wire makes electricity. Spinning a coiled wire around a magnet makes electricity too.

When a magnet is moved, its magnetic field moves with it. And changing a magnetic field produces electricity. The faster the coiled wire or the magnet is moved, the stronger the electric current it makes. In contrast, the slower the movement, the weaker the current. The number of coiled loops also affects the strength of the current. Having more coiled loops of wire near a moving magnet creates a stronger current.

6. **Circle** the meter that shows that an electric current is flowing.

7. **Apply** How could you increase the amount of current flowing through the meter?

....

....

....

....

....

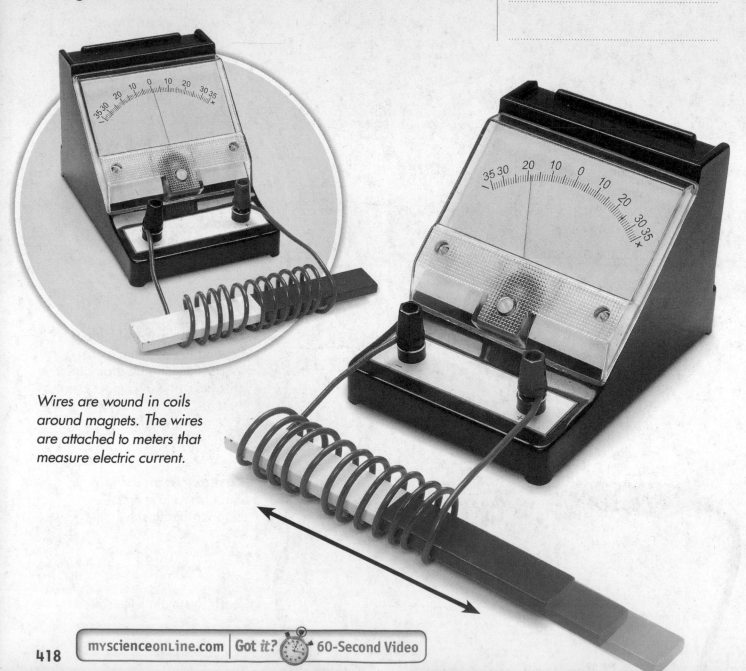

Wires are wound in coils around magnets. The wires are attached to meters that measure electric current.

myscienceonline.com | Got it? | 60-Second Video

Generators

A **generator** is a machine that produces electric energy by turning coils of wire around powerful magnets. A generator turns the energy of motion into electrical energy. The energy needed to turn the coils of wire can come from many sources. For example, water flowing through a dam can supply the motion that spins the generator.

Most homes, schools, and businesses today get their electricity from huge generators. The electricity travels over wires from the generators to buildings in a community.

A wind turbine contains a generator. Energy of motion from the wind turns the generator to produce electricity.

8. [CHALLENGE] In a wind turbine, how does the energy of motion produce electricity?

....

....

....

Got it?

9. **Summarize** How does electric current produce magnetism?

....

....

10. **UNLOCK THE BIG ?** Identify two characteristics that make electromagnets useful.

....

....

....

⊓ **Stop!** I need help with ....

⊔ **Wait!** I have a question about ....

▷ **Go!** Now I know ....

What is an electromagnet?

Follow a Procedure

☑ **1.** Start 25 centimeters from one end of a wire. Wrap the wire 30 times around a bolt near its head.

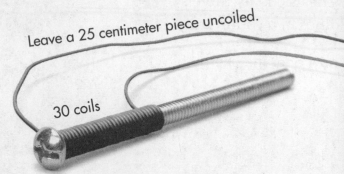

Leave a 25 centimeter piece uncoiled.

30 coils

☑ **2.** Hold the bolt's head near a paper clip. **Record** your **observations.**

☑ **3.** Make a circuit. Put a battery in a holder. Attach both ends of the wire to it. Find how many paper clips your electromagnet can pick up. Record. Then disconnect one wire.

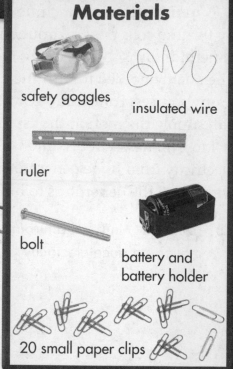

Materials

safety goggles

insulated wire

ruler

bolt

battery and battery holder

20 small paper clips

Be careful! **Wear safety goggles.**

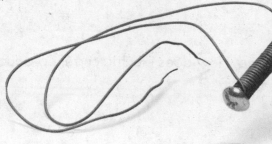

30 coils (no battery)

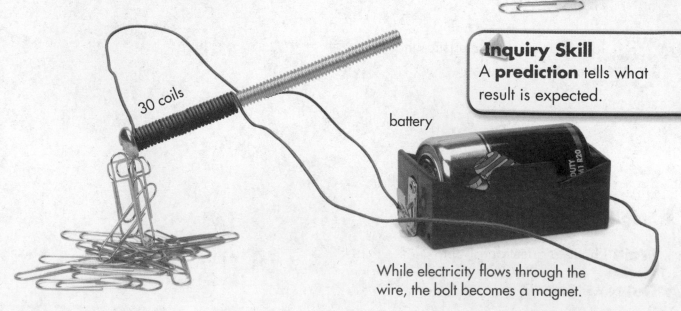

30 coils

battery

Inquiry Skill
A **prediction** tells what result is expected.

While electricity flows through the wire, the bolt becomes a magnet.

4. Add 20 more coils. **Predict** how many paper clips you can lift. Test your prediction.

5. Record your results with a bar graph or chart.

Observations of Electromagnetism

Number of Coils	Number of Paper Clips Picked Up
30 coils (no battery)	
30 coils	
50 coils	

Graph: Number of Paper Clips Picked Up (y-axis, 0–10) vs. Number of Coils (x-axis: 30 coils (no battery), 30 coils, 50 coils)

Analyze and Conclude

6. Draw a Conclusion What makes your electromagnet stronger?

7. UNLOCK THE BIG ? Infer How does an electromagnet use electrical energy?

Electrician

You flip a switch and a light goes on. Every time this happens, you have an electrician to thank.

Electricians run the wires that carry current throughout your home, your school, and any building that has electricity. Some electricians work mainly in houses and other small buildings. Others work in office buildings, where they might install telephones and cables for computers as well as electrical wiring. Still others work in large factories, where they might repair robots or fix machine tools.

Electricians check to make sure that electrical systems are safe. They usually spend much of the workday on their feet. Sometimes they need to climb ladders or crawl into small spaces to put up or repair wires. They must work carefully because poor wiring can cause electrical shocks and fires.

If you like to work with your hands and are good at problem solving, you might like to become an electrician.

Apply Why do you think it is important for electricians to be good at problem solving?

....

....

....

Vocabulary Smart Cards

static electricity
electric current
conductor
insulator
series circuit
parallel circuit
filament
magnetism
electromagnet
generator

Play a Game!

Cut out the Vocabulary Smart Cards.

Work with a partner. Choose a Vocabulary Smart Card. Do not let your partner see your card.

Draw a picture to show what the word means. Have your partner guess the word. Take turns drawing and guessing.

insulator

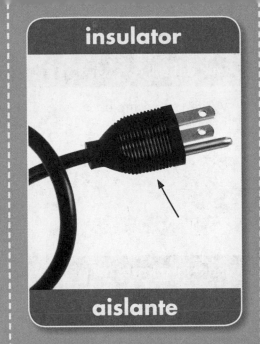

aislante

static electricity

electricidad estática

series circuit

circuito en serie

electric current

corriente eléctrica

parallel circuit

circuito en paralelo

conductor

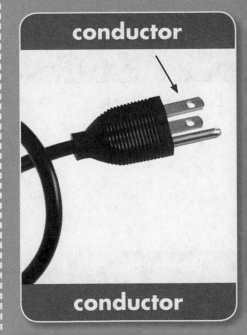

conductor

an excess of positive or negative charge in an object

Write another definition for this term.

....

....

....

exceso de carga positiva o negativa en un objeto

---

a material through which an electric charge moves with difficulty

Write an example.

....

....

....

material a través del cual una carga eléctrica se mueve con dificultad

---

Gold is one of the best conductors.

conductor
material through which an electric charge can move easily

Make a Word Pyramid!

Choose a vocabulary word and write the word and definition in the base of the pyramid. Write a sentence in the middle of the pyramid. Draw a picture of an example, or of something related, at the top.

---

an electric charge in motion

Write a sentence using this term.

....

....

....

carga eléctrica en movimiento

---

a circuit in which electric charge can only flow in one circular path

Draw an example.

circuito en el cual las cargas eléctricas sólo pueden fluir en una trayectoria circular

---

a material through which an electric charge can move easily

Draw an example.

material a través del cual las cargas eléctricas se mueven fácilmente

---

a circuit that has two or more paths through which electric charges may flow

Write an example.

....

....

....

circuito que tiene dos o más vías por las que pueden fluir las cargas eléctricas

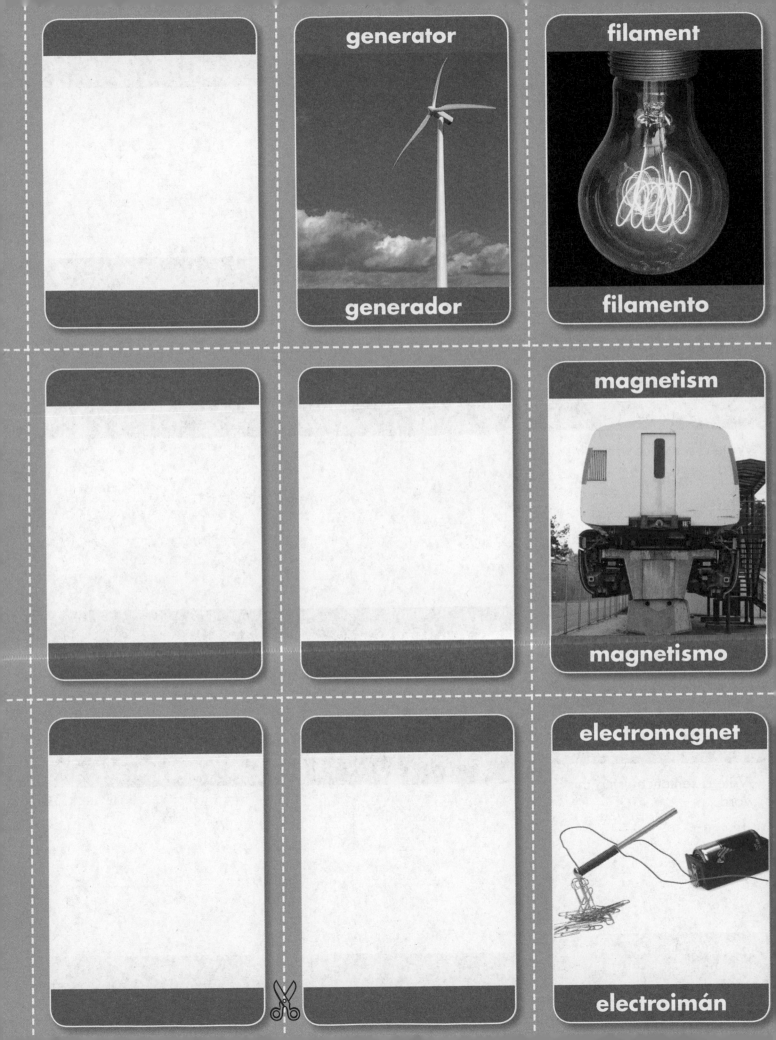

generator

generador

filament

filamento

magnetism

magnetismo

electromagnet

electroimán

a thin, coiled wire that can get very hot without melting

Write a sentence using this word.

....

....

....

alambre fino y enrollado que puede calentarse mucho sin derretirse

a machine that produces electric energy by turning coils of wire around powerful magnets

Write an example.

....

....

....

máquina que genera energía eléctrica al girar una bobina alrededor de imanes de gran potencia

....

....

....

a force that acts on moving electric charges and magnetic materials

Write a sentence using this word.

....

....

....

fuerza que actúa sobre cargas eléctricas en movimiento y materiales magnéticos

....

....

....

....

....

....

a magnet that only works when electricity is provided

Write a sentence using this word.

....

....

....

imán que funciona solamente cuando se aplica una corriente eléctrica

....

....

....

....

....

....

Lesson 1

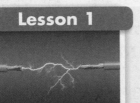

What is static electricity?

- An excess charge in an object is called static electricity.
- Objects with the same charge repel. Objects with opposite charges attract.

Lesson 2

How do electric charges flow in a circuit?

- An electric charge flows through conductors easily.
- An electric charge flows through insulators with difficulty.
- For a current to flow, electric charges must complete a circuit.

Lesson 3

How does electricity transfer energy?

- Electrical energy, light energy, and energy of motion are some forms of energy.
- Electrical energy can change to light energy and give off heat.

Lesson 4

What is magnetism?

- Magnetism is a force that works on moving electric charges and magnetic materials.
- Magnets can attract and repel magnetic materials and other magnets.

Lesson 5

How are electricity and magnetism transformed?

- An electromagnet is made by passing an electric current through coiled wire.
- Moving a magnet within coiled wire produces electricity.

Lesson 1

What is static electricity?

1. **Explain** Why might you feel a shock when you walk across a carpet and then touch a metal knob?

....

....

....

....

....

....

Lesson 2

How do electric charges flow in a circuit?

2. ◎ **Cause and Effect** (Circle) a cause and **underline** its effect in the paragraph below.

> Electric charges move more easily through some materials than others. Conductors are materials with atoms that easily become charged. As a result, an electric charge can move easily through a conductor. Most metals are good conductors.

Lesson 3

How does electricity transfer energy?

3. **Vocabulary** The resistor in an incandescent light bulb is called
   A. an insulator.
   B. an electric charge.
   C. a filament.
   D. a power source.

4. **Apply** List three appliances that transform electrical energy into another form of energy. Identify the form or forms of energy each produces.

....

....

....

....

....

Do the
math!

5. **Calculate** About 75 percent of the energy that passes through a fluorescent bulb becomes light. If a fluorescent bulb uses 2,000 kilowatt-hours, how much energy becomes light?

....

....

....

Lesson 4

What is magnetism?

6. **Describe** What is the structure of a magnet?

....

....

7. **Conclude** What happens if you put the north pole of one magnet next to the north pole of a second magnet? Why?

....

....

....

....

8. **Write About It** How does magnetism make this train move?

....

....

....

....

Lesson 5

How are electricity and magnetism transformed?

9. **Predict** Suppose that you are using a battery, some wire, and a nail to make an electromagnet. What will happen to the electromagnet if the battery runs out of power? Why?

....

....

....

....

10. **APPLY THE BIG ?** **How are electricity and magnetism used?**

· ·

Explain how a wind turbine transforms energy to produce electricity.

....

....

....

....

....

Fill in the bubble next to the answer choice you think is correct for each multiple-choice question.

1 Electrical energy is released when

Ⓐ an object is neutral.
Ⓑ charged particles move.
Ⓒ objects repel each other.
Ⓓ matter changes state.

2 A material through which an electric charge can move easily is a(n)

Ⓐ resistor.
Ⓑ insulator.
Ⓒ filament.
Ⓓ conductor.

3 Which of the following is a device that uses a resistor to transform electrical energy into light and heat?

Ⓐ a radio
Ⓑ a telephone
Ⓒ a printer
Ⓓ a toaster

4 _____ is a force that acts on moving electric charges and magnetic materials.

Ⓐ Gravity
Ⓑ Magnetism
Ⓒ Friction
Ⓓ Magnetic field

5 Which of the following statements about electromagnets is true?

Ⓐ Electromagnets have few practical uses.
Ⓑ An electromagnet can be turned on and off.
Ⓒ Having an iron core weakens an electromagnet.
Ⓓ Strong electromagnets always have a magnetic field.

6 How does energy change as it moves through this circuit?

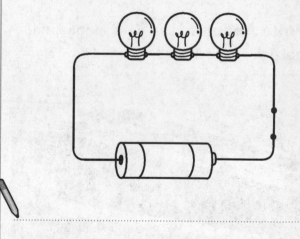

....

....

....

....

....

....

UNPLUG IT!

Did you know that a television continues to use energy, even when it is turned off? Computers, cell phone chargers, and electric toothbrushes do too. These devices continue to use energy because they are still plugged into a power source. The energy that flows through them, even when they are off, is called phantom energy. Phantom energy makes up part of a household's energy use. A household may spend about $100 each year on phantom energy.

You can make a difference. To conserve energy, plug your computer and other electronics into a power strip. When you are not using the electronics, switch off the power strip. Or unplug the electronics altogether. This simple step will stop phantom energy from flowing. Conserving energy will help the environment. It will also save your family money.

Analyze The toothbrush in the picture above is turned off. How can you tell that it is still using energy?

....

....

What
affects
motion?

Motion

 Try It!   How can you measure motion?

Lesson 1   What is motion?

Lesson 2   What is speed?

Investigate It!   How does friction affect motion?

 Predict   These cyclists are riding on a circular racing track. This track has curves and banks so that the cyclists can move very quickly. What might affect the cyclists' motion?

....

....

....

THE BIG ?   How can motion be described and measured?

How can you measure motion?

Motion is a change in the position of an object. In this activity you determine a way to measure motion.

☑ **1.** Look at the wind-up toy, timer, and masking tape.

☑ **2.** Think of a way to **measure** the motion of the toy.

Materials

wind-up toy

timer or stopwatch

masking tape

metric ruler

Inquiry Skill You can use a chart to help you **collect and record data.**

☑ **3. Collect and Record Data** Conduct your test. Repeat it twice. Average your data.

Data Table			
Trial			
1			
2			
3			
Average			

Explain Your Results

4. Interpret Data Was your data the same each time? Explain why your data may have varied. Compare your data with that of other groups.

....

....

5. How did you **measure** motion?

....

....

Sequence

- **Sequence** refers to the order in which events happen.
- Words such as *first, next, then, after,* and *finally* signal sequence.

Ramp and Marble

First, my friend gave me a ruler with a groove in the center. Next, I put one end of the ruler on the floor. Then, I propped the other end on a book to form a ramp. Finally, I put a marble in the groove at the high end of the ruler and let it go.

Practice It!

Circle clue words in the above reading. Then complete the graphic organizer to show the sequence in which things happened.

First

Next

Then

Finally

What is motion?

Draw the path that the bouncing ball takes.

my planet diary

//// MISCONCEPTION ////

Have you ever felt sick in a car, boat, train, or airplane? You may have had motion sickness. Some people think that motion sickness is a problem related to the stomach. However, motion sickness happens when a person's sense of balance is thrown off. Balance is controlled by the inner ear. Sometimes the inner ear and the eyes process riding in something, such as a car or airplane, in different ways. This can cause a person to get pale, to get sweaty, or to vomit.

What do you think people with motion sickness could do to feel better?

....

....

....

UNLOCK THE BIG ?

I will know what motion is. I will know that motion is relative and is affected by forces.

Words to Know

motion   force
reference   gravity
point

Motion

All kinds of things around you move in different ways. Objects can move in a straight line, in a curved path, back and forth as a vibration, or as a rotation. You can describe and measure their motion in different ways. **Motion** is a change in the position of an object.

Look at the toy car and track in the picture to the right. First, the car moves in a straight path. Next, the car moves in curves around the track. Finally, the car moves back to the starting line.

Sometimes toy cars move in a curved path.

Sometimes the cars move in a straight path on the track.

1. ◎ **Sequence** Describe the sequence of events of the yellow race car as it travels around the track.

2. **Identify** Of the types of motion discussed in this section, which types are not shown in the picture above?

....

....

First

Next

Finally

Relative Motion

As you ride your bicycle or walk down a street, you pass trees, buildings, and other things that do not move. They are fixed in place. When you pass a fixed object, you know you are moving. When you stand still, you can tell that a car you see moves if it changes position. Every day, you compare objects that change position with objects that do not. The change in one object's position compared with another object's position is called relative motion.

In the picture above, the three people are passing many trees. They also have different motions compared to each other, because they probably do not always have the same speed.

3. Infer If the bikers move at the same speed and the biker in the back uses only the biker in front as a reference, what might the biker in the back conclude about his or her own motion?

....

....

Frame of Reference

How do you know if a person on a water slide moves? How do you know if the water moves? You look at the changing positions of the person and the water. You compare the person's changing positions with the fixed position of the slide. You use the relative motion of the objects around you to decide what is moving and what is not moving.

Objects that do not seem to move define your frame of reference. Your frame of reference is like your point of view. How an object seems to move depends on your frame of reference.

One way to help you describe your motion is to find a reference point. A **reference point** is a place or object used to determine if an object is in motion. For example, when you ride in a car, you can tell your car is moving by observing a sign, a tree, or a building. Many objects can be reference points.

4. ◉ **Sequence Underline** the steps you take to tell if a person on a water slide moves. Then number each step.

5. **Locate Draw** an ✗ on a reference point for the girl. **Circle** a moving object.

439

A moving marble hits a blue marble that is standing still.

6. Explain What do you think the contact force will do to the yellow marble above?

....

....

....

Forces Affect Objects

Forces make objects move or stop. A **force** is any push or pull. Force can make an object that is standing still start to move in the direction of the force. It can also make a moving object move faster, slow down, stop, or change direction.

Some forces act only on contact. A contact force must touch an object to affect it. A marble on a level surface will not move until you hit it with your finger or another object.

Pushing or pulling can change both the position and motion of an object. The size of the change depends on the strength of the push or pull. For example, the harder you push a swing, the higher and faster it will move.

All forces have size and direction. Notice the dogs pulling on the rubber toy. They are pulling in opposite directions, but with the same amount of force. As long as they pull with forces that are the same size, the forces are balanced, and the toy will not move. If one dog pulls with more force, the forces will be unbalanced. The toy will move toward the dog pulling with greater force.

7. Locate <u>Underline</u> in the first paragraph the five ways a force can affect motion.

A person applies a force to bike pedals. The pedals transfer this force to the chain and then to the tires. This causes the bike to move.

The brakes produce a force that slows or stops the bike when necessary.

Force and Motion

Force causes a change in motion in an object. The amount of force acting on an object affects how that object changes speed, direction, or both. When you ride a bike, you push the pedals. If you push harder, the bike goes faster. You turn the handlebars. The bike changes direction. Pedaling and turning change the bike's motion.

A moving object changes its motion only when a force acts on it. If balanced forces are applied to a moving object, it will keep moving at the same speed and in the same direction. The moving object will not slow, speed up, or turn until the forces acting on it become unbalanced. An example is when you continue to pedal your bike with the same force. The bike will continue to move at the same speed because the same force is acting on it.

Balanced forces that act in opposite directions cancel each other. For example, if you apply the same force to the brake and pedal at the same time, the motion of the bike will not change.

8. **Demonstrate** Describe an example of balanced forces that cancel each other.

....

....

....

Lightning Lab

The Wrecking Ball
Work with a partner. Roll a ball across the floor. Note what is changing — the ball's position, its direction, or both. Roll the ball again. Have your partner roll another ball at it so that they collide. Note what is changing — the first ball's position, its direction, or both.

Force and Mass

How an object moves also depends on how much mass it has. More force is needed to change the motion of an object with more mass. You can easily move an empty shopping cart. As you fill the cart with groceries, the cart gains mass. So, you have to use more force to move the cart.

9. Evaluate Suppose one pumpkin is taken out of the wagon. How will the force needed to pull the wagon change?

....

....

....

Force of Gravity

The force that pulls all objects toward each other is **gravity.** The strength of the force of gravity depends on the masses of the objects and how much distance is between them. You do not notice or feel the force of gravity between everyday objects. The force of gravity increases as objects increase in mass. It also increases as objects get closer.

Gravity and Mass

Gravity is the force that makes an object such as a ball fall to the ground. When you drop a ball, it falls to the ground because Earth's large mass pulls on it. The ball pulls on Earth, too, but the ball's mass is too small to affect Earth in any noticeable way.

10. Apply Gravity keeps Earth orbiting the sun. Earth is about 150,000,000 km (93,205,679 miles) from the sun. What does this distance tell you about the masses of Earth and the sun?

....

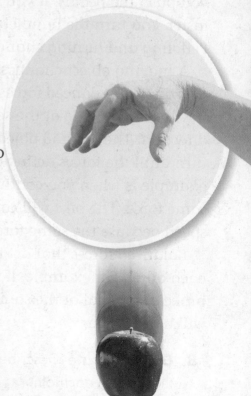

Gravity pulls this apple to the ground.

myscienceonline.com | Got it? 60-Second Video

Mass and Weight

Mass and weight are not the same thing. Mass measures how much matter is in an object. Weight measures how strong the force of gravity is on an object. Mass stays the same from one place to the next, but weight can change. For example, an object's weight is greater on Earth than it is on the moon because Earth's mass is greater than the moon's mass. But the object's mass is the same on Earth and on the moon because the amount of matter does not change.

bowling ball

tennis ball

11. Which ball pictured does Earth attract more?

12. [CHALLENGE] Suppose Earth had twice the mass that it has now, but kept the same size. How would this affect the mass and the weight of objects on its surface?

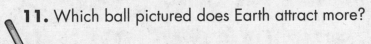

Got it?

13. Describe How are the amount of force needed to change the motion of an object and the mass of the object related?

14. Explain How does Earth's force of gravity affect objects at or near its surface?

⏹ **Stop!** I need help with ....

⏸ **Wait!** I have a question about ....

▶ **Go!** Now I know ....

What is speed?

Envision It!

Which animal do you think would win a 100-meter race?

Inquiry Explore It!

What can change a marble's speed?

☑ **1.** Roll a marble down a ramp. Time how long it takes the marble to move 180 cm.

_____ sec

Find the speed.

_____ cm/sec

speed = distance ÷ time

Place marble at end of ruler.

start

Use tape to label the start and the finish.

Materials

2 books

masking tape

metal marble

ruler

meterstick

calculator or computer (optional)

timer

☑ **2. Predict** how raising the ramp would change the speed.

Test your prediction by adding 1 book.

Time to move 180 cm = _____ sec

Speed = _____ cm/sec

Explain Your Results

3. Draw a Conclusion How did raising the ramp change the marble's speed?

myscienceonline.com | Explore It! Animation

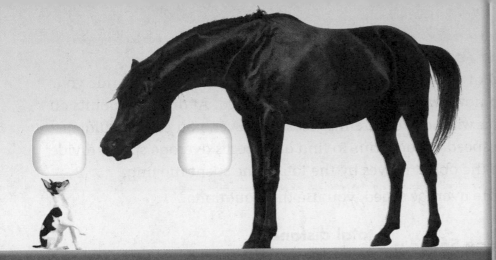

Rank the animals from fastest to slowest. Put a *1*, *2*, or *3* next to each animal.

Words to Know

speed
velocity

Speed

The rate at which an object changes position is called **speed.** Speed measures how fast an object moves. For example, a car moving at a high speed changes position faster than a car moving at a slow speed. The unit for speed is a unit of distance divided by a unit of time, such as kilometers per hour.

Many animals run faster than humans. The fastest land mammal is the cheetah. It can run at speeds around 70 miles per hour or 112 kilometers per hour. A peregrine falcon is also very fast. When it swoops to capture prey, the falcon moves at almost 275 miles per hour! In the pictures above, which animals do you think are faster than you?

1. **Locate** (Circle) the main idea in the second paragraph above. **Underline** the details.

2. **Compute** How much faster is the top speed of a peregrine falcon than that of the cheetah?

3. **Tell** Describe the speed of this rowboat.

Calculate Average Speed

The speed of most objects changes. For example, when you ride your bike, you do not always travel at the same speed. At different points on your trip, you will have different speeds. However, you can calculate the average speed of your trip. To find an object's average speed, divide the distance the object moves by the total time spent moving.

To calculate average speed, you use this equation:

$$\text{Average Speed} = \frac{\text{total distance}}{\text{total time}}$$

Look at the map on these pages. The map shows the route a car traveled from point A to point D.

Point A

Point B

The car traveled from point A to point B in 2 hours (hr). The distance from point A to point B is 120 kilometers (km). To calculate the car's average speed for this trip, divide 120 km by 2 hr.

$$\text{Average Speed} = \frac{120 \text{ km}}{2 \text{ hr}}$$

$$\text{Average Speed} = \frac{60 \text{ km}}{1 \text{ hr}}$$

$$\text{Average Speed} = 60 \frac{\text{km}}{\text{hr}}$$

So the car traveled at an average speed of 60 kilometers per hour from point A to point B.

At-Home Lab

On a Roll
Work in an open area. Mark a starting point. Roll a ball from the starting point. Mark where the ball stopped. Roll the ball from the starting point again. Use more force. Make a statement about the speed of the ball. Base your statements on your observations.

20 mi

20 km

The car traveled 231 kilometers from point B to point C in 3 hours.

$$\text{Speed} = \frac{231 \text{ km}}{3 \text{ hr}}$$

4. Calculate What was the average speed for this leg of the trip? Show your work.

The car traveled 90 kilometers from point C to point D in 2 hours.

5. Calculate What was the average speed for this leg of the trip? Show your work.

Point D

Point C

6. CHALLENGE What was the average speed for the entire trip from point A to point D? Show your work.

Velocity and Acceleration

Some objects change speed and direction. **Velocity** combines both the speed and the direction an object is moving. Some words that describe direction are *north, south, east,* and *west.* Others are *left, right, up,* and *down.*

Any change in the speed or direction of an object's motion is acceleration. Starting, speeding up, and slowing down are accelerations. The roller coaster accelerates as it speeds up or slows down. It is changing speed. A roller coaster on a curved path accelerates even if its speed does not change. That is because it changes direction as it moves around the curve.

7. **Summarize** What are two things that must be measured in order to find an object's velocity?

....

....

....

8. **Illustrate** Look at the roller coaster on the opposite page. **Draw** a solid arrow where the roller coaster slows down, and a dotted arrow where the coaster speeds up.

Do the math!

Make a Graph

The chart shows the distance a cyclist has traveled in 4 hours. Use the data in the chart to graph the distance traveled by the cyclist.

Distance Traveled by a Cyclist				
Time (hours)	1	2	3	4
Distance (kilometers)	15	32	40	60

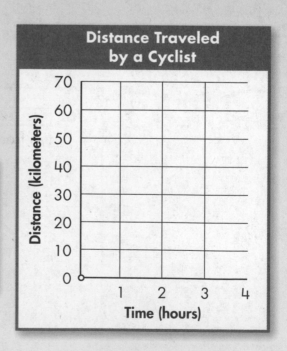

Distance Traveled by a Cyclist

9. ◎ Sequence

First, the roller coaster slows as it moves up to the top of the loop. Write what happens next.

....

....

....

....

....

....

Got it?

10. Produce How do you calculate average speed?

....

....

....

11. **UNLOCK THE DOOR** How do speed and velocity help to describe and measure motion?

....

....

....

⬛ **Stop!** I need help with ....

⏸ **Wait!** I have a question about ....

▶ **Go!** Now I know ....

How does friction affect motion?

Follow a Procedure

☑ **1.** Tape sandpaper to a piece of cardboard.

☑ **2.** Put a toy car and eraser at the top of the ramp. Have another student hold the Ramp Angle Protractor.

☑ **3.** Slowly raise the ramp by hand. When each object reaches the bottom of the ramp, **record** the angle. Repeat 2 more times.

Materials

sandpaper

tape

scissors

cardboard

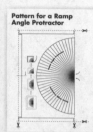
Pattern for a Ramp Angle Protractor

waxed paper

calculator or computer (optional)

eraser

toy car

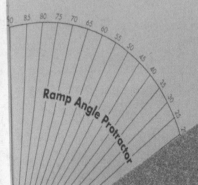
Ramp Angle Protractor

Inquiry Skill
You can use a bar graph to help you **interpret data.**

4. Tell what would happen if you used waxed paper instead of sandpaper. Test your **prediction** 3 times. Record your results.

Effect of Friction on Motion				
Trial	**Angle When Object Reached Bottom of Ramp** (degrees)			
	Sandpaper Surface		**Waxed-Paper Surface**	
	Car	**Eraser**	**Car**	**Eraser**
1				
2				
3				
Average				

5. Find the average angles. Make a bar graph of your results.

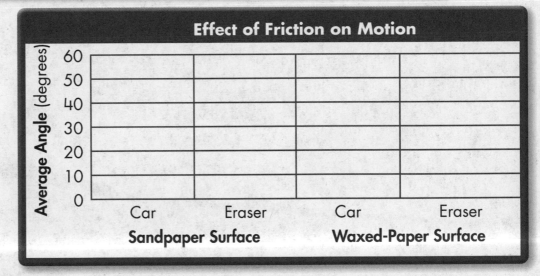

Analyze and Conclude

6. Interpret Data How did changing surfaces affect the angle you recorded?

....

7. Describe how friction affected the motion of the objects on each surface.

....

....

....

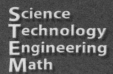

SmartPlane™

What if an airplane became damaged in mid-flight? What if software could help control the damaged airplane? Engineers are working on just such software! It is called the Intelligent Flight Control System. This technology helps damaged airplanes fly. For example, if a bird flew into an engine and damaged the engine, the software could help the pilot safely land the plane. The software technology would know how an airplane should fly. If the airplane started having problems, the system would adjust controls, such as engine thrust.

Determine How do you think engineers might use science and math to develop the software?

....

....

....

Future commercial airplanes could use this technology to avoid crashes and to save lives.

Vocabulary Smart Cards

motion
reference point
force
gravity
speed
velocity

Play a Game!

Cut out the Vocabulary Smart Cards.

Work with a partner. Choose a Vocabulary Smart Card. Write several sentences using the vocabulary word. Have your partner repeat using a different Vocabulary Smart Card.

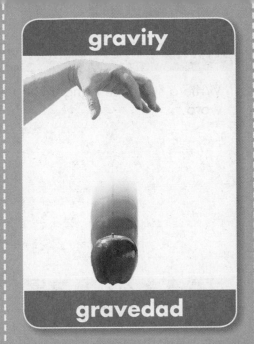

gravity

gravedad

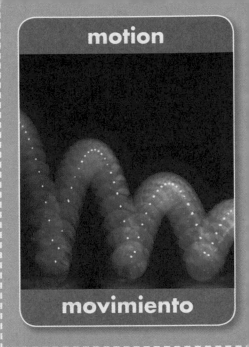

motion

movimiento

speed

rapidez

reference point

punto de referencia

velocity

velocidad

force

fuerza

a change in the position of an object

Write an example.

....

....

....

....

cambio en la posición de un objeto

---

the force that pulls all objects toward each other

Write a sentence using this word.

....

....

....

fuerza que atrae a todos los objetos entre sí

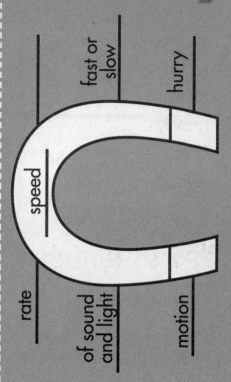

fast or slow

hurry

speed

rate

of sound and light

motion

Make a Word Magnet

Choose a vocabulary word and write it in the Word Magnet. Write words that are related to it on the lines.

---

a place or object used to determine if an object is in motion

Draw an example.

lugar u objeto usado para determinar si algo está en movimiento

---

the rate at which an object changes position

Write a sentence using this word.

....

....

....

....

ritmo al cual cambia la posición de un objeto

---

any push or pull

Draw an example.

empujón o jalón

---

the speed and the direction an object is moving

Write a sentence using this word.

....

....

....

....

rapidez y dirección en que se mueve un objeto

Chapter 10
Study Guide

REVIEW THE BIG ? How can motion be described and measured?

Physical Science

Lesson 1

What is motion?

- Objects move in straight lines, in curved paths, or back and forth.
- The mass of an object affects the force needed to change its motion.
- The force of gravity pulls objects to Earth.

Lesson 2

What is speed?

- Speed is the rate at which an object changes position.
- Velocity describes the speed and direction of a moving object.
- Acceleration is the change in speed or direction of an object.

Chapter Review

REVIEW THE BIG ?

How can motion be described and measured?

Lesson 1

What is motion?

1. **Vocabulary** Motion occurs when one object changes _____ in relation to another object.
   A. reference
   B. position
   C. force
   D. time

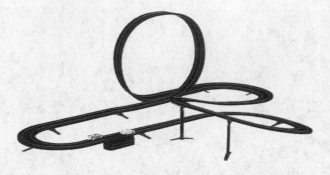

2. **Predict** If you are in a car that is going to the supermarket, how do you know when the car is moving?

....

....

....

3. **Analyze** What makes objects move? How would you make a lawnmower move?

....

....

....

....

4. ⊙ **Sequence** Read the paragraph. Then, fill in the graphic organizer to show the sequence of events.

> The car that I saw was really cool. First, it drove in my direction while I was on the sidewalk. Next, it drove past me and messed up my hair. Before going out of sight, it moved away from me.

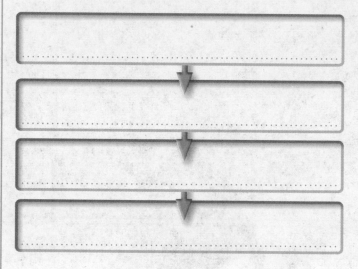

5. **Write About It** Why do you need to use force to move a ball up a ramp when it moves downward by itself?

....

....

....

....

Lesson 2

What is speed?

6.  The chart shows how far a runner races in 4 minutes. Use the data in the chart to graph the distance traveled by the runner.

Time (minutes)	Distance (meters)
1	200
2	400
3	600
4	800

Distance Traveled by a Runner

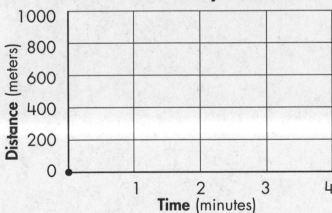

7. **Explain** What is velocity?

8. **Infer** What units might you use to measure and record the speed of a paper airplane?

9. **Apply** Circle the place on the ruler where the marble has the greatest speed.

10. **APPLY THE BIG ?** **How can motion be described and measured?**

Think about the motion of an airplane. Describe its speed and acceleration before and during takeoff.

Benchmark Practice

Fill in the bubble next to the answer choice you think is correct for each multiple-choice question.

1 Gravity is a force that makes objects

Ⓐ push apart.
Ⓑ pull toward each other.
Ⓒ stop moving.
Ⓓ move uphill.

2 A high-speed train travels 1,000 kilometers in 4 hours. What is the train's average speed?

Ⓐ 4,000 km/hr
Ⓑ 1,000 km/hr
Ⓒ 250 km/hr
Ⓓ 150 km/hr

3 What happens to the force of gravity between two objects when the mass of one of the objects is increased?

Ⓐ It increases.
Ⓑ It decreases.
Ⓒ It stays the same.
Ⓓ It pushes the objects apart.

4 Which of the following is an example of velocity?

Ⓐ walking 28 km
Ⓑ walking 28 km/hr quickly
Ⓒ walking 28 km/hr north
Ⓓ walking 28 km/hr

5 This picture shows the brakes on a bicycle. Explain how the use of the brakes changes the motion of the bicycle. How does the mass of the bicycle affect the force that needs to be applied to the brakes?

A Trip Along the San Juan Skyway

GoGreen!

The San Juan Skyway is a scenic road in Colorado. The road winds through national forests and through the San Juan Mountains. Drivers must travel slowly and carefully in places where the road gets steep. Drivers may also go slowly to enjoy the views of the mountains.

There is, however, another reason to travel at or below the speed limit. Did you know that most cars use less gas when they are traveling more slowly? Cars are most efficient when they are moving at a certain speed. A car's gas mileage decreases rapidly when it travels faster than 60 mph. For most cars, the most efficient speed is between 35 and 45 mph.

Place a check mark next to the items that your family does to save fuel.

Save Fuel in an Automobile

- [ ] Do not accelerate too quickly from stoplights or stop signs.
- [ ] Keep tires filled with the right amount of air.
- [ ] Have the vehicle serviced on a regular basis.
- [ ] Use bicycles or walk when the distance is not far.

Materials

ice cubes

3 plastic cups

newspaper

wool cloth

masking tape

clock

Inquiry Skill

Before starting a scientific investigation, make sure to **identify and control variables.**

Which is the best way to slow the rate at which ice melts?

Ask a question.

Which insulator is better at slowing the rate at which ice melts?

State a hypothesis.

1. Write a **hypothesis** by circling one choice and finishing the sentence.

   If cups containing identical ice cubes are wrapped in wool cloth or wrapped in newspaper, or unwrapped, then the ice cube

   (a) *wrapped in wool cloth*

   (b) *wrapped in newspaper*

   (c) *unwrapped*

   will take longest to melt because

   ....

   ....

Identify and control variables.

2. In this **experiment** you will measure the time it takes for each ice cube to melt. You will change only one **variable.** Everything else must remain the same. What should stay the same? List two examples.

   ....

   ....

3. Tell the one change you will make.

   ....

   ....

   ....

Design your test.

☑ **4.** Draw how you will set up your test.

☑ **5.** List your steps in the order you will do them.

☐ **6.** Follow the steps you wrote.

☐ **7. Record** your results in the table.

☐ **8.** Scientists repeat their tests to improve their accuracy.
Repeat your test if time allows.

Collect and record your data.

☑ **9.** Fill in the chart.

Work Like a Scientist
Scientists work with other scientists. Communicate with other groups to compare the results of your investigation.

Interpret your data.

☑ **10.** Use your data to make a bar graph.

☑ **11.** Look at your graph closely. Compare the effectiveness of the insulating materials.

....

....

....

....

....

☑ **12.** Identify the evidence you used to answer the question.

....

....

....

....

....

....

....

Technology Tools
Your teacher may want you to use a computer (with the right software) or a graphing calculator to help collect, organize, analyze, and present your data. These tools can help you make tables, charts, and graphs.

First, look at the trend shown by your bar graph. Then, conclude which material was the best insulator.

State your conclusion.

13. Communicate your conclusion. Compare your **hypothesis** with your results. How did your results compare with others?

....

....

....

....

....

....

Height and Potential Energy

Find out how the height of an object affects its potential energy. Use modeling clay to make three balls of the same size. Place a ball in a plastic bag and put it on the floor. Hold a thick book flat above the ball. Release the book so it lands on the clay. Remove the flattened ball from the bag and trace its outline on a sheet of paper. Repeat the procedure using the other balls of clay, but drop the book from different heights. Record your procedures and your observations. Draw conclusions based on your information.

Cooking up Science

Write a "scientific recipe" for a simple meal you like to eat. What physical or chemical changes do the ingredients go through as the food is prepared? What happens to the mass of the ingredients? What types of energy are used to prepare the meal?

Write a Poem

Write a poem about conductors and insulators. Include some examples of each type of material. Tell how they may be useful or dangerous. Here are some tips to help you write your poem:

- A poem often has words that repeat.
- The words can be recited in rhythm, and they often rhyme.

Using Scientific Methods

1. Ask a question.
2. State your hypothesis.
3. Identify and control variables.
4. Test your hypothesis.
5. Collect and record your data.
6. Interpret your data.
7. State your conclusion.
8. Try it again.

Measurements

Metric and Customary Measurements

The metric system is the measurement system most commonly used in science. Metric units are sometimes called SI units. SI stands for International System. It is called that because these units are used around the world.

These prefixes are used in the metric system:

kilo- means *thousand*
1 kilometer = 1,000 meters

milli- means *one thousandth*
1,000 millimeters = 1 meter, or 1 millimeter = 0.001 meter

centi- means *one hundredth*
100 centimeters = 1 meter, or 1 centimeter = 0.01 meter

1 liter

1 cup

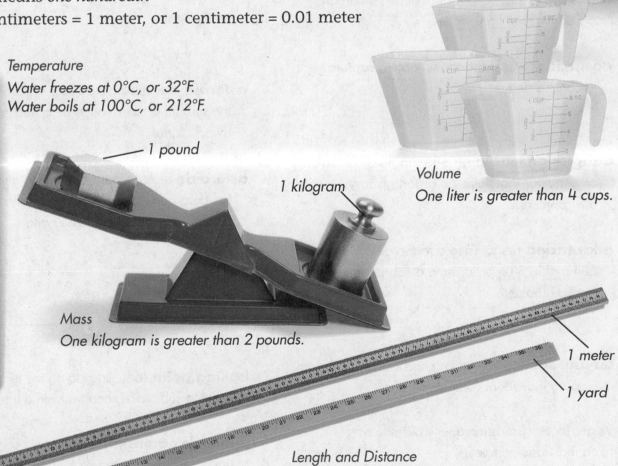

Temperature
Water freezes at 0°C, or 32°F.
Water boils at 100°C, or 212°F.

1 pound

1 kilogram

Volume
One liter is greater than 4 cups.

Mass
One kilogram is greater than 2 pounds.

1 meter

1 yard

Length and Distance
One meter is longer than 1 yard.

Glossary

The glossary uses letters and signs to show how words are pronounced. The mark ′ is placed after a syllable with a primary or heavy accent. The mark ′ is placed after a syllable with a secondary or lighter accent.

To hear these vocabulary words and definitions, you can refer to the AudioText CD, or log on to the digital path's Vocabulary Smart Cards.

Pronunciation Key

a in hat	ō in open	sh in she
ā in age	ȯ in all	th in thin
â in care	ô in order	ŦH in then
ä in far	oi in oil	zh in measure
e in let	ou in out	ə = a in about
ē in equal	u in cup	ə = e in taken
ėr in term	ů in put	ə = i in pencil
i in it	ü in rule	ə = o in lemon
ī in ice	ch in child	ə = u in circus
o in hot	ng in long	

A

absorption (ab sôrp′ shən) occurs when an object takes in light waves

absorción ocurre cuando un objeto captura las ondas de luz

adaptation (ad′ ap tā′ shən) a physical feature or behavior that helps an organism survive in its environment

adaptación rasgo físico o forma de conducta que ayuda a un organismo a sobrevivir en su medio ambiente

advantage (ad van′ tij) a characteristic that can help an individual compete

ventaja característica que le permite a un individuo competir

amplitude (am′ plə tüd) the height of a wave measured from its midline

amplitud altura de una onda medida desde su punto medio

asteroid (as′ tə roid′) a rocky object that orbits the sun but is too small to be called a planet or a dwarf planet

asteroide masa rocosa que orbita alrededor del Sol pero que es demasiado pequeña para ser llamada planeta o planeta enano

B

boiling point (boi′ ling point) the temperature at which a substance changes from a liquid to a gas

punto de ebullición temperatura a la cual una sustancia cambia de líquido a gas

C

carnivore (kär′ nə vôr) animal that gets food by eating other animals

carnívoro animal que se alimenta al comerse otros animales

characteristics (kar′ ik tə ris′ tiks) the qualities an organism has

rasgos cualidades que tiene un organismo

chemical change (kem′ ə kəl chānj) a change that produces a completely different kind of matter

cambio químico cambio por el cual se produce un tipo de materia completamente diferente

chlorophyll (klôr′ ə fil) the substance in plants that makes their parts green and captures energy from sunlight

clorofila sustancia que se encuentra en las plantas y que da color verde a sus partes y capta energía de la luz solar

classify (klas′ ə fī) to arrange or sort objects or living things according to their properties or characteristics

clasificar ordenar o agrupar objetos o seres vivos según sus propiedades o características

cleavage (klē′ vij) property of minerals to break along smooth, flat surfaces

fractura propiedad que les permite a los minerales romperse por superficies lisas y planas

comet (kom′ it) a frozen object that orbits the sun

cometa objeto helado que orbita alrededor del Sol

competition (kom′ pə tish′ ən) occurs when two or more living things need the same resources in order to survive

competencia situación en la que dos o más seres vivos necesitan los mismos recursos para sobrevivir

condensation (kon′ den sā′ shən) the process of a gas changing into a liquid

condensación proceso por el cual un gas se convierte en líquido

conduction (kən duk′ shən) the transfer of heat that occurs when one thing touches another

conducción transmisión de calor que ocurre cuando un objeto toca otro objeto

conductor (kən duk′ tər) a material through which an electric charge can move easily

conductor material a través del cual las cargas eléctricas se mueven fácilmente

constellation (kon′ stə lā′ shən) star pattern

constelación patrón estelar

consumer (kən sü′ mər) living thing that eats other living things

consumidor ser vivo que se alimenta de otros seres vivos

convection (kən vek′ shən) the transfer of thermal energy as matter moves

convección transferencia de energía térmica mientras se mueve la materia

decomposer (dē′ kəm pō′ zər) organism that breaks down plant and animal waste and remains

descomponedor organismo que destruye residuos y desechos de animales y vegetales

density (den′ sə tē) the property of matter that compares an object's mass to its volume

densidad propiedad de la materia que compara la masa de un objeto con su volumen

design process (di zīn′ pros′ es) a set of steps for developing products and processes that solve problems

proceso de diseño serie de pasos para desarrollar productos y procesos que resuelven problemas

E

eclipse (i klips´) event in which one object in space gets between the sun and another object

eclipse fenómeno en el que un objeto del espacio se interpone entre el Sol y otro objeto

ecosystem (ē´ kō sis´ təm) all the living and nonliving things in an environment and the many ways they interact

ecosistema todos los seres vivos y las cosas sin vida que hay en un medio ambiente y las múltiples interacciones entre ellos

electric current (i lek´ trik kėr´ ənt) an electric charge in motion

corriente eléctrica carga eléctrica en movimiento

electromagnet (i lek´ trō mag´ nit) a magnet that only works when electricity is provided

electroimán imán que funciona solamente cuando se aplica una corriente eléctrica

ellipse (i lips´) a shape that is like a circle stretched out in opposite directions

elipse forma que parece un círculo alargado

energy (en´ ər jē) the ability to cause motion or create change

energía capacidad de producir movimiento o causar cambio

erosion (i rō´ zhən) process of carrying away weathered bits of rock

erosión proceso por el cual se transportan pedacitos de roca desgastada

evaporation (i vap´ ə rā´ shən) the change from a liquid into a gas

evaporación cambio de líquido a gas

evidence (ev´ ə dəns) observations and facts gained from experiments

evidencia observaciones y datos obtenidos de experimentos

extinct (ek stingkt´) no longer existing as a species

extinto ya no existe más como especie

F

fault (fȯlt) a break or crack in rocks where Earth's crust can move suddenly

falla fisura o grieta en las rocas donde la corteza terrestre puede desplazarse en forma repentina

fertilization (fėr′ tl ə zā′ shən) the process in which a sperm cell and an egg cell combine

fertilización proceso por el cual se unen un óvulo y un espermatozoide

filament (fil′ ə mənt) a thin, coiled wire that can get very hot without melting

filamento alambre fino y enrollado que puede calentarse mucho sin derretirse

filtration (fil trā′ shən) the process of separating substances with a filter

filtración proceso de separar sustancias con un filtro

food chain (füd chān) the transfer of energy from one organism to another by eating and being eaten

cadena alimentaria transmisión de energía de un organismo a otro al comerlo o al ser comido

food web (füd web) system of overlapping food chains in which the flow of energy branches out in many directions

red alimentaria sistema de cadenas alimentarias que se sobreponen, en el cual la energía fluye en muchas direcciones

force (fôrs) any push or pull

fuerza empujón o jalón

fossil (fos′ əl) remains or mark of an animal or plant that lived long ago

fósil restos o marca de un ser vivo que existió hace mucho tiempo

frequency (frē′ kwən sē) number of waves that pass a point in a certain amount of time

frecuencia número de ondas que pasan por un punto en un tiempo determinado

G

generator (jen′ ə rā′ tər) a machine that produces electric energy by turning coils of wire around powerful magnets

generador máquina que genera energía eléctrica al girar una bobina alrededor de imanes de gran potencia

germinate (jèr′ mə nāt) to start to grow

germinar empezar a crecer

gravity (grav′ ə tē) the force that pulls all objects toward each other

gravedad fuerza que atrae a todos los objetos entre sí

groundwater (ground′ wȯ′ tər) any water that is underground

agua subterránea agua que está debajo del suelo

H

habitat (hab′ ə tat) area or place where an organism lives in an ecosystem

hábitat área o lugar de un ecosistema donde vive un organismo

hardness (härd′ nis) how easily the surface of a mineral can be scratched

dureza facilidad con la que se puede rasgar la superficie de un mineral

herbivore (ėr′ bə vôr) animal that eats plants

herbívoro animal que come plantas

hypothesis (hī poth′ ə sis) a possible answer to a question

hipótesis respuesta posible a una pregunta

igneous (ig′ nē əs) rocks that form from molten rock

ígnea rocas que se forman a partir de roca derretida

inference (in′ fər əns) a conclusion drawn from data and observations

inferencia conclusión que se saca de los datos y de las observaciones

inherit (in her′ it) to receive characteristics from an organism's parents

heredar recibir rasgos de los padres de un organismo

inquiry (in kwī′ rē) the process of asking questions and searching for answers

indagación proceso que consiste en preguntar y buscar respuestas

instinct (in′ stingkt) a behavior that is inherited

instinto conducta que se hereda

insulator (in′ sə lā′ tər) a material through which an electric charge moves with difficulty

aislante material a través del cual una carga eléctrica se mueve con dificultad

invertebrates (in vėr′ tə brits) animals without backbones

invertebrados animales que no tienen columna vertebral

investigation (in ves′ tə gā′ shən) a careful way of looking for something

investigación manera cuidadosa de buscar algo

kinetic energy (ki net′ ik en′ ər jē) energy of motion

energía cinética energía de movimiento

L

landform (land′ fôrm′) a natural land feature on Earth's surface

accidente geográfico formación natural en la superficie terrestre

lunar eclipse (lü′ nər i klips′) event in which the moon passes through Earth's shadow

eclipse lunar fenómeno en el que la Luna pasa por la sombra de la Tierra

luster (lus′ tər) the way the surface of a mineral reflects light

brillo reflejo de la luz en la superficie de un mineral

M

magnetism (mag′ nə tiz′ əm) a force that acts on moving electric charges and magnetic materials

magnetismo fuerza que actúa sobre cargas eléctricas en movimiento y materiales magnéticos

mass (mas) the measure of the amount of matter that makes up an object

masa medida de la cantidad de materia de la que está compuesto un objeto

melting point (mel′ ting point) the temperature at which a substance changes from a solid to a liquid

punto de fusión temperatura a la cual una sustancia cambia de sólido a líquido

metamorphic (met′ ə môr′ fik) rocks that have changed as a result of heat and pressure

metamórfica rocas que han cambiado a causa del calor y la presión

mineral (min′ ər əl) natural, nonliving solid crystals that make up rocks

mineral cristal natural, sólido y sin vida del que se componen las rocas

mixture (miks′ chər) a combination of two or more substances

mezcla combinación de dos o más sustancias

motion (mō′ shən) a change in the position of an object

movimiento cambio en la posición de un objeto

omnivore (om′ nə vôr′) animal that eats plants and other animals

omnívoro animal que come plantas y otros animales

orbit (ôr′ bit) path an object follows as it revolves around another object

órbita camino que sigue un objeto mientras gira alrededor de otro objeto

paleontologist (pā′ lē on tol′ ə jist) a scientist who studies fossils

paleontólogo científico que estudia los fósiles

parallel circuit (par′ ə lel sėr′ kit) a circuit that has two or more paths through which electric charges may flow

circuito en paralelo circuito que tiene dos o más vías por las que pueden fluir las cargas eléctricas

phase of matter (fāz ov mat′ ər) the form in which particles are arranged and move

fase de la materia manera en que están dispuestas y se mueven las partículas

photosynthesis (fō′ tō sin′ thə sis) the process in which plants make sugar

fotosíntesis proceso en el cual las plantas producen azúcar

pistil (pis′ tl) a female structure in plants that produces egg cells

pistilo estructura femenina de las plantas donde se producen los óvulos

pitch (pich) how high or low a sound is

tono cuán agudo o grave es un sonido

planet (plan′ it) a very large, round object that moves around a star

planeta cuerpo grande y redondo que orbita una estrella

....

pollination (pol′ ə nā′ shən) the movement of pollen from stamen to pistil

polinización proceso por el cual el polen se mueve del estambre al pistilo

....

population (pop′ yə lā′ shən) all the members of one species that live within an area of an ecosystem

población todos los miembros de una especie que viven en un área de un ecosistema

....

potential energy (pə ten′ shəl en′ ər jē) energy that is stored in an object

energía potencial energía que está almacenada en un objeto

....

precipitation (pri sip′ ə tā′ shən) any form of water that falls to Earth

precipitación cualquier forma de agua que cae a la Tierra

procedure (prə sē′ jər) a set of step-by-step instructions

procedimiento instrucciones paso por paso

....

producer (prə dü′ sər) living thing that makes its own food

productor ser vivo que genera su propio alimento

....

property (prop′ ər tē) a characteristic of an object

propiedad característica de un objeto

....

prototype (pro′ tə tīp) first fully working product that uses a design solution

prototipo el primer producto que demuestra una solución de diseño

R

radiation (rā′ dē ā′ shən) energy that is sent out in waves

radiación energía transmitida a través de ondas

reference point (ref′ ər əns point) a place or object used to determine if an object is in motion

punto de referencia lugar u objeto usado para determinar si algo está en movimiento

reflection (ri flek′ shən) occurs when light rays bounce off a surface

reflexión ocurre cuando los rayos de luz rebotan en una superficie

refraction (ri frak′ shən) the bending of light when it passes into a new medium

refracción desviación que sufre la luz cuando pasa de un medio a otro

revolution (rev′ ə lü′ shən) movement of one object around another

traslación movimiento de un objeto alrededor de otro objeto

rotation (rō tā′ shən) spinning of a planet, moon, or star around its axis

rotación giro de un planeta, una luna o una estrella sobre su propio eje

S

scientific methods (sī′ ən tif′ ik meth′ ədz) organized ways to answer questions and solve problems

métodos científicos maneras organizadas de responder a preguntas y resolver problemas

sedimentary (sed′ ə men′ tər ē) rocks that form when layers of sediments settle on top of one another and harden

sedimentaria rocas que se forman cuando varias capas de sedimento se acumulan, una sobre otra, y se endurecen

sepal (sē′ pəl) one of the leaflike parts that cover and protect the flower bud

sépalo una de las partes en forma de hoja que cubren y protegen el botón de las flores

series circuit (sir′ ēz sėr′ kit) a circuit in which electric charge can flow in only one circular path

circuito en serie circuito en el cual las cargas eléctricas sólo pueden fluir en una trayectoria circular

solar eclipse (sō′ lər i klips′) event in which the moon passes between the sun and Earth

eclipse solar fenómeno en el que la Luna pasa entre el Sol y la Tierra

solar system (sō′ lər sis′ təm) the sun, the planets and their moons, and other objects

sistema solar el Sol, los planetas y sus lunas, y otros objetos

sound (sound) energy in the form of vibrations passing through matter

sonido energía en forma de vibraciones que pasa a través de la materia

speed (spēd) the rate at which an object changes position

rapidez ritmo al cual cambia la posición de un objeto

stamen (stā′ mən) male structure in plants that makes pollen

estambre estructura masculina de las plantas que produce el polen

static electricity (stat′ ik i lek′ tris′ ə tē) an excess of positive or negative charge in an object

electricidad estática exceso de carga positiva o negativa en un objeto

stimulus (stim′ yə ləs) something that causes a reaction in a living thing

estímulo algo que provoca una reacción en un ser vivo

streak (strēk) color of the powder that a mineral leaves when it is scratched across a special plate

surco color del polvo que sale de un mineral cuando se le rasga en una placa especial

technology (tek nol′ ə jē) the knowledge, processes, and products that solve problems and make work easier

tecnología el conocimiento, los procesos y los productos con que se resuelven los problemas y se facilita el trabajo

three-dimensional (thrē/ də men/ shə nəl) describes objects that have length, width, and height

tridimensional describe objetos que tienen largo, ancho y altura

tool (tül) an object or device used to perform a task

instrumento objeto o herramienta que se usa para hacer un trabajo

two-dimensional (tü/ də men/ shə nəl) describes something that has length and width, but not height

bidimensional describe algo que tiene largo y ancho, pero no tiene altura

velocity (və los/ ə tē) the speed and the direction an object is moving

velocidad rapidez y dirección en que se mueve un objeto

vertebrates (vėr/ tə brits) animals that have backbones

vertebrados animales que tienen columna vertebral

volume (vol/ yəm) the amount of space that matter takes up

volumen cantidad de espacio que la materia ocupa

volume (vol/ yəm) a measure of how strong a sound seems to us

volumen medida de cuán fuerte nos parece un sonido

water cycle (wȯ′ tər sī′ kəl) the movement of water from Earth's surface to the atmosphere and back again

ciclo del agua recorrido de ida y vuelta que realiza el agua entre la atmósfera y la superficie de la Tierra

wavelength (wāv′ lengkth) distance between a point on one wave and a similar point on the next wave

longitud de onda distancia entre un punto de una onda y un punto similar de la onda que sigue

weathering (weŦH′ ər ing) process of rocks in Earth's crust slowly being broken into smaller pieces

meteorización proceso de las rocas de la corteza terrestre que se van rompiendo en trozos más pequeños

Index

and electricity, 409
and friction, 377
and light, 371, 376
movement of, 372
and phase changes, 322
radiation, 375
solar cooking, 389
sources of, 376–377
Heat lamps, *393*
Helium, 319
Hematite, 205
Herbivore, 149–151, 183–186
Heredity, 113
Hibernation, 108, 121
Horsetail plants, *176*
House cat, *85*
Hovercraft, 46
Humans, 115, 123
Hunger, 119
Hybrid cars, 71
Hypothesis, 17–19, 23, 35–38
Hypothesize, 17–19, 34–38, 176, 358, 359

Ice, 221, 222, 231, 319–320
melting, 323, 460–463
and water, 305
Ice caps, *233*
Icebergs, *231*
Iceland, *225*
Identify, 14, 18, 22, 49, 55, 56, 60, 61, 69, 95, 99, 122, 123, 146, 147, 151, 159, 163, 171, 173, 213, 214, 228, 232, 235, 250, 279, 282, 332, 362, 415, 437
Identify variables, 32, 460
Igneous, 209–211, 214–215, 245–248
Illustrate, 43, 111, 251, 322, 397, 448
Incandescent light bulb, *408*
Independent variables, 18, 296
Indianapolis 500, 48

Infer, 9, 11, 14, 28, 32, 33, 53, 56, 59, 63, 68, 69, 94, 96, 99, 100, 101, 105, 106, 113, 116, 124, 125, 140, 143, 147, 148, 149, 150, 155, 162, 171, 173, 178, 180, 181, 188, 207, 208, 218, 227, 229, 230, 234, 236, 241, 243, 266, 272, 282, 292, 304, 330, 336, 337, 350, 366, 372, 377, 378, 379, 396–397, 401, 403, 409, 410, 413, 421, 438, 457
Inference, 25, 28, 35–38
Inherit, 113–114, 127–132
Inherited characteristics, 112–117
and advantages, 117
and competition, 116
Inner ear, 436
Inner planets, *280–281*
Inquiries. *See* Apply It!; At-Home Lab; Design It!; Explore It!; Go Green; Investigate It!; Lightning Lab; Try It!
Inquiry, *7,* 35–38
Inquiry Skills
choose materials, 46
classify, 82, 84, 125, 200, 304, 392
communicate, 24, 33, 46, 54, 112, 195, 299, 366, 394, 414, 463
design, 46, 63, 72–77
draw conclusions, 10, 24, 54, 76, 125, 270, 318, 394, 400, 421, 444
estimate, 140, 310
experiment, 192, 296, 460
hypothesize, 192, 296, 299, 460, 463
identify and control variables, 32, 296, 460
infer, 32, 33, 63, 100, 106, 124, 125, 140, 148, 162, 180, 181, 208, 218, 230, 236, 243, 266, 304, 330, 336, 337, 350, 366, 372, 378, 379, 410, 421
interpret data, 46, 84, 154, 284, 285, 310, 337, 434, 450, 451
make and use models, 54, 62, 106, 154, 162, 208, 230, 256, 270, 285
measure, 16, 33, 124, 230, 284, 298, 310, 318, 434

observe, 4, 10, 62, 63, 76, 82, 100, 106, 112, 124, 148, 181, 200, 218, 236, 243, 256, 266, 270, 285, 304, 318, 330, 336, 337, 350, 366, 372, 379, 392, 394, 400, 410, 414, 420
predict, 3, 45, 62, 63, 81, 100, 139, 199, 236, 255, 303, 310, 349, 391, 392, 400, 420, 421, 433, 444, 451
record data, 16, 24, 33, 54, 62, 82, 84, 106, 125, 162, 181, 236, 242, 266, 298, 310, 318, 330, 336, 337, 350, 372, 379, 392, 410, 414, 420, 434, 450, 451, 462
redesign, 46
test, 74, 76
Instinct, 119–121, 123, 127–132
Insulator, 401, 403, 423–426, 462
Intelligent Flight Control System, 452
International Crane Foundation (ICF), 126
Interpret, 316, 326
Interpret data, 46, 84, 154, 284, 285, 310, 337, 434, 450, 451
Invertebrates, 85, 90, 127–132
Investigate, 269
Investigate It!, 3, 32–33, 45, 62–63, 81, 124–125, 139, 180–181, 199, 242–243, 255, 284–285, 303, 336–337, 349, 378–379, 391, 420–421, 433, 450–451
Investigation, *7,* 8, 35–38
Irises, 101
Iron, 202, 309, *323,* 328, 334
Iron filings, *412*

Jellyfish, *90*
Judge, 9, 15, 61
Jupiter, *278, 282*
Justify, 28, 335

Kansas, *177*
Kilauea Volcano, *226*

Credits

Staff Credits

The people who made up the *Interactive Science* team—representing core design digital and multimedia production services, digital product development, editorial, manufacturing, and production—are listed below.

Geri Amani, Alisa Anderson, Jose Arrendondo, Amy Austin, Lindsay Bellino, Charlie Bink, Bridget Binstock, Holly Blessen, Robin Bobo, Craig Bottomley, Jim Brady, Laura Brancky, Chris Budzisz, Mary Chingwa, Sitha Chhor, Caroline Chung, Margaret Clampitt, Karen Corliss, Brandon Cole, Mitch Coulter, AnnMarie Coyne, Fran Curran, Dana Damiano, Nancy Duffner, Amanda Ferguson, David Gall, Mark Geyer, Amy Goodwin, Gerardine Griffin, Chris Haggerty, Laura Hancko, Jericho Hernandez, Autumn Hickenlooper, Guy Huff, George Jacobson, Marian Jones, Kathi Kalina, Chris Kammer, Sheila Kanitsch, Alyse Kondrat, Mary Kramer, Thea Limpus, Dominique Mariano, Lori McGuire, Melinda Medina, Angelina Mendez, Claudi Mimo, John Moore, Phoebe Novak, Anthony Nuccio, Jeffrey Osier, Julianne Regnier, Charlene Rimsa, Rebecca Roberts, Camille Salerno, Manuel Sanchez, Carol Schmitz, Amanda Seldera, Sheetal Shah, Jeannine Shelton El, Geri Shulman, Greg Sorenson, Samantha Sparkman, Mindy Spelius, Karen Stockwell, Dee Sunday, Dennis Tarwood, Jennie Teece, Lois Teesdale, Michaela Tudela, Oscar Vera, Dave Wade, Tom Wickland, James Yagelski, Tim Yetzina, Diane Zimmermann

Illustrations

xiii, 102, 129, 234, 244, 247, 356 Precision Graphics; **103, 129, 144** Robert Ulrich; **162** Rich Foreman; **170, 171, 178** Alan Male; **227, 247** Adam Benton; **271, 405, 440, 453** Peter Bollinger; **278, 289** Paul Oglesby; **320** Big Sesh Studios
All other illustrations Chandler Digital Art

Photographs

Every effort has been made to secure permission and provide appropriate credit for photographic material. The publisher deeply regrets any omission and pledges to correct errors called to its attention in subsequent editions.

Unless otherwise acknowledged, all photographs are the property of Pearson Education, Inc.

Photo locators denoted as follows: Top (T), Center (C), Bottom (B), Left (L), Right (R), Background (Bkgd)

COVER: Robert Harding Picture Library/Alamy Images

vi (TR) ©Alexis Rosenfeld/Photo Researchers, Inc.; **vii** (TR) ©Neo Edmund/Shutterstock; **viii** (TR) Alan & Linda Detrick / Photo Researchers, Inc./Photo Researchers, Inc.; **ix** (TR) ©Larisa Lofitskaya/Shutterstock; **x** (TR) ©Savanah Stewart/ Danita Delimont/Alamy; **xii** (TR) ©Corbis/Jupiter Images; **xiv** (TR) ©Jeffrey Van Daele/Shutterstock; **xv** (TR) ©Peter Cade/ Getty Images; **1** (Bkgrd) ©James Thew/Shutterstock, (Bkgrd) ©niderlander/Shutterstock, (B) Nathan Denette/The Canadian Press/AP Images, (T) ©Morgan Lane Photography/Shutterstock; **2-3** (C) ©Morgan Lane Photography/Shutterstock; **6** (T) ©Inga Spence/Alamy Images, (B) Demetrio Carrasco/©DK Images; **7** (CR) ©Harald Sund/Getty Images; **8** (Bkgrd) ©Linda Sikes/Alamy Images, (TL) ©Robbie Shone/Alamy Images; **9** (TR) Colin Keates/Courtesy of the Natural History Museum, London/©DK Images; **12** (BR) Getty Images; **14** (CR) ©Photoroller/Shutterstock, (BR) Steve Shott/©DK Images; **15** (CR) Mike Dunning/©DK Images; **16** (T) ©Grant Faint/ Getty Images; **17** (BR) ©Maria Stenzel/National Geographic Image Collection; **22** (BL) ©Tim Ridley/DK Images, (TL) Robert F. Bukaty/AP Images; **24** (T) ©Alexis Rosenfeld/ Photo Researchers, Inc.; **25** (R) ©Photoroller/Shutterstock; **28** (TL) ©Leslie Banks/iStockphoto, (BC) Jupiter Images, (BL) Tim Ridley/©DK Images; **29** (BL) ©Alyda De Villers/ iStockphoto, (BC) ©DK Images; **30** (TR) ©image100/Alamy; **34** (C) ©Cultura Limited/SuperStock, (CR) ©fStop/Alamy; **35** (TR) ©Harald Sund/Getty Images, (TC) ©Maria Stenzel/ National Geographic Image Collection, (CR) ©Robbie Shone/ Alamy Images; **37** (TC) ©Leslie Banks/iStockphoto, (CR) ©Tim Ridley/DK Images, (TR) Robert F. Bukaty/AP Images; **43** (Bkgrd) ©Alexey Stiop/Shutterstock, (CL) ©Image Source ; **44** (C) Nathan Denette/The Canadian Press/AP Images; **47** (C) ©Andrew Holt/Getty Images, (TR) ©Gary Crabbe/Alamy Images; **48** (BL) ©Dieter Wanke/Alamy Images, (T) ©Neo Edmund/Shutterstock, (CL) ©Steve Allen/Jupiter Images, (TL) URC Media; **49** (CR) ©Anthony Berenyi/Shutterstock; **50** (TR) ©China Images/Alamy Images, (TCL) ©Deco/Alamy Images, (TL) ©Pictorial Press Ltd./Alamy Images; **51** (TR) ©Artostock/ Alamy Images, (CR) ©David R. Frazier Photolibrary, Inc./ Alamy Images; **52** (BR) ©Thomas Northcut/Thinkstock, (BL) Jupiterimages/Thinkstock; **53** (TR) Khromov Alexey/Shutterstock, (CR) Nicola Armstrong/Alamy; **54** (TR) Stefan Wackerhagen/ Alamy Images; **55** (TL) Bayne Stanley/Alamy Images; **56** (BR, BL) Library of Congress; **57** (CR) Goolia Photography/ Alamy, (TR) Library of Congress, (BC) Tomas Kopecny/Alamy Images, (CL) Weberfoto/Alamy Images; **58** (B) LaRC/NASA; **59** (TR) Library of Congress; **60** (BR) Library of Congress; **61** (TR) Peter Bowater/Alamy Images; **64** (CR) ©Amos Nachoum/ Corbis, (B) ©Dante Fenolio/Photo Researchers, Inc.; **65** (TR) ©Anthony Berenyi/Shutterstock, (BR) LaRC/NASA; **67** (Bkgd) Nathan Denette/The Canadian Press/AP Images, (TL) ©Neo Edmund/Shutterstock, (CL) Bayne Stanley/Alamy; **71** (C) ©Masterfile Royalty-Free; **80** (C) ©Darryl Torckler/Getty Images; **84** (TR) ©Insuratelu Gabriela Gianina/Shutterstock; **85** (CC) ©Dwight Smith/Shutterstock, (TL) ©Getty Images/ Jupiter Images, (CR) Terry Whittaker/Alamy Images; **86** (CR) ©John Durham/Photo Researchers, Inc., (BL) Sue Atkinson/ DK Images; **87** (BR) ©Maslov Dmitry/Shutterstock, (TR) ©Nigel Cattlin / Alamy/Alamy Images, (CR) Dr. Keith Wheeler / Photo Researchers, Inc./Photo Researchers, Inc., (C) Nigel Cattlin / Photo Researchers, Inc./Photo Researchers, Inc.; **88** (CR) ©Gregory G. Dimijian /Photo Researchers, Inc., (CL) ©Joseph T. Collins/Photo Researchers, Inc., (C) ©Larry Miller /Photo Researchers, Inc.; **89** (BL) ©Jeffrey Lepore /Photo Researchers, Inc., (CL) ©Joseph T. and Suzanne L. Collins /Photo Researchers, Inc., (CR) ©Millard H. Sharp /Photo Researchers, Inc.; **90** (CC) ©Richard Whitcombe/123RF, (CR) ©Wong Hock weng/

This is your book.

You can write in it.

Take Note

This space is yours. It is great for drawing diagrams and making notes.

This is your book.

You can write in it.

This is your book.

You can write in it.

This is your book.

You can write in it.

interactive SCIENCE

This is your book.

You can write in it.

interactive
SCIENCE

This is your book.

You can write in it.